M000101081

UNAUTHORIZED COPYING OR REUSE OF ANY PART OF THIS PAGE IS ILLEGAL

Published in 2018 by Rockridge edu. enterprise & services. inc.
ALL RIGHTS RESERVED.
COPYRIGHT @2016
BY SAN YOO

NO part of this book may be reproduced in any form, by phtosat, Microfilm, PDF or any other means, or incorporated into any information retrieval system, electronic or mechanical, without the written permission of the copyright owner

All inquiries should be addressed to:
Rockridge edu. enterprise & services inc.
869 SEYMOUR BLVD. NORTH VANCOUVER B.C. CANADA V7J 2J7
satvancouver@gmail.com

HOW TO USE THIS BOOK

Why Is It So Hard to Improve Reading and Verbal Scores?

San: Do you feel you're stuck in the reading and Verbal scores, Jimin?

Do you know why you can't improve your score?

Jimin: I know. I know.

Because I'm turkey.

That's why they eat me alive.

San: It's because what you do is what everybody does every day!: buying a book, solving a bunch of questions, looking at the answer keys, and feeling yourself guilty like a trapped miserable turkey.

Isn't it true at the midpoint of your practice, you don't pay attention to your errors and incorrect choices? You know why? Because you grow more an more frustrated to look at your faults.

From the beginning to the end of practice, you rely on your own judgment and avoid looking at your mistakes!

It's because in our DNA we avoid looking at what we hate, what we don't like, and what is our own faults.   NEVER will you be able to improve if you continue this old method!

Jimin: Any suggestion not to be a freaking turkey?

San: Ya! Sure! I can instantly and dramatically improve your scores.

I can get you out of the pungent smell of turkey within your innocent soul!

First, know that solving bunch of meaningless questions and looking at the answer keys won't work. (It's not because you're a turkey.) It's a part of human survival instincts to avoid and deny our mistakes.   Focus on Chapter 1 in this book. It doesn't start with the test questions. It starts with the answer explanations that show how the passage is created, how the question is created, what type of question you are dealing with, and in which line the answer (or clue) is located,

So just relax and read the answer explanation. Make sure to absorb every tiny bit of tricks.

Check the tick mark on each question when you're done.

HOW TO USE THIS BOOK

Why Is It So Hard to Improve Reading and Verbal Scores?

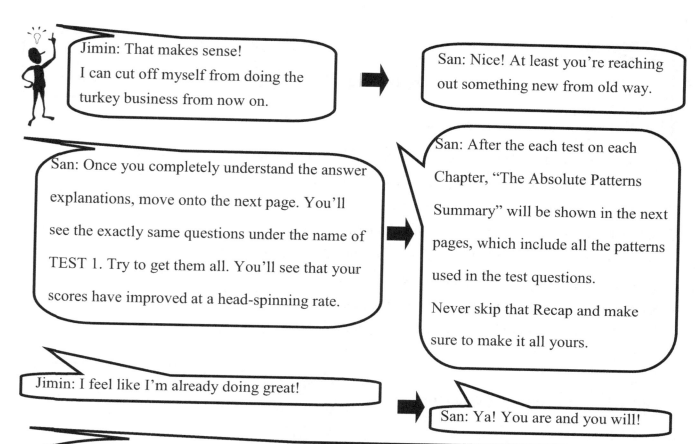

Jimin: That makes sense! I can cut off myself from doing the turkey business from now on.

San: Nice! At least you're reaching out something new from old way.

San: Once you completely understand the answer explanations, move onto the next page. You'll see the exactly same questions under the name of TEST 1. Try to get them all. You'll see that your scores have improved at a head-spinning rate.

San: After the each test on each Chapter, "The Absolute Patterns Summary" will be shown in the next pages, which include all the patterns used in the test questions. Never skip that Recap and make sure to make it all yours.

Jimin: I feel like I'm already doing great!

San: Ya! You are and you will!

San: The following chapter 2, however, begins with the actual test 2.

If you still feel uncomfortable, it's your book, do the same process as you did in Chapter 1.

Move onto the next Chapter 3, 4, 5,…until you feel confident about what you're doing.

By the time you finish this book, you will acknowledge yourself you were in fact an eagle believing yourself you are a turkey.

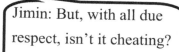

Jimin: But, with all due respect, isn't it cheating?

San: I know! When you do this you might feel a sort of wearing a brand-new underwear, a bit uncomfortable inside. But soon will you find it comfortable like it becomes a part of your skin.

HOW TO USE THIS BOOK

How to Read the Chapter 1. Reading Answer Explanations

San: Do you know, Jimin, that every single reading and analogy question is created by the unique but repeating pattern?

Jimin: You won't believe me, but I don't. What are they like?

San: The entire Reading and Analogy Sections use the unique but repeating patterns.

The official SSAT creates the questions based on these patterns.

This book is created by focusing on these facts: categorizing the entire questions into 10 Reading Absolute Patterns and 12 Analogy Absolute Patterns.

Instead of practicing each individual question endlessly without knowing the patterns and logic behind it, please work with these hidden patterns.

Memorize these Absolute Patterns in this book and check to see if you are following the patterns. Practice until every pattern becomes natural to you.

Chapter 1: Test 1 Answer Explanations

San: Each passage indicates two information: Underline (the questions); Boldface (the answer location)

Questions 1-6 are based on the following passage.

Brain Research through Advancing Innovative Neurotechnologies (BRAIN) Initiative has (Q9:B) **the potential to do for neuroscience what the Human Genome Project did for genomics** by supporting the development and application of innovative technologies that can create (Q7:C & Q8:E) **a dynamic understanding of brain function. It aims to help researchers uncover the mysteries of brain disorders,** such as Alzheimer's and Parkinson's diseases.

<u>These technologies will shed light on the complex links between brain function and behavior.</u>
While <u>these technological innovations have contributed substantially to our expanding knowledge of the brain,</u> **significant breakthroughs** in how we treat neurological and psychiatric disease will require a new generation of <u>tools to enable researchers to record signals from brain cells</u> in much greater numbers and at even faster speeds. (Q10:A) **That's where the BRAIN Initiative comes in.** <u>A Scientific Vision,</u> which articulates the (Q11:E) **scientific goals** of The BRAIN Initiative at the NIH charts (Q12:C) **a multi-year scientific plan** for achieving these

San: Following these underlines and boldfaces can you avoid sharp swings between the lines without direction, while observing from where the question and answer are created.

HOW TO USE THIS BOOK

How to Read the Chapter 1. Reading Answer Explanations

> Next to the question number—Q9 (question 9) will you see the Pattern number—**Absolute Pattern 9: Relationships Question.**
>
> Q9 is formulated and categorized by the Absolute Pattern 9. At the end of each chapter will you discover the summery of Absolute Patterns applied in each test questions.

> Check the tick mark to make sure everything is understood!

Q9. **Absolute Pattern 9: Relationships Question**	Got It!	No
Finding relations between the cause-effect, comparison-contrast, characters, and ideas	✓	

Question Pattern: The author mentioned **Human Genome project** mainly to

A) celebrates what it did to genomics
B) compare what BRAIN Initiative can do to neuroscience
C) introduce neurotechnology
D) present complexity of neurotechnolgy
E) present achievement of BRAIN Initiative

Initiative has **the potential to do for neuroscience what the Human Genome Project did for genomics** by supporting the development

> **Question Pattern** can be divided into two parts: the question pattern,—which never changes in the actual test—and the keywords that makes the each question unique. The keywords are boldfaced.

> (B) is the answer here. You will find from where the answer came with a simple explanations

Knowing the question patterns will reward you several advantages:

√ you will be familiar with tricky terms within the questions so that you can save time in the actual test.

√ you will be able to guess what the question is basically seeking even without reading the passage.

√ you can avoid possible confusion or mistakes such as "EXCEPT" or "Unlike"

UNAUTHORIZED COPYING OR REUSE OF ANY PART OF THIS PAGE IS ILLEGAL

HOW TO USE THIS BOOK

Chapter 1. Reading Test 1

After practicing the answer explanation part in this chapter, try to solve these identical questions without the answers, but by relying on your memory. You will get close to, if not 100 percent, the perfect scores.

This process will give you an in-depth, stress free training.

Questions 16-21 are based on the following passage.

Line

Each year, CDER approves hundreds of new medications, most of which are variations of previously existing products, such as new dosage forms of already-approved products, or cost-saving generics. These new products contribute to quality of care, greater access to medication, more consumer choice that enhances affordability and public health.

5   However, products in a small subset of these new approvals, that we refer to as <u>novel drugs</u>, are among the more truly innovative products that often help advance clinical care to another level. Every year, CDER summarizes these new products. <u>The annual summary</u> reports the quantity of novel drugs that it approved.

However, it also focuses on the high quality of many of these new drugs, their contributions to enhanced patient care. This year, we approved many new drugs to treat various forms of cancer, including myeloma,

10 lung, skin, breast. This year's field also includes new drugs to treat reversal agent for a blood thinner.

For the first year, we approved more "<u>orphan</u>" drugs for rare diseases than any previous year in our history.

16

In the 1st paragraph, the author emphasizes that new medications will enhance all of the followings EXCEPT

A) they will completely replace existing products

B) they will contribute to quality of care

C) they will allow greater accessibility to mediation

D) they will give more consumer choices

E) they will give cost-saving alternatives

19

Novel drug is characterized as the one with?

A) advanced and innovative drug

B) less expensive

C) more concerned with public health

D) less known previously

E) barely passed the regulations

HOW TO USE THIS BOOK

How to Read the Chapter Summary: The Absolute Patterns

San: 12 Absolute Patterns for Analogy are equally divided at the end of each chapter. You may read and practice all of them at once.

Absolute Pattern 1. Category Pattern
Finding Part/Whole, Same Type/Kind, Association

Q1.Smell is to pungent as
A) sight is to strong
B) hear is to Mozart
C) touch is to fire
D) taste is to sweet
E) sense is to anger

San: This Pattern is the Category Pattern.
You should find a part from the whole, a same type or kind, or an associated category with the question.

The correct answer is D

San: The question focuses on our five sensory devices (touch, smell, hearing, sight, taste).
The pungent smell is a strong smell. It is very strong smell like you fart after eating a lot of onions because they're cheap. Pungent is associated with a smell as sweet is associated with a taste.
You can also say like pungent is a part of or a type of smell.
A) strong, B) Mozart, and C) fire and E) anger are all unrelated words.

Jimin: But I didn't know what pungent was.

San: If the question contains a word that you don't know, look for the most meaningful pair from the five choices.

Jimin: For me, Mozart in B) is more meaningful though.

San: "pungent"—even though you don't know its meaning—is adjective. You can tell that much, can't you? You should find the same adjective from the five choices.
B) and C) are nouns and A) doesn't make sense.

Jimin: What is this pungent smell! Did you eat onions?

UNAUTHORIZED COPYING OR REUSE OF ANY PART OF THIS PAGE IS ILLEGAL

HOW TO USE THIS BOOK

How to Read the Chapter Summary: The Absolute Patterns

San: 10 Absolute Patterns for Reading are equally divided at the end of each chapter. You may read and practice all of them at once.

Chapter 1

10 Absolute Patterns for the Reading Section

Category A: Content Question has five patterns:

San: The Content question may also be called the local question.
Either with the line reference number (i.e., line 5) or without it, the content question normally asks localized, detailed information from only one or two sentences in the passage.

The question may ask explicitly stated keywords in the sentences, or, in more complex level, implicitly analogous (similar) situations within a sentence.

San: Neither of the cases requires the holistic understanding of the entire passage. Reading only the target sentence will save your precious time and mental horsepower. Now. Let's talk about the Content Question Patterns.

Absolute Pattern 2: Summary Question

The basic technique to find the answer is almost the same as pattern 1: Main Idea Question.
The major difference, however, —especially in the literary passage—can be seen in its focusing on the manner of voice, tone, and style of the sentence.

In literary passage, the answer often carries more subjective words, such as "criticize", "emphatic", "celebrate"—contrary to the main idea pattern that maintains a neutral tone and objective view.

HOW TO USE THIS BOOK

Almost all students preparing for the SSAT put enormous intellectual effort to achieve their goals.

However, when they receive the test results, they soon find themselves disappointing scores.

The Verbal and Reading, most often than not, are the main culprits.

That is what delays your score improvement.

This book focuses mostly on Verbal and the Reading sections.

Please practice with the ABSOLUTE PATTERNS until you thoroughly understand the logic behind each question. You will get the score you want on your upcoming test!

CAN THIS BOOK GUARANTEE MY SCORE?

Yes. If you understand all the ABSOLUTE PATTERNS in the reading and verbal section and maintain the minimum vocabulary level. But remember! There's no overnight scheme.

You should work very hard to memorize vocabulary first.

WHAT IS THE MINIMUM VOCABULARY AND IS IT IN THIS BOOK?

For the students aiming the 99% on the reading and Verbal section, I recommend:

SSAT Upper Level: ……….1500 vocabulary

SSAT Middle Level: …….. .1000 vocabulary

SSAT Elementary Level……..600 vocabulary

I made bunches of uninspiring, difficult-to-memorize vocabularies into a pretty Absolute Vocabulary book with photos. Please email me for free copy: satvancouver@gmail.com (with proof of purchase of this book)

WHAT IF I FAIL ON MY SSAT, WHAT CAN I DO? SUPPOSE I MEMORIZED ALL THE VOCABULARY YOU RECOMMENDED AND UNDERSTOOD ALL THE LOGIC IN THIS BOOK, BUT STILL FAILED.

If you failed on your SSAT, you should try again! In fact, there are eight chances to try again every year! Nobody reaches to the goal in one shot!

If you believed in yourself that you had memorized all the vocabularies I recommended, you are wrong! It took me many years to store all the vocabularies into my long-term memory.

Try to review the vocabularies up to the point that you feel comfortable. You will soon forget what you memorized, but keep going, don't stop.

Your reward won't stop at the SSAT, but beyond the SAT.

CONTENTS

CONTENTS

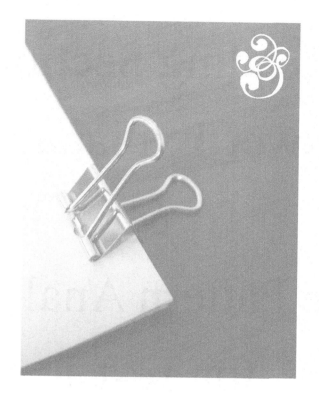

Chapter 1

1. ANSWER EXPLANATIONS for TEST 1

2. CHAPTER SUMMARY

3. TEST 1

UNAUTHORIZED COPYING OR REUSE OF ANY PART OF THIS PAGE IS ILLEGAL

SSAT
Reading Section
Answer Explanations
&
The Pattern Analyses
for Test 1

Test 1 starts with the Answer Explanations using

the Absolute Patterns.

Please understand each question according to the Patterns

before taking Test 1

There's no Time Limit for this Practice.

ALL THE LOGIC AND RULES BEHIND EVERY

SINGLE SSAT QUESTION

Questions 1-6 are based on the following passage.

(4) **The family of Dashwood had long been** settled in Sussex, where, for many generations, they had lived in so respectable a manner as to engage the general good opinion of their surrounding acquaintance. The old Dashwood was a single man, who lived to a very advanced age, and who for many years of his life, had a (2) **constant companion and housekeeper in his sister.**

But her death, which happened ten years before his own, produced a great alteration in his home; (1) **for to supply her loss, he invited and received into his house the family of his nephew** (4) **Mr. Henry Dashwood, the legal inheritor of the Norland estate, and the person to whom he intended to bequeath it.** But by his own marriage Mr. Henry added to his wealth. To him therefore the <u>succession to the Norland estate</u> was not so really important as to his <u>Sisters</u>, and could be (3) **but small.**

He was (6) **neither so unjust, nor so ungrateful,** as to leave his estate to Mr. Henry Dashwood on such terms as (4 & 5) **destroyed half the value of the bequest to his Sisters.**

Q1. Absolute Pattern 2: Summary Question Summarizing a sentence, or entire passage
Question Pattern: According to paragraph 2 (lines 5-10), **the old Dashwood invited Mr. Henry Dashwood for**

	Got It!	No
	✓	

A) he had a contemptuous feeling to Mr. Henry B) Mr. Henry had some financial issue **C) he had more than one reason** D) he needed to repent his wrongdoings E) Mr. Henry was still single	for **to supply her loss,** he invited and received into his house the family of his nephew Mr. Henry Dashwood, the legal inheritor of the Norland estate, and the person to whom he intended **to bequeath it.**

Q2. Absolute Pattern 2: Summary Question
Question Pattern: All of the following correctly **describe the Old Dashwood EXCEPT**

	Got It!	No
	✓	

A) he lived in the parents' house B) his family was well respected from the neighbors C) he did not have a wife **D) he lived all alone as a single man** E) he wanted to be grateful as he leaves his estate	Dashwood was a single man, who lived to a very advanced age, and who for many years of his life, had a **constant companion and housekeeper in his sister**

Q3. Absolute Pattern 3: Inference Question Finding an indirect suggestion (or guessing)
Question Pattern: To **Mr. Henry, the succession to the Norland estate** mentioned in line 8 was

	Got It!	No
	✓	

A) significant B) a gift to strengthen distinctive family tie C) important to satisfy his greed D) a seed of foreboding family feud **E) insignificant**	To him therefore the <u>succession to the Norland estate</u> was not so really important as to his <u>Sisters,</u> and could be **but small**

Q4. Absolute Pattern 1: Main Idea Question
Finding the main idea of the entire passage, a specific paragraph, or sentences
Question Pattern: The **primary purpose** of the passage is to

	Got It!	No
	✓	

A) define a legal custom related to inheritance B) emphasize the benefits of having good neighbors **C) introduce the settings of the story** D) show a prolonged family feud E) betray cunning tricks of Mr. Henry Dashwood	**The family of Dashwood had long been** settled in Sussex, where, for many generations, they had lived in so respectable a manner ... * The first sentence describes where the character lives, who he is,.... Or the settings of the story.

Q5. Absolute Pattern 3: Inference Question Finding an indirect suggestion (or guessing)
Question Pattern: It can be inferred from the passage that the **"Sisters" in line 9**

Got It! ✓ | No

A) had amassed great wealth B) had some difficulties with the Old Dashwood **C) were not the legal inheritors** D) brought joy to the family E) were preferred inheritors to Mr. Henry Dashwood	his house the family of his nephew **Mr. Henry Dashwood, the legal inheritor of the Norland estate**, and the person to whom he intended to bequeath it. destroyed half the value of the **bequest to his Sisters** *The legal inheritor is Mr. Henry Dashwood, but the Old Dashwood wanted to destroy the inheritance for his sister.

Q6. Absolute Pattern 3: Inference Question Finding an indirect suggestion (or guessing)
Question Pattern: It can be inferred from lines 10-11 that **in his will, the Old Dashwood tried to?**

Got It! ✓ | No

A) balance and appease every heir B) condescend every heir C) earn profits from every heir D) defend his estate from every heir E) remove Mr. Henry from his family	He was **neither so unjust, nor so ungrateful,** as to leave his estate. *In other words, he tried to balance and appease every heir.

Questions 7-12 are based on the following passage.

Brain Research through Advancing Innovative Neurotechnologies (BRAIN) Initiative has (9) **the potential to do for neuroscience what the Human Genome Project did for genomics** by supporting the development and application of innovative technologies that can create (7 & 8) **a dynamic understanding of brain function. It aims to help researchers uncover the mysteries of brain disorders,** such as Alzheimer's and Parkinson's diseases.
These technologies will shed light on the complex links between brain function and behavior.
<u>While</u> these technological innovations have contributed substantially to our expanding knowledge of the brain, **significant breakthroughs** in how we treat neurological and psychiatric disease will require a new generation of tools to enable researchers to record signals from brain cells in much greater numbers and at even faster speeds.
(10) **That's where the BRAIN Initiative comes in.** <u>A Scientific Vision</u>, which articulates the (11) **scientific goals** of The BRAIN Initiative at the NIH charts (12) **a multi-year scientific plan** for achieving these goals, including timetables, milestones, and **cost estimates.** and focused effort across the agency.

Q7. Absolute Pattern 8: Understanding True Purpose
Question Pattern: The **primary purpose of the BRAIN Initiative** is to help researchers

Got It! ✓ | No

A) advance Human Genome Project **B) understand brain function and disorder** C) sequence the human genome D) develop better human brain E) develop medicines for brain disorder	a dynamic **understanding of brain function**. It aims to help researchers uncover the mysteries of **brain disorders,..**

Q8. Absolute Pattern 3: Inference Question Finding an indirect suggestion (or guessing)
Question Pattern: The **"mysteries" in line 4?**mplies that at **the current stage,** the research of brain disorders

Got It! ✓ | No

A) is dynamically improving B) is expected to be unlocked pretty soon **C) is still at understanding level** D) requires huge financial support E) has seen mysterious breakthrough recently	a dynamic **understanding of brain function**. It aims to help researchers uncover the mysteries of **brain disorders,..**

Q9. Absolute Pattern 9: Relationships Question

Got It!	No
✓	

Finding relations between the cause-effect, comparison-contrast, characters, and ideas

Question Pattern: The author mentioned **Human Genome project** mainly to

A) celebrates what it did to genomics **B) compare what BRAIN Initiative can do to neuroscience** C) introduce neurotechnology D) present complexity of neurotechnolgy E) present achievement of BRAIN Initiative	Initiative has **the potential to do for neuroscience what the Human Genome Project did for genomics** by supporting the development

Q10. Absolute Pattern 8: Understanding True Purpose

Got It!	No
✓	

Finding the true purpose of statement, sentences, or the entire paragraph

Question Pattern: The author uses **"While these...brain,"** (lines 6-7) to make which of the following points?

A) BRAIN Initiatives is even more pivotal B) BRAIN Initiative may succeed without these technological innovations C) These technological innovations are outmoded D) These technological innovations are beyond our understanding E) These technological innovations are role models	**While** these technological innovations have contributed substantially to our expanding knowledge of the brain, **significant breakthroughs** in how we treat...**That's where the BRAIN Initiative comes in.** *"While," is used the same way as like 'however' or 'but.' It cancels out the previous phrase, giving more importance to the following clause

Q11. Absolute Pattern 8: Understanding True Purpose

Got It!	No
✓	

Finding the true purpose of statement, sentences, or the entire paragraph

Question Pattern: In line 9, the author mentions "**A Scientific Vision**" mainly to

A) present scientific goals of the BRAIN Initiative B) voice doubt about its undertaking C) raise over-budget issue in a single project D) celebrate goals of BRAIN that are achieved E) acclaim efforts made by the agency	A Scientific Vision, which articulates the **scientific goals** of The BRAIN

Q12. Absolute Pattern 2: Summary Question

Got It!	No
✓	

Summarizing a sentence or entire passage

Question Pattern: Which of the following objectives is committed by BRAIN Initiative

I. **Multi-year scientific plan for the Working Group** I. **Financial estimates for the research** II. Developing medicines for the brain disorder A) I only B) II only C) III only **D) I and II only** E) I, II, and III	The BRAIN Initiative at the NIH charts **a multi-year scientific plan** for achieving these goals, including timetables, milestones, and **cost estimates**.

Questions 13-17 are based on the following passage.

The United Kingdom European Union membership referendum took place on Thursday 23 June 2016 in the United Kingdom to gauge support for the country's continued membership in the European Union.
The referendum result was (14) **not legally binding**. The result was split with the constituent countries of the United Kingdom, with a majority in (15) **England and Wales voting to leave**, and a majority in **Scotland voting to remain.**
   (17) To start the **process to leave the EU, which is expected to take several years, the British government** (13 &16) **will have to invoke Article 50 of the Treaty on Europe an Union.**   The UK government has announced formal process of leaving the EU although revoking the vote might be possible. Britain Stronger in Europe was the official group campaigning for the UK to remain in the EU and was led by the Prime Minister David Cameron.
   Other campaign groups, political parties, businesses, trade unions, newspapers and prominent individuals were also involved, and each side had supporters from across the political spectrum.

	Got It!	No
Q13. Absolute Pattern 3: Inference Question Finding an indirect suggestion (or guessing) **Question Pattern:** The phrase "**not legally binding**" (line 3) implies that	✓	

A) there's a theoretical fallacy with the referendum result B) the referendum was in fact for an entertainment **C) there's a final Article 50 confirmation waiting** D) such a revolutionary process itself requires no legality E) the referendum should be held once more	...will have to invoke **Article 50 of the Treaty** on Europe an Union. Because the referendum is not legally binding.

Q14. Absolute Pattern 3: Inference Question Finding an indirect suggestion (or guessing)
Question Pattern: Which of the following phrases directly **undermines the result of referendum**?

A) to gauge support (line 2) **B) not legally binding (line 3)** C) split with the constituent countries (line 3) D) England and Wales voting to leave (line 4) E) Scotland voting to remain (line 4)	The referendum result was not legally binding. *If the referendum were not legally binding, it can undermine the result.

	Got It!	No
Q15. Absolute Pattern 9: Relationships Question Finding relations between the cause-effect, comparison-contrast, characters, and ideas **Question Pattern:** The **geographical reference** in lines 3-4 (The result…voting to remain) serves to underscore	✓	

A) different customs among the United Kingdom **B) contradictions to the referendum** C) essentially unified voice to the referendum D) countries that traditionally supported EU E) countries that traditionally disfavored EU	England and Wales **voting to leave**, and a majority in Scotland **voting to remain**

	Got It!	No
Q16. Absolute Pattern 3: Inference Question Finding an indirect suggestion (or guessing) **Question Pattern:** "**Article 50**" mentioned in line 6 would probably contain	✓	

A) compilations of EU countries' population statistics **B) sources of formal treaty to disjoin EU** C) studies of UK's trade projection with EU D) analyses of Referendum results E) measurements of EU countries' wealth	will have to invoke Article 50 of the Treaty on Europe an Union. D) is impossible.

Q17. **Absolute Pattern 2: Summary Question** Summarizing a sentence or entire passage **Question Pattern: After the referendum result**, the British government needs to undergo a process of	Got It! ✓	No

A) **disjoining treaty with EU** B) referendum cancelation C) announcement for immediate leaving EU D) official campaign for rejoining EU E) dividing economic spectrum from the politics	will have to invoke Article 50 of the Treaty on Europe an Union… C) is opposite. The passage says "To start the process to leave the EU, which is expected to **take several years**"

Questions 18-23 are based on the following passage.

(23) **No man can fully grasp how far and how fast we have come**, but condense, if you will, the 50,000 years of man's recorded history in a time span of but a half-century. Stated in these terms, we know very little about the first 40 years, except at the end of them advanced man had learned to use the skins of animals to cover them. Then, only last week did we develop television, and (18) **now if America's new spacecraft succeeds** in reaching Venus, we will have literally reached the stars **before midnight tonight**.

This is a breathtaking pace, and such a pace cannot help but create new ills as it dispels old, (19) new **ignorance, new problems, new dangers.** Surely the opening vistas of space promise **high costs** and **hardships**, as well as high reward. So it is not surprising that some would have us stay where we are a little longer to rest, to wait.

But why, some say, the moon? We choose to go to the moon not because they are easy, (21) **but because they are hard.** We have seen facilities greatest and most complex exploration in man's history: Saturn C-1 booster rocket, (20) **generating power equivalent to 10,000 automobiles**, the F-1 rocket engines, each one as powerful as all **eight engines** of the Saturn combined, Saturn missile as tall as a **48 story structure, as wide as a city block**.

But if I were to say, my fellow citizens, that we shall send to the moon and then return it safely to earth, re-entering the atmosphere at speeds of over 25,000 miles per hour, causing heat about half that of the temperature of the sun--(22) **almost as hot as it is here today**. I'm the one who is doing all the work, **so we just want you to stay cool for a minute.**

Q18. **Absolute Pattern 4: Example Question** **Question Pattern: "but condense 50,000...before midnight tonight," Kennedy alludes** to the audience	Got It! ✓	No

A) **a support the space program** B) a precondition for public approval of the program C) reasons for the low level of public awareness D) some limitations that block space program E) major assignments during his incumbency	now if America's new spacecraft succeeds in reaching Venus, we will have literally reached the stars **before midnight tonight.** B) precondition makes the sentence negative. E) is too vague

Q19. **Absolute Pattern 2: Summary Question** **Question Pattern:** In lines 6-8, Kennedy mentions despite of rapid advancement in space program certain **obstacles should be overcome** EXCEPT	✓	

A) demand from some people to delay the project B) ignorance due to lack of information C) high expenditure D) **restrictive government policy** E) hardships	new **ignorance, new problems, new dangers.** Surely the opening vistas of space promise **high costs** and **hardships**, D) is opposite because Kennedy administration supports the program

Q20. Absolute Pattern 2: Summary Question

Got It!	No
✓	

Summarizing a sentence or entire passage

Question Pattern: In lines 10-12 (We have seen...a city block), Kennedy mainly describes the space project's

A) undeterred persistence **B) immensity** C) probable challenges D) impact on society E) contribution to the community in Texas	**generating power equivalent to 10,000 automobiles**, the F-1 rocket engines, each one as powerful as all **eight engines** of the Saturn combined, Saturn missile as tall as a **48 story structure, as wide as a city block**.

Q21. Absolute Pattern 8: Understanding True Purpose

Got It!	No
✓	

Finding the true purpose of statement, sentences, or the entire paragraph

Question Pattern: In line 9, "But why, some say, the moon?" President Kennedy makes which of the following assumptions?

A) The progress must be made in small, gradual steps B) Had we tried earlier, the Moon would have been conquered already **C) We must welcome challenges** D) With the right equipment and audacity, any nations can tap the untried mission E) With our effort, we will soon conquer the universe	We choose to go to the moon not because they are easy, but **because they are hard.**

Q22. Absolute Pattern 7: Understanding Attitude (Tone) Question

Got It!	No
✓	

Finding tone such as positive-negative, active-passive, mental-physical, subjective-objective

Question Pattern: The tone of Kennedy in line 15 (so we just...for a minute) is

A) anger **B) humorous** C) didactic D) profound E) irate	**almost as hot as it is here today**. I'm the one who is doing all the work, so we just want you to stay cool for a minute. *Hot and cool juxtapose the situation that creates humor.

Q23. Absolute Pattern 1: Main Idea Question

Got It!	No
✓	

Finding the main idea of the entire passage, a specific paragraph, or sentences

Question Pattern: The primary purpose of the first paragraph (lines 1-5) is to

A) show some of the impressive scientific achievement in human history B) show human history through condensed time **C) introduce the speaker's main speech** D) explain the importance of history study E) educate some dramatic history to the audience	**No man can fully grasp** how far and how fast we have come The speaker's main purpose is to introduce his speech, the space program. if you will, the 50,000 years .... is an example to clarify his main purpose, therefore, A) and B) are incorrect.

Questions 24-29 are based on the following passage.

> Black ice, sometimes called clear ice, refers to a thin coating of glaze ice on a surface, especially on roads. The ice itself is not black, (24 & 25) **but visually transparent,** allowing the often black road below to be seen through it. The typically low level of noticeable ice pellets, snow means that areas of the ice are often practically invisible to drivers stepping on it. There is, thus, a risk of skidding and subsequent accidents due to the unexpected loss of traction. (29) **Black ice is formed on relatively dry roads,** rendering it invisible to drivers. Deicing with (28) **salt (sodium chloride) is effective to down temperatures of about −18 °C (0 °F).**
>
> (26) **At below −18 °C, black ice can form on roadways** when the moisture from automobile exhaust condenses on the road surface. Such conditions caused multiple accidents in Minnesota when the temperatures dipped below −18 °C for a prolonged period of time in December 2008. With salt's ineffectiveness at melting ice at these temperatures compounds the problem. Black ice (27) **may form even when the ambient temperature** is several degrees above the freezing point of water 0 °C (32 °F), if the air warms suddenly after a prolonged cold spell that has left the surface of the roadway well below the freezing point temperature.

Q24. Absolute Pattern 8: Understanding True Purpose

Got It! ✓ No

Question Pattern: The passage describes that **black ice makes drivers more difficult because**

A) black road below the ice freezes B) of snow compaction **C) of its transparency** D) of unexpected accidents E) of unexpected loss of traction	The ice itself is not black, **but visually transparent**

Q25. Absolute Pattern 2: Summary Question

Got It! ✓ No

Question Pattern: All of the following are referred to as the **characteristics of black ice** EXCEPT

A) it causes sudden traction issues while driving B) it is often invisible to drivers **C) its black pigment absorbs the surface heat faster** D) it is also dubbed as clear ice E) it covers the thin road surface	The ice itself is not black, **but visually transparent.** Therefore, (C) is opposite. The other choices are all mentioned.

Q26. Absolute Pattern 4: Example Question

Got It! ✓ No

Finding the true purpose behind a specific name or idea within a sentence

Question Pattern: What **caused the significant multiple accidents** in Minnesota in line 8?

A) the low temperature B) salt C) excessive moisture on roads D) reckless driving E) standing water	**At below −18 °C, black ice can form on roadways** when the moisture from automobile exhaust condenses on the road surface. Such conditions caused multiple accidents C) is opposite. ...when the moisture from automobile exhaust condenses on the road surface.

Q27. Absolute Pattern 2: Summary Question

✓

Question Pattern: The paragraph 3 (lines 7-13) indicates that one of the **difficulties in dealing with black ice is** that

A) it should not be treated with salt B) it increases road surface temperature C) it turns snow into water **D) it may form even in mild weather** E) it forms even when weather is below −18 °C	Black ice **may form even when the ambient temperature** is several degrees above the freezing point of water 0 °C (32 °F),

---

UNAUTHORIZED COPYING OR REUSE OF ANY PART OF THIS PAGE IS ILLEGAL

Q28. Absolute Pattern 2: Summary Question

Got It!	No
✓	

Question Pattern: The discussion of **accidents in Minnesota** (line 8) primarily suggests that

A) Minnesota is typically susceptible to black ice **B) only at above 18 °C can salt prevent such multiple accidents** C) black ice is more visible in Minnesota D) we know very little about the characteristics of black ice E) typical black ice causes multiple accidents	**salt (sodium chloride) is effective to down temperatures of about −18 °C (0 °F). At below −18 °** Such conditions caused multiple <u>accidents in Minnesota</u> when the temperatures dipped below −18 °C

Q29. Absolute Pattern 6: Analogy Question Finding a similar situation

Got It!	No
✓	

Question Pattern: Which of the following areas would most likely be **affected by black ice accident**?

A) open roads in Hawaii during rainy seasons B) mountain regions in Alaska covered with perennial snow C) dangerously spiraling hiking tracks in Utah D) humid coastal highways in Florida **E) cold and dry bridges in British Columbia**	**Black ice is formed on relatively dry roads,** rendering it invisible to drivers.

Questions 30-35 are based on the following passage.

Many scientists believe we are not alone in the universe. (30) **It's probable that life** could rise on at least the billions of planets thought to exist in our galaxy alone (31 &32) **just as it did here on planet Earth.**

 <u>This basic question</u> about our place in the Universe is one that may be answered by scientific investigations. Experts from NASA addressed this question at a public talk held at NASA Headquarters. (35) **They outlined NASA's roadmap to the search for life in the universe.** In the near future, people will be able to point to a star and say, 'that star has a planet like Earth'," says Sara Seager, the professor at Harvard. However, the impression of how common planets are in the Milky way adversely creates backlash among scientists. NASA's quest to study planetary systems around other stars started with ground-based observatories, then moved to Hubble Space Telescope. Today's telescopes can look at many stars and tell if they have one or more orbiting planets. (33) **But it can't determine if the planets are the right distance away from the star to have liquid water** [QUESTION 34]

Q30. Absolute Pattern 7: Understanding Attitude (Tone) Question

Got It!	No
✓	

Question Pattern: The passage suggests that many scientists' belief in line 1 is based on

A) professional speculation B) investigated conviction C) personal intuition D) ongoing survey E) determination from the history	**It's probable that life** could rise on at least some of the billions of planets thought to exist in our galaxy alone just as it did here on planet Earth. *"probable" implies professional (scientific) speculation. C) is too extreme

Q31. Absolute Pattern 6: Analogy Question Finding a similar situation

Got It!	No
✓	

Question Pattern: Which of the following statements is **analogous to "many scientists' belief"** in lines1-2

A) a rebellion will occur soon because it occurred ten years ago B) many ISIS members will be disillusioned just as were some members C) our company can't find hope this quarter because the new boss is lousy D) biologists deny microbes 100 meters beneath the earth surface just as they do to 200 meters **E) the island will grow orange because similar island grows orange**	**It's probable that life** could rise on at least some of the billions of planets thought to exist in our galaxy alone **just as it did here on planet Earth.**

Q32. Absolute Pattern 3: Inference Question Finding an indirect suggestion (or guessing)

Question Pattern: "**This basic question**" in line 3 directly refers to

Got It!	No
✓	

A) the history of universe
B) the civilizations of the earth
C) the evolutionary condition similar to the earth
D) the number of planets in our galaxy
E) the accuracy of scientific investigations

just as it did here on planet Earth. This basic question...
"This" is called an amplifier that emphasizes the previous sentence. The concept of amplifier is very important.
*"it did" refers to the life arose on Earth. Or, the evolutionary condition.

Q33. Absolute Pattern 3: Inference Question Finding an indirect suggestion (or guessing)

Question Pattern: It can be inferred that the **upcoming future telescopes would probably focus on finding**

Got It!	No
✓	

A) the orbiting planetary systems that measure the right distance to have liquid
B) the living things like us
C) any planets in universe
D) only the orbiting planets in our galaxy
E) any inhabitable planets exactly look like the earth

But it can't determine if the planets are the right distance away from the star to have liquid water

Q34. Absolute Pattern 5: Word-In-Context Question
Finding a clue word and the keyword from the sentence in question

Question Pattern: Which of the following phrases would the author **add after the last sentence** "to have liquid water"?

Got It!	No
✓	

A) that can be the key ingredient to life.
B) that invalidates scientists' previous theory.
C) that puzzles our knowledge about universe.
D) that explains the origin of the universe.
E) that supports other forms do not require water.

the star to have liquid water **A) that can be the key ingredient to life.**

Only (A) contains the keyword "life," the main focus of the passage.

Q35. Absolute Pattern 1: Main Idea Question
Finding the main idea of the entire passage, a specific paragraph, or sentences

Question Pattern: The **passage primary describes**

Got It!	No
✓	

A) a well-known theory of life in the universe
B) the reasons some planets are inhabitable
C) mysterious universe
D) searching for life in our galaxy
E) statistical analysis of similar planets in the solar system

They outlined NASA's roadmap to the search for life in the universe.

A) is incorrect because the passage is relatively a new discovery.

Questions 36-40 are based on the following passage.

We hold these **truths** to be **self-evident**, that all men are created equal, that they are endowed by their Creator with certain (Q36) **unalienable Rights**, that among these are Life, Liberty, and the pursuit of Happiness. That to secure these rights, Governments are instituted among Men, But when a long train of (Q39) **abuses and usurpations**, pursuing invariably the same Object evinces a design to reduce them under absolute **Despotism**, it is their right, it is their duty, (Q37 & Q38) **to throw off such Government, and to provide new Guards for their future security.** Such has been the patient sufferance of these Colonies; and (Q40) **such is now** the necessity which constrains them to alter their former Systems of Government.

Q36. Absolute Pattern 5: Word-In-Context Question   Got It! ✓ | No

Finding a clue word and the keyword from the sentence in question

Question Pattern: The phrase "**self-evident**" in line 1 can be understood that some truths are

A) beyond our judgment B) morally perfect C) beyond the political interpretation D) open-ended debate E) determined by ourselves	We hold these truths to <u>be self-evident,</u> that all men are created equal, that they are endowed by their Creator with certain <u>unalienable Rights,</u> *The phrase "self-evident" in line 1 can be understood as some truths are perfect and cannot be questioned. Self-evident = unalienable Rights. The word 'unalienable,' meaning something that cannot be taken away because it is natural further clarifies the hidden meaning of 'self-reliance.' B) it's not about morality. C) it's not limited to "the political" D) is Opposite

---

Q37 Absolute Pattern 2: Summary Question   Got It! ✓ | No

Summarizing a sentence or entire passage

Question Pattern: The **unalienable Rights** in line 2 include all of the following EXCEPT

A) Right to establish sovereign government B) Right to live a life C) Right to pursue happiness D) Equal Right E) Right to enjoy freedom	...to throw off such Government, and to provide new Guards for their future security. *Should all these rights in (B),(C),(D), and (E) be rejected, then (A) necessarily comes along.

Q38. Absolute Pattern 2: Summary Question   Got It! ✓ | No

Summarizing a sentence or entire passage

Question Pattern: The author defines that the **government**

A) has the absolute power above all men **B) is instituted to secure the rights of all men** C) is created by God D) should not reduce its power E) can do whatever to protect the life of the citizen	**to throw off such Government, and to provide new Guards for their future security...that** whenever any Form of Government becomes destructive of these ends, it is the <u>Right of the People to alter or to abolish it, and to institute new Government.</u> A), D), E) are Opposite C) is not stated

Q39. **Absolute Pattern 7: Understanding Attitude (Tone) Question**		Got It!	No
Finding tone such as positive-negative, active-passive, mental-physical, subjective-objective		✓	
Question Pattern: The author's attitude to "**Despotism**" in line 4 is best described as			

A) admiration B) appreciation C) enthusiasm **D) warning** E) necessity	Despot = cruel ruler But when a long train of **abuses and usurpations**, pursuing invariably the same Object evinces a design to **reduce them under absolute Despotism**, The author's tone is grave and negative. Therefore, all the other choices are wrong

Q40. **Absolute Pattern 7: Understanding Attitude (Tone) Question**		Got It!	No
Finding tone such as positive-negative, active-passive, mental-physical, subjective-objective.		✓	
Question Pattern: The statement "**such is now**" (**line 6**) serves to indicate the			

A) courage B) anger C) excitement D) forecast **E) urgency**	--Such has been the patient sufferance of these Colonies; and such is now the necessity which constrains them to alter their former Systems of Government. "Such is now" implies the urgency.

SSAT
Verbal Section
Answer Explanations
&
The Pattern Analyses
for Test 1

Test 1 starts with the answer explanations using the Absolute

Patterns. Please understand each question according to the

Patterns before taking test 1

There's no Time Limit for this Practice.

ALL THE LOGIC AND RULES BEHIND EVERY

SINGLE SSAT QUESTION

Test 1 Absolute Patterns for the Analogy Section

Absolute Pattern 5. Degree Pattern
Finding a Degree and a Shape in person, place, thing, and emotion

Q31. D is the Best Answer. Global is bigger than nation as city is to village. (E) is flipped.

Absolute Pattern 1. Category Pattern
Finding Part/Whole, Same Type/Kind, Association

Q32. B is the Best Answer. Wave, mollusk, cliff, and seagull are all found in beach, hence the same nature category. The other choices are not as close as the question.

Absolute Pattern 4. Characteristic Pattern
Finding Characteristic of Person, Place, Object, or Idea and its Associated Action

Q33. A is the Best Answer.
Headache is a short-term illness that comes and goes. On the other hand, cancer is a chronic (constant) pain.

Absolute Pattern 6. Definition Pattern
Finding Definition/Concept of person, place, thing, and emotion

Q34. D is the Best Answer. Bear belongs to Ursine category. Fish belongs to piscine category.
Horse = equine; pig = porcine; cow=bovine; dog=canine

Absolute Pattern 1. Category Pattern
Finding Part/Whole, Same Type/Kind, Association

Q35. B is the Best Answer. Security system (whole) contains video (part), audio (part), and alarm (part)

Absolute Pattern 3. Purpose (Tool) Pattern
Finding Relationships between the Purpose of Individual to Object, to its Function, its User, its Use, and its Association

Q36. D is the Best Answer. Napkin is used in restaurant; tissue is used in toilet.

Absolute Pattern 3. Purpose (Tool) Pattern
Finding Relationships between the Purpose of Individual to Object, to its Function, its User, its Use, and its Association

Q37. A is the Best Answer. Home uses appliance such as refrigerator or washing machine; factory uses machine. (B), (E) are both synonym category. For (C), both parts are the electronics category.

Absolute Pattern 3. Purpose (Tool) Pattern
Finding Relationships between the Purpose of Individual to Object, to its Function, its User, its Use, and its Association

Q38. D is the Best Answer. Defense force protects enemy as screen door protects mosquitoes.

Absolute Pattern 2. Synonym/Antonym
Finding a similar or an opposite meaning between words

Q39. B is the Best Answer. Affluent and prosperous are synonym; sufficient and enough are synonym.

Absolute Pattern 2. Synonym/Antonym
Finding a similar or an opposite meaning between words

Q40. D is the Best Answer.   Censure is an antonym to praise as is cerebral to unintellectual.

Absolute Pattern 3. Purpose (Tool) Pattern
Finding Relationships between the Purpose of Individual to Object, to its Function, its User,
its Use, and its Association

Q41. C is the Best Answer. Dishwasher uses detergent; fire uses oxygen.
(A) is flipped over. (B) is a part-whole pattern.

Absolute Pattern 6. Definition Pattern
Finding Definition/Concept of person, place, thing, and emotion

Q42. A is the Best Answer. Definition question often asks how people think about something or define based on our feeling or emotion. Surgery is characteristically sophisticated. Tea characteristically gives relaxation.

Absolute Pattern 3. Purpose (Tool) Pattern
Finding Relationships between the Purpose of Individual to Object, to its Function, its User,
its Use, and its Association

Q43. A is the Best Answer. Peace treaty is to make peace; commerce is to make money.
(B) is very, very remotely related if not unrelated. (C), (D) are flipped over. (E) is absolutely unrelated.

Absolute Pattern 3. Purpose (Tool) Pattern
Finding Relationships between the Purpose of Individual to Object, to its Function, its User,
its Use, and its Association

Q44. B is the Best Answer. Library is to read as exam is to pass.

Absolute Pattern 4. Characteristic Pattern
Finding Characteristic of Person, Place, Object, or Idea and its Associated Action

Q45. C is the Best Answer. Guerrilla fights in jungle as boxer fights in the ring, the location characteristics.
All the other choices are based on our perception that can't be measured or quantified.

Absolute Pattern 4. Characteristic Pattern
Finding Characteristic of Person, Place, Object, or Idea and its Associated Action

Q46. C is the Best Answer. Kid characteristically shows curiosity. Mother characteristically shows nurture.
(B) is incorrect because betrayal is not the dominant factor in friend. (E) is flipped over.

Absolute Pattern 3. Purpose (Tool) Pattern
Finding Relationships between the Purpose of Individual to Object, to its Function, its User, its Use, and its Association

Q47. C is the Best Answer. The purpose of forum is to give a speech. The purpose of tutoring is to give guidance.

Absolute Pattern 5. Degree Pattern
Finding a Degree and a Shape in person, place, thing, and emotion

Q48. D is the Best Answer. Laugh is greater degree than smile so is Devour than lick.
The others are all synonyms.

Absolute Pattern 5. Degree Pattern
Finding a Degree and a Shape in person, place, thing, and emotion

Q49. D is the Best Answer.   Approximation is greater degree than detail just as is Winter sports than hockey.
The other choices are all flipped over.

Absolute Pattern 5. Degree Pattern
Finding a Degree and a Shape in person, place, thing, and emotion

Q50. E is the Best Answer. This question asks aboutdegree as well as synonyms. Grievance is greater degree than melancholy so as Sad is than moody. They are all synonyms too.
(A), (B) are flipped over in degree pattern. (C), (D) are synonyms only, not following the question category.

Absolute Pattern 5. Degree Pattern
Finding a Degree and a Shape in person, place, thing, and emotion

Q51. D is the Best Answer. Wheel and eye glasses are both round shape, same as (D).
(A) is characteristic pattern. (B) is production pattern.

Absolute Pattern 4. Characteristic Pattern
Finding Characteristic of Person, Place, Object, or Idea and its Associated Action

Q52. D is the Best Answer. Deception is characteristically hidden. Compliment is characteristically exposed.

Absolute Pattern 8. Production Pattern
Finding Cause-and-Effect in Person, Concept, and Object

Q53. C is the Best Answer.
When Angry makes you scream; boredom makes you yawn. (A) and (B) are flipped. (E) is synonym

Absolute Pattern 8. Production Pattern
Finding Cause-and-Effect in Person, Concept, and Object

Q54. C is the Best Answer. Championship player produces lucrative contract. Coach produces strategy.
(A) is flipped. (B) is antonym. (D) is category pattern.

Absolute Pattern 3. Purpose (Tool) Pattern
Finding Relationships between the Purpose of Individual to Object, to its Function, its User, its Use, and its Association

Q55. D is the Best Answer. The purpose of flyer is for sales. The purpose of advertisement is for promotion. (A) is category patterns. (B) is cause-effect pattern. (C) is not the question category or unassociated with the question. (E) is a part-whole pattern.

Absolute Pattern 3. Purpose (Tool) Pattern
Finding Relationships between the Purpose of Individual to Object, to its Function, its User, its Use, and its Association

Q56. B is the Best Answer. Broker earns commission. Waiter earns tip.
They are both human and money related jobs. (A) is purpose category but non-human concept.
(C), (D) are a part-whole patterns. (E) synonyms.

Absolute Pattern 3. Purpose (Tool) Pattern
Finding Relationships between the Purpose of Individual to Object, to its Function, its User, its Use, and its Association

Q57. C is the Best Answer. In nest is egg found so as in web we find prey. (A), (D), and (E) are predator-prey, the category patterns. (B) is same bird category.

Absolute Pattern 1. Category Pattern
Finding Part/Whole, Same Type/Kind, Association

Q58. C is the Best Answer. The question and all five choices are part/whole pattern, which means there's a subdivision within the choices that meets the question category.
River contains fish as (C) ocean contains whale. They are associated with water.
All the other choices are not associated with water.

Absolute Pattern 11. Subjective-Objective Pattern
Finding Quality-Quantity, Tangible-Intangible Association

Q59. C is the Best Answer. The question is objective view with no quantifier.
60 miles per hour is widely accepted a normal speed. (C) air ticket should apply standard price, therefore, objective view. (A) "Jason is to average kid" is personal statement, therefore subjective view.
(B) "40 percent," (D) "100," and (E) "160" are all numeric quantifiers, therefore different from objective view.

Absolute Pattern 11. Subjective-Objective Pattern
Finding Quality-Quantity, Tangible-Intangible Association

Q60. B is the Best Answer. 60 mile per hour is economical and (B) above B is to ideal grade point are all objective view. The other choices all apply numeric quantifiers.

Chapter 1 Summary

The Chapter Summary contains equal portions of

12 Absolute Patterns for Analogy Section and

10 Absolute Patterns for Reading Section.

You may study all at once to significantly

improve your understanding and your scores.

Chapter 1

How SSAT Analogy Section is Created

Jimin: Analogy is really confusing! I sometimes experience brain freeze when I deal with these guys.

San: To improve your score in Analogy, we must first understand how SSAT people actually create the questions! Look at the chart below.

Elementary Level	Middle Level/Upper Level
1. Antonyms	1. Antonyms
2. Synonyms	2. Synonym
3. Degree	3. Degree
4. Part/Whole	4. Part/Whole
5. Characteristic	5. Whole/Part
6. Category	6. Type/Kind
7. Product to Producer	7. Association
8. Uses	8. Cause-Effect
9. Users	9. Function
10. Homonyms	10. Purpose
	11. Defining relationships
	12. Individual to Object
	13. Word
	14. Noun/Verb

Jimin: Wait a minute!

San: I know. I know. You're going to say why we're even looking at the Elementary level while we are studying the Upper level. Right?

San: The reason we're looking at these levels is that they use the identical formats.

The Upper level use different terminologies, but its fundamental concept and the way each question is made are no different at all.

One of the greatest advantages in learning the Foundational level is that it gives us the concrete concept that can greatly improve our understanding with the higher level.

I see there are so many students who are scared of analogy.

Chapter 1

How SSAT Analogy Section is Created

Jimin: If all three levels use the same Analogy patterns, why would they use different names?

San: Good question. Analogy is made of human thoughts, logic, and reasoning that rely heavily on linguistics (the study of language).

San: Because very profound are the principles of human thoughts and, logic, analogy uses scientifically precise terms just like philosophy does, often, very difficult vocabularies.

Elementary Level	Middle Level/Upper Level
1. Antonyms	1. Antonyms
2. Synonyms	2. Synonym
3. Degree	3. Degree
4. Part/Whole	4. Part/Whole
5. Characteristic	5. Whole/Part
6. Category	6. Type/Kind
7. Product to Producer	7. Association
8. Uses	8. Cause-Effect
9. Users	9. Function
10. Homonyms	10. Purpose
	11. Defining relationships
	12. Individual to Object
	13. Word
	14. Noun/Verb

As you can see most analogy patterns are overlapping in all levels.

Jimin: So, you're saying that because the Upper Level is difficult, they use difficult language like philosophy does?
Cool! Then, are all SSAT creators profound philosophers?

San: Highly doubt that! Some say they have a tendency to think very, very hard for simple matters like analogy. For instance, they separate Part/Whole from Whole/Part because they think they are different. How they are different?

Chapter 1

How SSAT Analogy Section is Created

San: Now, let's take a look how each analogy and its basic concept is working.

Elementary Level

Antonyms: expensive is to cheap as cold is to hot

Explanation: expensive is an antonym to cheap as cold is an antonym to hot

Synonyms: man is to male as feeling is emotion

Explanation: man is a synonym to male as feeling is a synonym to emotion

Characteristic: beaver is to build as bee is to sting

Explanation: beaver has a characteristic of building dam as bee has a characteristic of sting.

Homonyms: sand is to sandwich as sunny is to sun.

Explanation: sand and sandwich make the same sound as sunny and sun make the same sound.

Degree: dime is to cent as kilogram is to gram.

Explanation:: dime is greater than cent as kilogram is greater than gram.

Part/Whole tire is to car as keypad is to cell phone

Explanation: tire is a part of car as keypad is a part of cell phone

Category: chicken is to bird as bear is to mammal

Explanation: chicken belongs to bird category as bear belongs to mammal category.

Product to Producer: pig is to bacon as chicken is to egg

Explanation: pig produces bacon as chicken produces egg.

Uses: knife is to cut as hammer is to pound

Explanation: we use knife to cut as we use hammer to pound.

Users: professor is to projector as student is to paper

Explanation: professor uses projector as student uses paper.

Chapter 1

How SSAT Analogy Section is Created

Middle/Upper Level

Defining relationships: chef is to meal as plumber is to water pipe.
Explanation: The job of chef is to make meal as the job of plumber is to fix water pipe.

Type/Kind: poetry is to reading as whisky is to drink
Explanation: poetry is a type of reading as whisky is a type of drink.

Whole/Part: car is to tire as cell phone is to speaker.
Explanation:: car includes a tire as cell phone includes a speaker.

Word: fly is to flew as go is to went
Explanation: flew is the past tense of fly as went is the past tense of go

Noun/Verb: dance is to dancer as sing is to singer
Explanation: dancer dances as singer sings.

Individual to Object: professor is to projector as student is to paper
Explanation: professor uses a projector as student uses a paper

Function: knife is to cut as hammer is to pound
Explanation: we use a knife to cut as we use hammer to pound.

Cause-Effect: pig is to bacon as chicken is to egg
Explanation: we raise pig for bacon as we raise chicken for egg

Purpose: bike is to ride as radio is to listen
Explanation: The purpose of bike is to ride as the purpose of radio is to listen

Association: chameleon is to change as skunk is to odor
Explanation: chameleon is known to change its skin colors for protection as skunk is known to use its odor for protection.

The Absolute Patterns for Analogy summary continues in the following chapters.

UNAUTHORIZED COPYING OR REUSE OF ANY PART OF THIS PAGE IS ILLEGAL

Chapter 1

10 Absolute Patterns for the Reading Section

San: Do you know one of the worst mistakes that you make while solving the reading questions, Jimin?

Jimin: I know. Before I select the wrong choice, I should have fired the SSAT guys who created such a dumb question. That's one of my worst mistakes!

San: You should understand the question type by separating into two main parts: the pattern and the keywords.

Question Pattern never changes in the actual test, while the keywords make the each question unique. The keywords are boldfaced ones in the explanation section.

	Got It!	No
Q28. Absolute Pattern 2: Summary Question **Question Pattern:** The discussion of **accidents in Minnesota** (line 8) primarily suggests that	✓	

A) Minnesota is typically susceptible to black ice **B) only at above 18 °C can salt prevent such multiple accidents** C) black ice is more visible in Minnesota D) we know very little about the characteristics of black ice E) typical black ice causes multiple accidents	**salt (sodium chloride) is effective to down temperatures of about −18 °C (0 °F). At below −18 °** Such conditions caused multiple <u>accidents in Minnesota</u> when the temperatures dipped below −18 °C

Question Pattern is the main frame of the question, and the frame never changes. The number of these unchanging question patterns is very limited. In fact, there are only 10 of them. These patterns will appear in your test by slightly modifying some words-if not exactly written as shown in this book.

By understanding these 10 patterns, several advantages will reward you:

√ you will be familiar with tricky terms within the question so that you can save time in the actual test.

√ you will be able to guess what the question is basically seeking even without reading the passage.

√ you can avoid possible confusion or mistakes such as "EXCEPT" questions.

Question Keywords are the most important words in the question.

Test creators look for keywords from the passage and then plug the keywords into the question patterns to create each question.

The most common question keywords in the reading passage and the question are nouns and verbs.

<u>Adjectives and adverbs seldom provide answer</u>, although they provide some clues for the answer such as "always," "only."

Chapter 1

10 Absolute Patterns for the Reading Section

Category A: Content Question has five patterns:

San: The entire 40 questions in the reading section, both literary and informational passages, can be categorized into two parts:
Category A: Content Question;
Category B: Technique Question

10 Absolute Patterns—mostly one pattern per question —plus incorrect patterns will be absolutely the most effective and systemic way to improve your scores.

Jimin: I sometimes don't even understand the meaning of the question.

San: Your humble vocabulary could be one of the two reasons. Email me: satvancouver@gmail.com
I will give you the FREE SSAT ABSOLUTE Vocabulary with a picture book.

Category A: Content Question has five patterns:

▶ **Absolute Pattern 2: Summary Question**
Summarizing a sentence, or entire passage

▶ **Absolute Pattern 4: Example Question**
Finding the true purpose behind a specific name or idea within a sentence

▶ **Absolute Pattern 5: Word-In-Context Question**
Finding a clue word and the keyword from the sentence in question

▶ **Absolute Pattern 8: Understanding the True Purpose**
Finding the true purpose of statement

▶ **Absolute Pattern 9: Relationships Question**
Finding relationships between the cause-effect, comparison-contrast, characters, and ideas

Chapter 1

10 Absolute Patterns for the Reading Section

Category A: Content Question has five patterns:

San: The Content question may also be called the local question.
Either with the line reference number (i.e., line 5) or without it, the content question normally asks localized, detailed information from only one or two sentences in the passage.

The question may ask explicitly stated keywords in the sentences, or, in more complex level, implicitly analogous (similar) situations within a sentence.

San: Neither of the cases requires the holistic understanding of the entire passage. Reading only the target sentence will save your precious time and mental horsepower. Now. Let's talk about the Content Question Patterns.

Absolute Pattern 2: Summary Question

The basic technique to find the answer is almost the same as pattern 1: Main Idea Question.
The major difference, however, —especially in the literary passage—can be seen in its focusing on the manner of voice, tone, and style of the sentence.

In literary passage, the answer often carries more subjective words, such as "criticize", "emphatic", "celebrate."

The summary question in the informational passage (Science, History, Social) is quite similar to the main idea question in that they both tend to apply broad and neutral tone in the keywords. That is, informational passage does not carry emotional tone like "blame," "criticize," or "celebrates." Instead, it uses "approve" or disapprove." Also, the Summary question in the Informational passage relies heavily on the introduction and the conclusion. In the Informational, don't forget to re-read the introduction and conclusion sentence.

The Absolute Patterns for Reading summary continues in the following chapters.

SSAT
Reading & Verbal
Test 1

Inside Test 1 will you see the exactly same questions that you've just finished.

Your goal is to get 100 percent with the crystal clear logic behind each question.

Test 1 Reading Section
Time: 40 Minutes, 40 Questions

Directions: Each reading passage is followed by questions about it. Answer the questions that follow a passage on the basis of what is stated or implied in that passage.

Questions 1-6 are based on the following passage.

Line

The family of Dashwood had long been settled in Sussex, where, for many generations, they had lived in so respectable a manner as to engage the general good opinion of their surrounding acquaintance. The old Dashwood was a single man, who lived to a very advanced age, and who for many years of his life, had a constant companion and housekeeper in his sister.

5   But her death, which happened ten years before his own, produced a great alteration in his home; for to supply her loss, he invited and received into his house the family of his nephew Mr. Henry Dashwood, the legal inheritor of the Norland estate, and the person to whom he intended to bequeath it. But by his own marriage Mr. Henry added to his wealth. To him therefore the succession to the Norland estate was not so really important as to his Sisters, and could be but small.

10   He was neither so unjust, nor so ungrateful, as to leave his estate to Mr. Henry Dashwood on such terms as destroyed half the value of the bequest to his Sisters.

1

According to paragraph 2 (lines 5-9), the old Dashwood invited Mr. Henry Dashwood for

A) he had a contemptuous feeling to Mr. Henry
B) Mr. Henry had some financial issue
C) he had more than one reason
D) he needed to repent his wrongdoings
E) Mr. Henry was still single

2

All of the following correctly describe the Old Dashwood EXCEPT

A) he lived in the parents' house
B) his family was well respected from the neighbors
C) he did not have a wife
D) he lived all alone as a single man
E) he wanted to be grateful as he leaves his estate

3

To Mr. Henry, the succession to the Norland estate mentioned in line 8 was

A) significant
B) a gift to strengthen distinctive family tie
C) important to satisfy his greed
D) a seed of foreboding family feud
E) insignificant

4

The primary purpose of the passage is to

A) define a legal custom related to inheritance
B) emphasize the benefits of having good neighbors
C) introduce the settings of the story
D) show a prolonged family feud
E) betray cunning tricks of Mr. Henry Dashwood

5

It can be inferred from the passage that the "Sisters" in line 9

A) had amassed great wealth
B) had some difficulties with the Old Dashwood
C) were not the legal inheritors
D) brought joy to the family
E) were preferred inheritors to Mr. Henry Dashwood

6

It can be inferred from lines 10-11 that in his will, the Old Dashwood tried to?

A) balance and appease every heir
B) condescend every heir
C) earn profits from every heir
D) defend his estate from every heir
E) remove Mr. Henry from his family

Questions 7-12 are based on the following passage.

Line

Brain Research through Advancing Innovative Neurotechnologies (BRAIN) Initiative has the potential to do for neuroscience what the Human Genome Project did for genomics by supporting the development and application of innovative technologies that can create a dynamic understanding of brain function. It aims to help researchers uncover the <u>mysteries</u> of brain disorders, such as Alzheimer's and Parkinson's diseases.
5   These technologies will shed light on the complex links between brain function and behavior. <u>While these technological innovations have contributed substantially to our expanding knowledge of the brain,</u> significant breakthroughs in how we treat neurological and psychiatric disease will require a new generation of tools to enable researchers to record signals from brain cells in much greater numbers and at even faster speeds. That's where the BRAIN Initiative comes in.   <u>A Scientific Vision</u>, which articulates the
10   scientific goals of The BRAIN Initiative at the NIH charts a multi-year scientific plan for achieving these goals, including timetables, milestones, and cost estimates. and focused effort across the agency.

7

The primary purpose of the BRAIN Initiative is to help researchers

A) advance Human Genome Project
B) understand brain function and disorder
C) sequence the human genome
D) develop better human brain
E) develop medicines for brain disorder

8

The "mysteries" in line 4 implies that at the current stage, the research of brain disorders

A) is dynamically improving
B) is expected to be unlocked pretty soon
C) is still at understanding level
D) requires huge financial support
E) has seen mysterious breakthrough recently

9

The author mentions Human Genome project mainly to
A) celebrates what it did to genomics
B) compare what BRAIN Initiative can do to neuroscience
C) introduce neurotechnology
D) present complexity of neurotechnolgy
E) present achievement of BRAIN Initiative

10

The author uses the phrase "While these...brain," (lines 6-7) to make which of the following points?
A) BRAIN Initiatives is even more pivotal
B) BRAIN Initiative may succeed without these technological innovations
C) These technological innovations are outmoded
D) These technological innovations are beyond our understanding
E) These technological innovations are role models

11

In line 9, the author mentions "A Scientific Vision" mainly to
A) present scientific goals of the BRAIN Initiative
B) voice doubt about its undertaking
C) raise over-budget issue in a single project
D) celebrate goals of BRAIN that are achieved
E) acclaim efforts made by the agency

12

Which of the following objectives is committed by BRAIN Initiative
I. Multi-year scientific plan for the Working Group
I. Financial estimates for the research
II. Developing medicines for the brain disorder
A) I only
B) II only
C) III only
D) I and II only
E) I, II, and III

Questions 13-17 are based on the following passage.

Line

The United Kingdom European Union membership referendum took place on Thursday 23 June 2016 in the United Kingdom to gauge support for the country's continued membership in the European Union. The referendum result was not legally binding. The result was split with the constituent countries of the United Kingdom, with a majority in England and Wales voting to leave, and a majority in Scotland voting to remain.

5   To start the process to leave the EU, which is expected to take several years, the British government will have to invoke Article 50 of the Treaty on European Union.   The UK government has announced formal process of leaving the EU although revoking the vote might be possible. Britain Stronger in Europe was the official group campaigning for the UK to remain in the EU and was led by the Prime Minister David Cameron.

10   Other campaign groups, political parties, businesses, trade unions, newspapers and prominent individuals were also involved, and each side had supporters from across the political spectrum.

13

The phrase "not legally binding" (line 3) implies that
A) there's a theoretical fallacy with the
       referendum result
B) the referendum was in fact for an entertainment
C) there's a final Article 50 confirmation waiting
D) such a revolutionary process itself requires
       no legality
E) the referendum should be held once more

14

Which of the following phrases directly undermines the result of referendum?
A) to gauge support (line 2)
B) not legally binding (line 3)
C) split with the constituent countries (line 3)
D) England and Wales voting to leave (line 4)
E) Scotland voting to remain (line 4)

15

The geographical reference in lines 3-4 (The result… voting to remain) serves to underscore
A) different customs among the United Kingdom
B) contradictions to the referendum
C) essentially unified voice to the referendum
D) countries that traditionally supported EU
E) countries that traditionally disfavored EU

16

"Article 50" mentioned in line 6 would probably contain
A) compilations of EU countries' population statistics
B) sources of formal treaty to disjoin EU
C) studies of UK's trade projection with EU
D) analyses of Referendum results
E) measurements of EU countries' wealth

17

After the referendum result, the British government needs to undergo a process of
A) disjoining treaty with EU
B) referendum cancelation
C) announcement for immediate leaving EU
D) official campaign for rejoining EU
E) dividing economic spectrum from the politics

Questions 18-23 are based on the following passage.

Line

No man can fully grasp how far and how fast we have come, but condense, if you will, the 50,000 years of man's recorded history in a time span of but a half-century. Stated in these terms, we know very little about the first 40 years, except at the end of them advanced man had learned to use the skins of animals to cover them. Then, only last week did we develop television, and now if America's new spacecraft succeeds in
5 reaching Venus, we will have literally reached the stars before midnight tonight.

This is a breathtaking pace, and such a pace cannot help but create new ills as it dispels old, new ignorance, new problems, new dangers. Surely the opening vistas of space promise high costs and hardships, as well as high reward. So it is not surprising that some would have us stay where we are a little longer to rest, to wait.

But why, some say, the moon? We choose to go to the moon not because they are easy, but because they are
10 hard. We have seen facilities greatest and most complex exploration in man's history: Saturn C-1 booster rocket, generating power equivalent to 10,000 automobiles, the F-1 rocket engines, each one as powerful as all eight engines of the Saturn combined, Saturn missile as tall as a 48 story structure, as wide as a city block.

But if I were to say, my fellow citizens, that we shall send to the moon and then return it safely to earth, re-entering the atmosphere at speeds of over 25,000 miles per hour, causing heat about half that of the
15 temperature of the sun--almost as hot as it is here today. I'm the one who is doing all the work, so we just want you to stay cool for a minute.

18

In his speech, "but condense 50,000...before midnight tonight," Kennedy alludes to the audience
A) a support the space program
B) a precondition for public approval of the program
C) reasons for the low level of public awareness
D) some limitations that block space program
E) major assignments during his incumbency

19

In lines 6-8, Kennedy mentions despite of rapid advancement in space program certain obstacles should be overcome EXCEPT
A) demand from some people to delay the project
B) ignorance due to lack of information
C) high expenditure
D) restrictive government policy
E) hardships

20

In lines 10-12 (We have seen...a city block), Kennedy mainly describes the space project's
A) undeterred persistence
B) immensity
C) probable challenges
D) impact on society
E) contribution to the community in Texas

21

In line 9, "But why, some say, the moon?" President Kennedy makes which of the following assumptions?
A) The progress must be made in small, gradual steps
B) Had we tried earlier, the Moon would have been conquered already
C) We must welcome challenges
D) With the right equipment and audacity, any nations can tap the untried mission
E) With our effort, we will soon conquer the universe

22

The tone of Kennedy in line 15 (so we just...for a minute) is
A) anger
B) humorous
C) didactic
D) profound
E) irate

23

The primary purpose of the first paragraph (lines 1-5) is to
A) show some of the impressive scientific achievement in human history
B) show human history through condensed time
C) introduce speaker's main speech
D) explain the importance of history study
E) educate some dramatic history to the audience

Questions 24-29 are based on the following passage.

Line

Black ice, sometimes called clear ice, refers to a thin coating of glaze ice on a surface, especially on roads. The ice itself is not black, but visually transparent, allowing the often black road below to be seen through it.

The typically low level of noticeable ice pellets, snow means that areas of the ice are often practically invisible to drivers stepping on it. There is, thus, a risk of skidding and subsequent accidents due to the

5 unexpected loss of traction. Black ice is formed on relatively dry roads, rendering it invisible to drivers. Deicing with salt (sodium chloride) is effective to down temperatures of about −18 °C (0 °F).

At below −18 °C, black ice can form on roadways when the moisture from automobile exhaust condenses on the road surface. Such conditions caused multiple accidents in Minnesota when the temperatures dipped below −18 °C for a prolonged period of time in December 2008. With salt's ineffectiveness at melting ice at

10 these temperatures compounds the problem. Black ice may form even when the ambient temperature is several degrees above the freezing point of water 0 °C (32 °F), if the air warms suddenly after a prolonged cold spell that has left the surface of the roadway well below the freezing point temperature.

24

The passage describes that black ice makes drivers more difficult because

A) black road below the ice freezes

B) of snow compaction

C) of its transparency

D) of unexpected accidents

E) of unexpected loss of traction

25

All of the following are referred to as the characteristics of black ice EXCEPT

A) it causes sudden traction issues while driving

B) it is often invisible to drivers

C) its black pigment absorbs the surface heat faster

D) it is also dubbed as clear ice

E) it covers the thin road surface

26

What caused the significant multiple accidents in Minnesota in line 8?

A) the low temperature

B) salt

C) excessive moisture on roads

D) reckless driving

E) standing water

27

The paragraph 3 (lines 7-12) indicates that one of the difficulties in dealing with black ice is that it

A) should not be treated with salt

B) increases road surface temperature

C) turns snow into water

D) may form even in mild weather

E) forms even when weather is below −18 °C

28

The discussion of accidents in Minnesota (line 8) primarily suggests that

A) Minnesota is typically susceptible to black ice

B) only at above 18 °C can salt prevent such multiple accidents

C) black ice is more visible in Minnesota

D) we know very little about the characteristics of black ice

E) typical black ice causes multiple accidents

29

Which of the following areas would most likely be affected by black ice accident?

A) open roads in Hawaii during rainy seasons

B) mountain regions in Alaska covered with perennial snow

C) dangerously spiraling hiking tracks in Utah

D) humid coastal highways in Florida

E) cold and dry bridges in British Columbia

Questions 30-35 are based on the following passage.

Line

Many scientists believe we are not alone in the universe. It's probable that life could rise on at least some of the billions of planets thought to exist in our galaxy alone just as it did here on planet Earth.

This basic question about our place in the Universe is one that may be answered by scientific investigations. Experts from NASA addressed this question at a public talk held at NASA Headquarters. They outlined
5 NASA's roadmap to the search for life in the universe. In the near future, people will be able to point to a star and say, 'that star has a planet like Earth'," says Sara Seager, the professor at Harvard. However, the impression of how common planets are in the Milky way adversely creates backlash among scientists. NASA's quest to study planetary systems around other stars started with ground-based observatories, then moved to Hubble
10 Space Telescope. Today's telescopes can look at many stars and tell if they have one or more orbiting planets. But it can't determine if the planets are the right distance away from the star to have liquid water [QUESTION]

30

The passage suggests that many scientists' belief in line 1 is based on

A) professional speculation
B) investigated conviction
C) personal intuition
D) ongoing survey
E) determination from the history

31

Which of the following statements is analogous to "many scientists' belief" in lines 1-2

A) a rebellion will occur soon because it occurred ten years ago
B) many ISIS members will be disillusioned just as were some members
C) our company can't find hope this quarter because the new boss is lousy
D) biologists deny microbes 100 meters beneath the earth surface just as they do to 200 meters
E) the island will grow orange because similar island grows orange

32

"This basic question" in line 3 directly refers to

A) the history of universe
B) the civilizations of the earth
C) the evolutionary condition similar to the earth
D) the number of planets in our galaxy
E) the accuracy of scientific investigations

33

It can be inferred that the upcoming future telescopes would probably focus on finding

A) the orbiting planetary systems that measure the right distance to have liquid
B) the living things like us
C) any planets in universe
D) only the orbiting planets in our galaxy
E) any inhabitable planets exactly look like the earth

34

Which of the following phrases would the author add after the last sentence "to have liquid water"?

A) that can be the key ingredient to life
B) that invalidates scientists' previous theory
C) that puzzles our knowledge about universe
D) that explains the origin of the universe
E) that supports other forms do not require water

35

The passage primary describes

A) a well-known theory of life in the universe
B) the reasons some planets are inhabitable
C) mysterious universe
D) searching for life in our galaxy
E) statistical analysis of similar planets in the solar system

Questions 36-40 are based on the following passage.

Line

5

We hold these truths to be <u>self-evident</u>, that all men are created equal, that they are endowed by their Creator with certain <u>unalienable Rights,</u> that among these are Life, Liberty, and the pursuit of Happiness. That to secure these rights, Governments are instituted among Men, But when a long train of abuses and usurpations, pursuing invariably the same Object evinces a design to reduce them under absolute <u>Despotism</u>, it is their right, it is their duty, to throw off such Government, and to provide new Guards for their future security.

Such has been the patient sufferance of these Colonies; and <u>such is now </u>the necessity which constrains them to alter their former Systems of Government.

36

The phrase "self-evident" in line 1 can be understood that some truths are

A) beyond our judgment
B) morally perfect
C) beyond the political interpretation
D) open-ended debate
E) determined by ourselves

37

The unalienable Rights in line 2 include all of the following EXCEPT

A) Right to establish sovereign government
B) Right to live a life
C) Right to pursue happiness
D) Equal Right
E) Right to enjoy freedom

38

The author defines that the government

A) has the absolute power above all men
B) is instituted to secure the rights of all men
C) is created by God
D) should not reduce its power
E) can do whatever to protect the life of the citizen.

39

The author's attitude to "Despotism" in line 4 is best described as

A) admiration
B) appreciation
C) enthusiasm
D) warning
E) necessity

40

The statement "such is now" (line 6) serves to indicate the

A) courage
B) anger
C) excitement
D) forecast
E) urgency

Test 1 Verbal Section   30 MINUTES, 60 QUESTIONS

Directions: the synonym questions ask you to find the most appropriate synonym to the question.

The analogy questions ask you to find the most appropriate analogy to the question.
Select the answer that best matches to the question.

Synonym Sample Question:

Q: SUPERIOR

A higher rank

B inferior

C considerable

D supermarket

E supper

A) is the best answer because the synonym for superior is higher rank.

B) is incorrect because it applies the 'opposite concept.

C) and E) are irrelevant words.

D) is incorrect because it applies physical concept to mental concept

---

Test 1 Synonym questions 1 to 30

1. ACQUIESCE
(A) accept
(B) acquire
(C) quiet
(D) account
(E) acquisition

2. VIGOR
(A) victory
(B) strength
(C) model
(D) gorgeous
(E) great

3. PINNACLE
(A) fruit
(B) paint
(C) clever
(D) peak
(E) sharp

4. CITADEL
(A) tired
(B) delegate
(C) fortress
(D) city
(E) town

5. OMINOUS
(A) onion
(B) forbidding
(C) vocabulary
(D) agree
(E) manner

6. FRENZY

(A) easy

(B) fire

(C) fury

(D) freelance

(E) friend

7. ACRID

(A) harsh

(B) arcane

(C) agree

(D) accept

(E) accordance

8. VITAL

(A) vibration

(B) talent

(C) energetic

(D) state

(E) vision

9. TRANQUIL

(A) noise

(B) peace

(C) train

(D) automobile

(E) people

10. SYMBOL

(A) representation

(B) simple

(C) abnormal

(D) signature

(E) similarity

11. SHUN

(A) sun

(B) avoid

(C) wait

(D) sign

(E) copy

12. RESTORE

(A) fix

(B) shop

(C) make

(D) produce

(E) repeat

13. ADAMANT

(A) stubborn

(B) flexible

(C) address

(D) mantle

(E) adage

14. ADHERENT

(A) follower

(B) place

(C) inflexible

(D) advice

(E) addition

15. MOCK

(A) make fun of

(B) test

(C) modify

(D) mode

(E) pain

16. COLLABORATE

(A) university
(B) labor
(C) work together
(D) union
(E) toothpaste

17. FALTER

(A) pause
(B) palpitate
(C) parent
(D) continue
(E) fable

18. ADMONISH

(A) chastise
(B) teach
(C) add
(D) demonstrate
(E) monster

19. SOBER

(A) wet
(B) not drunk
(C) animal
(D) accept
(E) base

20. SURGE

(A) supplement
(B) surrogate
(C) upwelling
(D) doctor
(E) certificate

21. DRASTIC

(A) easy going
(B) draconian
(C) extreme
(D) design
(E) down

22. DISPLACE

(A) habitat
(B) get rid of
(C) relocation
(D) dance
(E) fix

23. SOMBER

(A) sad
(B) joy
(C) hate
(D) argue
(E) someday

24. ADROIT

(A) dexterous
(B) unskillful
(C) difficult
(D) add
(E) itinerary

25. ADULATION

(A) reintroduction
(B) praise
(C) deny
(D) boring
(E) refrain

26. STUBBORN

(A) obstinate

(B) yielding

(C) idea

(D) state

(E) strategy

27. UNIFORM

(A) vary

(B) dress

(C) official

(D) even

(E) colorful

28. OFFENSIVE

(A) defensive

(B) propensity

(C) belligerent

(D) skillful

(E) protect

29. TOXIC

(A) poisonous

(B) alcoholic

(C) transported

(D) excite

(E) healing

30. PRECISE

(A) exact

(B) loosen

(C) deviant

(D) similar

(E) cut

Analogy Sample Question:

Q: River is to Ocean as:

A better is to good

B rain is to cloud

C father is to mother

D city is to country

E fork is to spoon

D is the correct answer. Just as the river is smaller than the Ocean, the city is smaller than the country. The pattern applied in this question is the Degree Pattern (small to big)

A) is incorrect because the word order is flipped over.

B) is incorrect because it applies the production pattern (cloud produces rain) C),

E) are incorrect because they apply the Antonym patterns.

Test 1 Analogy questions 31 to 60

31. Global is to nation as

(A) street is to road

(B) passenger is to passerby

(C) universal is to one world

(D) city is to village

(E) city is to state

32. Wave is to mollusk as

(A) snorkeling is to swim vest

(B) cliff is to seagull

(C) oxygen tank is to goggle

(D) boat is to canoe

(E) kayak is to hotel

33. Headache is to cancer as chronic is to

(A) short term

(B) pills

(C) prescription

(D) pain

(E) stress

34. Ursine is to bear as piscine as

(A) horse

(B) pig

(C) cow

(D) fish

(E) canine

35. Security system is to video as

(A) protection is to hotel lounge

(B) audio is to alarm

(C) security guard is to traveling

(D) surveillance system is to maid

(E) police is to chef

36. Napkin is to toilet as tissue is

(A) paper

(B) wipe

(C) meal

(D) restaurant

(E) shelf

37. Appliance is to factory as

(A) home is to machinery

(B) step is to process

(C) T.V. is to radio

(D) automation is to security

(E) hacking is to attack

38. Enemy is to defense force as

(A) onslaught is to anxiety

(B) first-aid is to paramedic

(C) honor is to hero

(D) mosquitoes is screen door

(E) battle is to intervention

39. Affluent is to prosperous as sufficient is to

(A) rich

(B) enough

(C) vary

(D) suffering

(E) suffuse

40. Censure is to praise as

(A) criticize is to warn

(B) stigmatize is to disgrace

(C) acclaim is to claim

(D) cerebral is to unintellectual

(E) condemn is to blame

41. Dishwasher is to detergent as

(A) steam is to steam engine

(B) kitchen is to refrigerator

(C) fire is to oxygen

(D) love is to friendship

(E) cleaning is to floor

42. Surgery is to sophistication as
(A) tea is to relaxation
(B) grade 1 math is to complexity
(C) rocket science is to effortless
(D) ecosystem is to random
(E) capital punishment is to simplicity

43. Peace treaty is to peace as
(A) commerce is to money
(B) war is to politics
(C) reflect is to mirror
(D) breath is to air
(E) morality is to god

44. Exam is to library as read is to
(A) identify
(B) pass
(C) fail
(D) wise
(E) succeed

45. Guerrilla is to jungle as
(A) terrorist is to scary
(B) military is to destructive
(C) boxer is to ring
(D) market is to noise
(E) shop is to busy

46. Kid is to curiosity as
(A) friend is to betrayal
(B) enemy is to forgiveness
(C) mother is to nurture
(D) nature is to imagination
(E) comfort is to bed

47. Forum is to tutoring as
(A) play ground is to stadium
(B) mic is to facility
(C) guidance is to speech
(D) play is to rule
(E) crowd is to friend

48. Laugh is to smile as
(A) whimper is to whine
(B) foot is to paw
(C) claw is to nail
(D) devour is to lick
(E) cub is to baby

49. Approximation is to detail as
(A) solar system is to universe
(B) moon is to sun
(C) Los Angeles is to California
(D) winter sports is to hockey
(E) waltz is to dance

50. Grievance is to melancholy as
(A) shoplifting is to murder
(B) decline is to extinction
(C) reduction is to decrease
(D) increment is to amplification
(E) sadness is to moody

51. Wheel is to eye glasses as
(A) sugar is to sweet
(B) anniversary is to memento
(C) vehicle is to seatbelt
(D) moon is to earth
(E) rubber is to plastic

52. Deception is to hidden as
(A) hard work is to success
(B) saving is to rich
(C) pilgrimage is to religious
(D) compliment is to expose
(E) duplicity is to reveal

53. Scream is to angry as
(A) training is to exhaustion
(B) sleeping is to restoration
(C) yawn is to boredom
(D) love is to friendly
(E) gossip is to rumor

54. Championship player is to lucrative contract as
(A) final is to semifinal
(B) defending champ is to opponent
(C) coach is to strategy
(D) team is to captain
(E) quarterback is to injury

55. Flyer is to sales as
(A) salesman is to job
(B) defect is to fix
(C) hunting is to animal
(D) advertisement is to promotion
(E) school is to teacher

56. Broker is to tip as
(A) company is to stock
(B) waiter is to commission
(C) country is to government
(D) music is to melody
(E) tale is to story

57. Nest is to egg as
(A) cat is to mouse
(B) chicken is to duck
(C) web is to prey
(D) lion is to zebra
(E) tiger is to wild hog

58. River is to fish as
(A) factory worker is to worker
(B) car is to passenger
(C) ocean is to whale
(D) jungle is to banana
(E) bakery is to bread

59. 60 miles is to normal speed as
(A) Jason is to average kid
(B) income tax is to 40 percent
(C) air ticket is to standard price
(D) 32 Celsius is to 100 Fahrenheit
(E) 100 miles is to 160km

60. 60 mile per hour is economical as
(A) 100 pound per sack is to ten super-sack
(B) above B is to ideal grade point
(C) 100 degree is to optimum boiling point
(D) 100 years old is one centennial
(E) 1 dollar is ten dimes

TEST 1
READING SECTION

Please refer to the Reading Section Absolute Pattern Analyses

THE SYNONYM QUESTIONS TEST 1 NO.1 ~ 30		THE ANALOGY QUESTIONS TEST 1 NO. 31 ~ 60

Please refer to the Analogy Section Absolute Pattern Analyses

1	A	16	C
2	B	17	A
3	D	18	A
4	C	19	B
5	B	20	C
6	C	21	C
7	A	22	C
8	C	23	A
9	B	24	A
10	A	25	B
11	B	26	A
12	A	27	D
13	A	28	C
14	A	29	A
15	A	30	A

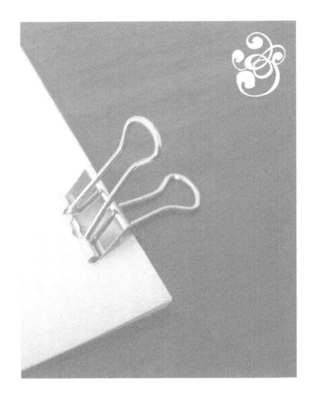

Chapter 2

1. TEST 2

2. ANSWER EXPLANATIONS for TEST 2

3. CHAPTER SUMMARY

SSAT
Reading & Verbal
Test 2

This chapter starts with the Actual Test 2

Your goal is not getting good enough scores, but 100%

It's your book

It's up to you to practice the Answer Explanations

and the Patterns first

UNAUTHORIZED COPYING OR REUSE OF ANY PART OF THIS PAGE IS ILLEGAL

Test 2 Reading Section
Time: 40 Minutes, 40 Questions

Directions: Each reading passage is followed by questions about it. Answer the questions that follow a passage on the basis of what is stated or implied in that passage.

Questions 1-9 are based on the following passage.

Line

   Greenhouse gas concentrations in the atmosphere will continue to increase unless the billions of annual tons decrease substantially. Increased concentrations are expected to increase Earth's average temperature, influence the patterns and amounts of precipitation, reduce ice and snow cover, as well as permafrost, raise sea level, and increase the acidity of the oceans. Temperature increases and other climate changes may directly
5 impact our food and water supply, ecosystems, coasts, and human health. The magnitude and rate of future climate change will primarily depend on many uncertain factors.
   Among many noted estimates, the IPCC's "SRES" scenarios have been frequently used to foresee future climate change. The SRES scenarios are "baseline" scenarios, which means that the current or future measures that limit GHG emissions are not to be rigidly defined. Emissions projections of the SRES scenarios are
10 widely comparable in range to the baseline emissions that have been developed by the scientific community.
   Many greenhouse gases stay in the atmosphere for long periods of time. As a result, even if emissions stopped increasing, atmospheric greenhouse gas concentrations would continue to increase and remain elevated for hundreds of years. This is because the oceans, which store heat, take many decades to fully respond to higher greenhouse gas concentrations.

1

Greenhouse gas concentration increase may cause all of the following EXCEPT

A) oceans' acidity level increase
B) sea level increase
C) snow cover reduction
D) altering the precipitation patterns
E) average temperature drop

2

Climate changes due to greenhouse gas may directly impact on all of the following EXCEPT

A) coasts
B) ecosystems
C) water supply
D) human health
E) the IPCC's SRES

3

The author introduces IPCC's "SRES" in line 7 as scenarios with

A) a mere projection
B) definite figures to follow
C) the only available model
D) unreliable estimation
E) widely accepted facts with accuracy

4

The author uses quotations in the word "baseline" in line 8 in order to emphasize that

A) the SRES is only the reference
B) the SRES should be strictly observed
C) GHG emission level should not be considered
D) GHG emission level should be the foundational scenario
E) the SRES should be abandoned

5

In the first paragraph (lines 1-6) the author defines the magnitude and the rate of future climate should be contingent on

A) divine will

B) ocean sea level

C) various uncertain factors

D) the government policies

E) acidity level in the oceans

6

The author's primary tone in line 11-13 (Many greenhouse gases...hundreds of years.) is one of

A) pessimistic

B) optimistic

C) futuristic

D) fantastic

E) fascinated

7

It can be inferred that if we stabilize and gradually reduce current greenhouse gas emission, surface air temperatures will

A) soon cool down

B) slowly cool down

C) spike with great magnitude

D) continue to warm

E) not to be known at present

8

The word "comparable" in line 10 most nearly means

A) applicable

B) limited

C) compatible

D) available

E) unavailable

9

According to the 3rd paragraph (lines 11-13), the main cause for the unresponsive greenhouse gas concentrations is due to

A) the characteristics of precipitation

B) the characteristics of the oceans

C) the characteristics of the earth

D) the characteristics of human

E) the characteristics of seasons

Questions 10-15 are based on the following passage.

Line

Emma Woodhouse was the youngest of the two daughters. Her mother had died too long ago for her to have more than an indistinct remembrance of her caresses; and her place had been supplied by an excellent woman as governess, who had fallen little short of a mother in affection. Sixteen years had Miss Taylor been in Mr. Woodhouse's family, less as a governess than a friend. Between *them* it was more the intimacy of sisters.

5   The real evils, indeed, of Emma's situation were the power of having rather too much her own way, and a disposition to think a little too well of herself; these were the disadvantages which threatened alloy to her many enjoyments.   Sorrow came--a happy sorrow. Miss Taylor married. It was on the wedding-day of this beloved friend that Emma first sat in mournful thought of any continuance. The want of Miss Taylor would be felt every hour of every day. She recalled her past kindness--the kindness--how she had taught and how she had played

10 with her from five years old—how she had devoted all her powers to attach and amuse her in health-and how nursed her through the various illnesses of childhood. A large debt of gratitude was owing here followed Isabella's marriage, on their being left to each other, was yet a dearer, tenderer recollection.

10

The relationship between Emma's family and Miss Taylor can be best summarized as that

A) Miss Taylor had been in romantic relations with Emma's father

B) Miss Taylor had a genuinely condescending view on Emma

C) Miss Taylor had a strong affinity to Emma

D) Miss Taylor had been a subservient governess

E) Emma and Miss Taylor shared no same affection

11

Which of the following examples is most analogous to Emma's character described in lines 5-7?

A) A girl bragging her cooking skills messes up the kitchen

B) A pizza delivery man grateful for a big tip

C) A store manager nonchalant about selling the goods

D) A teacher elated about one student who excelled on the test

E) A company president earning a huge salary and perk

12

Line 7 ("happy sorrow") make use of which of the following literary devices?

A) Oxymoron

B) Onomatopoeia

C) Metaphor

D) Literary allusion

E) simile

13

In line 8 "want" most nearly means?

A) Wish

B) Lack

C) Sympathy

D) Invoke

E) Obsession

14

The author uses parallel structures in lines 9-11 (how she…childhood) as a part of larger attempt to

A) convey the impact of separation

B) illustrate the advent of cheerful moments

C) honor Miss Taylor's contribution

D) describe she won't have the same experiences in the future

E) confess the relations had been exploited

15

After Isabella's marriage, both Emma and Miss Taylor realized

A) a strengthened unity after feeling abandoned

B) they were not real sisters and had no tender relations

C) a peculiar interest in marriage

D) Isabella left a large debt under their names

E) they should follow Isabella and soon to get married

Questions 16-21 are based on the following passage.

Line

Each year, CDER approves hundreds of new medications, most of which are variations of previously existing products, such as new dosage forms of already-approved products, or cost-saving generics. These new products contribute to quality of care, greater access to medication, more consumer choice that enhances affordability and public health.

5   However, products in a small subset of these new approvals, that we refer to as <u>novel drugs</u>, are among the more truly innovative products that often help advance clinical care to another level. Every year, CDER summarizes these new products. <u>The annual summary</u> reports the quantity of novel drugs that it approved.

However, it also focuses on the high quality of many of these new drugs, their contributions to enhanced patient care. This year, we approved many new drugs to treat various forms of cancer, including myeloma,

10 lung, skin, breast. This year's field also includes new drugs to treat reversal agent for a blood thinner.

For the first year, we approved more "<u>orphan</u>" drugs for rare diseases than any previous year in our history.

16

In the 1st paragraph, the author emphasizes that new medications will enhance all of the followings EXCEPT

A) they will completely replace existing products

B) they will contribute to quality of care

C) they will allow greater accessibility to mediation

D) they will give more consumer choice

E) they will give cost-saving alternatives

17

According to the 1st paragraph, which of the following medications would LEAST likely be approved by CDER?

A) Pills already-approved with new dosage forms

B) Cost-saving generic pills

C) Pills that allow greater access to the patients

D) Pills that enhance public health

E) Already-approved pills with more appealing name

18

Which of the following analogies most resembles the annual summary in line 7?

A) A boy reads over dozens of comics to kill time.

B) A respected physicist writes his autobiography

C) A chef buys over twenty boxes of only the highest quality tomatoes

D) A pianist renders music with a low quality piano

E) A grandma buys a generic drug to save money

19

Novel drug is characterized as the one with?

A) advanced and innovative drug

B) less expensive

C) more concerned with public health

D) less known previously

E) barely passed the regulations

20

In Line 11, "orphan" most nearly refers to

A) a drug for child without parent

B) a drug for rare diseases with a single purpose

C) illegal drug without name

D) highly replicable and affordable drug

E) a drug approved by the law enforcement

21

Paragraph 3 (lines 8—11) suggests that CDER has approved the new drugs available to the patients with or need of EXCEPT

A) multiple myeloma

B) skin cancer

C) lung cancer

D) a new blood thinner

E) breast cancer

Questions 22-27 are based on the following passage.

Line   The World Digital Library (WDL) is an international digital library operated by UNESCO. Its mission is to promote international and intercultural understanding, expand the volume and variety of cultural content on the Internet and build capacity in partner institutions to narrow the digital divide within and among countries.

5   The library intends to make available on the Internet, free of charge and in multilingual format, significant primary materials from cultures around the world, including manuscripts, maps, rare books, musical scores, recordings, films, prints, photographs, drawings. After almost 20 years without participation, the United States re-established its permanent delegation to the United Nations Educational, Scientific and Cultural Organization (UNESCO) in 2003. The WDL opened with 1,236 items. As of late 2015, it lists more than 12,000 items from nearly 200 countries, dating back to 8,000 BCE. Foremost was the belief that the World Digital Library should

10   engage partners in planning the four main project areas: technical architecture, selection, governance, and garnering funding. This was achieved in December 2006, that 45 national library directors and library technical directors from UNESCO met in Paris to discuss the development of the World Digital Library.

22

The mission of the World Digital Library includes all of the following EXCEPT

A) expand the volume of students participation

B) narrow the digital divide within countries

C) build partner institutions' capacity

D) expand volumes of the cultural content

E) promote intercultural understanding

23

Which of the following statements is true with "The library" in line 4 ?

A) it is accessible to mostly English language users

B) hardcopies and physical library are also available

C) free of charge policy with certain age limits

D) primary cultural materials are accessible with scholar I.D.

E) films are available

24

The role of the United States to UNESCO in the past 20 years can best be described as

A) sporadic at best

B) permanent

C) representative

D) significant

E) readily available

25

The author mentions *8,000 BCE* in line 9 in order to

A) impress the old history of the library

B) exemplify some of the materials readers can find

C) boast the rarity of the collection

D) establish the link between WDL and a specific collection

E) commend the superiority of the library collections

26

The passage mentions which of the following groups would play the significant role to advance the WDL?

A) the reader

B) the UNESCO Council

C) U.S. President

D) partners

E) librarians

27

The author mentions December 2006 UNESCO meeting in Paris primarily to

A) give an example of materialized goals of the WDL

B) suggest contrasting views among countries

C) suggest the significant role of the WDL in the world

D) impress the reader that even Paris is working with WDL

E) give an example of failed attempt of UNESCO

Questions 28-33 are based on the following passage.

Line

In the mid 1800's, hydraulic power performed diverse mechanical works that replaced workers' arduous labor, dawning the Industrial Revolution. Contemporary historians naively believed the industrialization in workplaces revolutionized the deprived lives of city dwellers. During this time, observing girls and married women flowing into factories, Adam Togason, an English economist, cautioned that women without femininity
5 would advent. politicians such as Ruth Henry, or Smith Tyler, however, saw the phenomenon as an opportunity to liberate women from the socioeconomic submission. Sociologists, adamantly questioned the early observers' beliefs. Their reasoning behind this was that such dramatic mechanical developments as spinning jenny, washing machine have not endowed better lives to women. Although women's participation in industry has changed a lot since the Industrial Revolution, glass ceiling by gender, low pay jobs that usually
10 require rudimentary skills gave little chance to women to advance in society. Historical investigation concerning the Industrial Revolution needs serious revision in that Industrial Revolution did not necessarily revolutionize women's status in society. Rather, Industrial Revolution may even have failed to secure women from their conventional roles.

28

Ruth Henry in line 5 would most likely respond to Sociologists in line 6 as they are
A) analytical
B) realistic
C) absolutely correct
D) misleading
E) amateurs

29

The author would most likely respond to Ruth Henry, or Smith Tylerin in line 5 by
A) approving that industrialization would improve womanhood in American society
B) approving that industrialization would liberate women from society
C) approving that industrialization would degrade womanhood
D) approving that women were primarily interested in industrialization
E) disapproving that industrialization would improve womanhood in American society

30

In line 10, the author views historical investigation as
A) a poorly drafted reference
B) a revolutionary scholarly work
C) a quintessential guidebook for feminism study
D) an erroneous theory
E) a typical history book with conventional idea

31

The description in line 7 (dramatic mechanical Developments) serves primarily to illustrate
A) that with the right equipment, women could enjoy good living
B) how women's livelihood was stagnant
C) many steps involving industrialization
D) the importance of having good equipment
E) specific examples endowed by industrialization

32

Which of the following characteristics would LEAST likely be attributed to "phenomenon" mentioned in line 5?
A) The usage of spinning jenny and washing machine
B) The employment of married women in industry
C) Laboring fewer hours
D) Women living with the traditional pattern of female society
E) Girls flowing into factories

33

It can be inferred that women's feelings toward the Industrialization may eventually have changed to that of
A) contemporary historians in line 2
B) politicians in line 5
C) Adam Togason in line 4
D) Ruth Henry in line 5
E) Smith Tyler in line 5

Questions 34-36 are based on the following passage.

Line | It would seem that Cicero's love for literature was inherited from his father.
Cicero's first systematic lessons in philosophy were given him by the Epicurean Phaedrus, whose lectures he attended at a very early age. At this time Cicero also heard the lectures of Diodotus the Stoic the art of dialectic. This art, which Cicero deems so important to the orator that he calls it "abbreviated
5 | eloquence," was then the monopoly of the Stoic school.

34

In line 1 ("It would…his father.") the author makes use of which of the following?

A) Speculation

B) Allusion

C) Analogy

D) Confirmation

E) Euphemism

35

Who would be most likely to learn "the art of dialectic" mentioned in line 4?

A) Merchant

B) Scientist

C) Poet

D) Farmer

E) Politician

36

In line 5, "the monopoly of the Stoic school" implies that the education system then was

A) cooperative

B) diversified

C) limited

D) expansive

E) underdeveloped

Questions 37-40 are based on the following passage.

Line | Sand constitutes from 1/3 of the volume of concrete; when a large amount of concrete is to be made a contractor cannot, therefore, afford to guess at his source of sand supply.
A long haul over poor roads can easily make the sand cost more than the stone of concrete.
Tests show conclusively that sand with rounded grains makes quite as strong a mortar as does sand with
5 | angular grains. The admixture with sand of a considerable percentage of loam or clay is also not the unmixed evil. These experiments demonstrate conclusively that loam and clay in sand to the amount of 10 to 15 per cent result in minimal material reduction in the strength of mortars made with this sand as compared with mortars made with the same sand after washing. There can be no doubt but that washing sand is an unnecessary one.

37

According to the author, using clay as a concrete material is

A) still debatable

B) an alternative

C) superior to sand

D) to be avoid

E) more expensive

38

The term "unmixed evil" in line 6 mainly indicates

A) thoroughly washed sand

B) concrete

C) rounded sand

D) sharp sand

E) loam

39

The passage states that when builders buy sand they should consider which of the following most?

A) the quality of loam

B) the quality of concrete

C) poor road condition

D) the quality of clay

E) the size of long haul

40

Which of the following makes the ideal concrete?

A) 1/3 of the best quality cleaned and sharp sand

B) 1/3 of cheap rounded sand

C) thoroughly washed cheap sand

D) 1/3 of clay

E) 1/2 of loam

Test 2 Verbal Section   30 MINUTES, 60 QUESTIONS

Directions: the synonym questions ask you to find the most appropriate synonym to the question.

The analogy questions ask you to find the most appropriate analogy to the question.
Select the answer that best matches to the question.

Synonym Sample Question:

Q: SUPERIOR

A higher rank

B inferior

C considerable

D supermarket

E supper

A) is the best answer because the synonym for superior is higher rank.

B) is incorrect because it applies the 'opposite concept.

C) and E) are irrelevant words.

D) is incorrect because it applies physical concept to mental concept

Test 2 Synonym questions 1 to 30

1. RAUCOUS
(A) harsh
(B) mellow
(C) deep
(D) flexible
(E) comfort

2. PROSPER
(A) advance
(B) propel
(C) unsuccessful
(D) profuse
(E) professional

3. ADULTERATE
(A) fully grown
(B) contaminate
(C) adultery
(D) pure
(E) adulate

4. TACTFUL
(A) skillful
(B) diplomatic
(C) fixed
(D) technique
(E) stream

5. REMOTE
(A) far away
(B) satellite
(C) orbit
(D) travel
(E) control

6. CONCISE

(A) short

(B) dictionary

(C) cut

(D) together

(E) skill

7. PRUDENT

(A) pure

(B) discreet

(C) ingenuity

(D) reckless

(E) provisional

8. AMPLE

(A) medium

(B) a lot

(C) fruit

(D) ambiguous

(E) scarce

9. AUDACIOUS

(A) hearing

(B) radio

(C) equipped

(D) audience

(E) bold

10. HINDER

(A) progress

(B) hindsight

(C) protect

(D) lofty

(E) delay

11. AESTHETIC

(A) beauty

(B) showy

(C) theoretic

(D) study

(E) funny

12. FOSTER

(A) terminate

(B) prevent

(C) promote

(D) stymie

(E) halt

13. PREVAIL

(A) Stipend

(B) defeat

(C) lonely

(D) premeditate

(E) win

14. AFFABLE

(A) friendly

(B) affectation

(C) fabulous

(D) disloyal

(E) easy

15. AFFECTATION

(A) artificial

(B) natural

(C) behavior

(D) impression

(E) intention

16. BROOD

(A) confident

(B) offspring

(C) bloody

(D) focus

(E) share

17. POTENT

(A) weak

(B) delivery

(C) powerful

(D) motionless

(E) great

18. ENTICE

(A) band

(B) tight

(C) engender

(D) tempt

(E) affinity

19. UNCANNY

(A) natural

(B) spontaneity

(C) sympathy

(D) affluent

(E) eerie

20. SUFFICIENT

(A) affluent

(B) poor

(C) good

(D) subversive

(E) prosper

21. AGENDA

(A) program

(B) book

(C) gender

(D) agrarian

(E) aggregation

22. FLOUNDER

(A) inundate

(B) flower

(C) stumble

(D) scent

(E) odor

23. AGNOSTIC

(A) believer

(B) non-believer

(C) adherent

(D) follower

(E) geology

24. EAGERNESS

(A) alacrity

(B) serendipity

(C) iconoclast

(D) pivot

(E) crestfallen

25. To assert without proof

(A) epicure

(B) cosmopolitan

(C) allege

(D) husbandry

(E) equanimity

26. SATURATE

(A) salt

(B) soak

(C) dry

(D) wet

(E) semiarid

27. UNINVOLVED

(A) halcyon

(B) juxtapose

(C) demagogue

(D) double entendre

(E) aloof

28. CLARIFY

(A) dubious

(B) hard to understand

(C) explain

(D) mirror

(E) nostalgia

29. TYRANT

(A) president

(B) king

(C) dictator

(D) medicine

(E) subject

30. MOBILIZE

(A) vehicle

(B) transport

(C) activate

(D) stop

(E) engine oil

Analogy Sample Question:

Q: River is to Ocean as:

A better is to good

B rain is to cloud

C father is to mother

D city is to country

E fork is to spoon

D is the correct answer. Just as the river is smaller than the Ocean, the city is smaller than the country. The pattern applied in this question is the Degree Pattern (small to big)

A) is incorrect because the word order is flipped over.

B) is incorrect because it applies the production pattern (cloud produces rain) C),

E) are incorrect because they apply the Antonym patterns.

Test 2 Analogy questions 31 to 60

31. Pedal is to bike as automobile is to

(A) mirror

(B) insurance

(C) engine

(D) driver

(E) highway

32. Hieroglyph is to alphabet as English is to

(A) telegraph

(B) text

(C) pictograph

(D) signal

(E) rhythm

33. Failure is to mistake as virus is to

(A) treatment

(B) bacteria

(C) hospital

(D) disease

(E) insurance

34. Factory is to product as business is to

(A) competition

(B) dedication

(C) society

(D) money

(E) products

35. Mercury is to Saturn as Jupiter is

(A) venus

(B) cupid

(C) astrology

(D) astronomy

(E) universe

36. Painting is to Modernism as

(A) Baroque is to music

(B) musician is to audience

(C) art is to Picasso

(D) Mozart is to Vivaldi

(E) classic is to hip-hop

37. Abstract is to abstruse as

(A) hypothesis is to fact

(B) opinion is to conviction

(C) belief is to steadfast

(D) conjecture is to convincing

(E) truth is to doubt

38. Allusion is to hint as

(A) reference is to inference

(B) Conviction is to convolution

(C) stout is to slim

(D) fancy is to fantasy

(E) indirect is to direct

39. Elephant is to cheetah as

(A) canine is to feline

(B) herbivore is to carnivore

(C) extinct is to endangered

(D) Africa is to Asia

(E) fast is to slow

40. Industry is to investment as

(A) hotel is to room

(B) savings account is to deposit

(C) restaurant is to reservation

(D) waitress is to tip

(E) waiter is to uniform

41. Sympathy is to love as

(A) smell is to odor

(B) pungent is to acrid

(C) tolerable is to overjoy

(D) climax is to anticlimax

(E) hate is to dislike

42. Trap is hunting as copyright is to

(A) plagiarism

(B) trademark

(C) protection right

(D) ownership

(E) proof

43. Infrastructure is to society as nature is to

(A) foundation

(B) nurture

(C) wild

(D) ecosystem

(E) animal

44. Spring is to rejuvenate as winter is to

(A) increase

(B) contract

(C) progress

(D) cold

(E) underground

45. Guerrilla is to atypical as military is

(A) typical

(B) command

(C) coup

(D) modern

(E) irregular

46. Laundry is to scent as

(A) cat is to soft

(B) wrapping paper is to corrugated

(C) heavy-metal music is to blasting

(D) baby face is to cute

(E) sock is to odor

47. Baseball is to taekwondo as

(A) soccer is to boxing

(B) cheerleader is to dancer

(C) homework is to assignment

(D) stalemate is to draw

(E) stick is to glove

48. Hunch is to conviction as

(A) conjecture is to guess

(B) intuition is to faith

(C) doubt is to dubious

(D) belief is to trust

(E) idea is to thinking

49. Career is to hobby as

(A) primary is to secondary

(B) independent is to cooperation

(C) city is to rural

(D) income is to revenue

(E) office is to money

50. Candle is to spear as

(A) cake is to celebration

(B) wish is to blow

(C) light is to dark

(D) chopping board is to T.V. monitor

(E) war is to battle

51. Book is to proofreading as

(A) symptom is to diagnose

(B) painting is to sketchy

(C) salesman is to sales

(D) choreography is to dancing

(E) regimen is to sport

UNAUTHORIZED COPYING OR REUSE OF ANY PART OF THIS PAGE IS ILLEGAL

52. Protest is to overthrow as

(A) delay is to expedite

(B) satisfaction is to guarantee

(C) follow is to support

(D) debate is to put forward

(E) rumor is to truth

53. Manner is to expression as privacy is to

(A) mistake

(B) out of the sight

(C) habit

(D) characteristic

(E) lifestyle

54. Olympic is to medal as

(A) winter is to snow

(B) athlete scorecard is to point

(C) player is to coach

(D) gold medal is to silver medal

(E) pack is to crowd

55. Diversity is to flexibility as

(A) radio is to music

(B) internet is to information

(C) uniformity is to agreement

(D) hard work is to success

(E) solid is to infirmity

56. Noise is to baby as

(A) injury is to accident

(B) construction is to demolition

(C) coffee is to sleeping

(D) reading is to knowledge

(E) flu shot is to disease

57. Music is to relaxation as

(A) driver is to driving

(B) bee is to honey

(C) spider is to web

(D) beaver is to dam

(E) movie is to entertainment

58. Travel is to memory as

(A) insect is to disease

(B) itinerary is to schedule

(C) lottery ticket is to gamble

(D) mother is to meal

(E) church is to pew

59. 150 pound child is to overweight as

(A) dance is to recreation

(B) child obesity is to social issue

(C) double-digit increase is to high

(D) gallon is to liquid

(E) 100° F is to 37° C

60. Shark is to sloth as

(A) snail is to tortoise

(B) chipmunk is to squirrel

(C) crow is to crane

(D) pit bull is to panda

(E) dolphin is to whale

Test 2

Answer Explanations

&

The Pattern Analyses

If your Test 2 scores are unsatisfactory,

Test 3, 4, 5... won't be satisfactory either.

Practice the Answer Explanations and then solve

the Actual Test 2 again.

ALL THE LOGIC AND RULES BEHIND EVERY
SINGLE SSAT QUESTION

UNAUTHORIZED COPYING OR REUSE OF ANY PART OF THIS PAGE IS ILLEGAL

TEST 2
READING SECTION

Please refer to the Reading Section Absolute Pattern Analyses

THE SYNONYM QUESTIONS TEST 2 NO.1 ~ 30   THE ANALOGY QUESTIONS TEST 2 NO. 31 ~ 60

1	A	16	B
2	A	17	C
3	B	18	D
4	A	19	E
5	A	20	A
6	A	21	A
7	B	22	C
8	B	23	B
9	E	24	A
10	E	25	C
11	A	26	B
12	C	27	E
13	E	28	C
14	A	29	C
15	A	30	C

Please refer to the Analogy Section Absolute Pattern Analyses

Questions 1-9 are based on the following passage.

Greenhouse gas concentrations in the atmosphere will continue to increase unless the billions of annual tons decrease substantially. Increased concentrations are expected to (1) **increase Earth's average temperature**, influence the patterns and amounts of precipitation, reduce ice and snow cover, as well as permafrost, raise sea level, and increase the acidity of the oceans. Temperature increases and other (2) **climate changes may directly impact our food and water supply, ecosystems, coasts, and human health**. The magnitude and rate of future climate change will primarily (5) **depend on many uncertain factors**.

Among many noted estimates, the IPCC's "SRES" scenarios was frequently used to foresee future climate change. The SRES scenarios are "baseline" scenarios, which means that the current or future measures that limit GHG emissions (3 & 4) **are not to be rigidly defined**. Emissions projections of the SRES scenarios are (8) **widely comparable** in range to the baseline emissions that have been developed by the scientific community. Many greenhouse gases stay in the atmosphere for long periods of time. As a result, (6 & 7) **even if emissions stopped increasing, atmospheric greenhouse gas concentrations would continue to increase and remain elevated for hundreds of years**. (9) **This is because the oceans, which store heat, take many decades to fully respond** to higher greenhouse gas concentrations.

Q1. Absolute Pattern 2: Summary Question
Summarizing a sentence or entire passage
Question Pattern: Greenhouse gas concentration increase may cause all of the following EXCEPT

A) oceans' acidity level increase B) sea level increase C) snow cover reduction D) altering the precipitation patterns **E) average temperature drop**	Increased concentrations are expected to **increase Earth's average temperature**, The other choices are all mentioned in above sentence.

Q2. Absolute Pattern 2: Summary Question
Question Pattern: Climate changes due to greenhouse gas may **directly impact** on all of the following EXCEPT

A) coasts B) ecosystems C) water supply D) human health **E) the IPCC's SRES**	climate changes may directly impact our food and water supply, ecosystems, coasts, and human health E) is a scientific scenario

Q3. Absolute Pattern 7: Understanding Attitude (Tone) Question
Finding tone such as positive-negative, active-passive, mental-physical, subjective-objective
Question Pattern: The author introduces **IPCC's "SRES"** in line 7 as scenarios with

A) a mere projection B) definite figures to follow C) the only available model D) unreliable estimation E) widely accepted facts with accuracy	The SRES scenarios are "baseline" scenarios, which means that the current or future measures that limit GHG emissions (3) **are not to be rigidly defined.** A), B), and E) are direct opposite. D) is too extreme

Q4. Absolute Pattern 8: Understanding True Purpose
Question Pattern: The author uses quotations in the word "**baseline**" in line 8 in order to **emphasize** that

A) the SRES is only the reference B) the SRES should be strictly observed C) GHG emission level should not be considered D) GHG emission level should be the foundational scenario E) the SRES should be abandoned	The SRES scenarios are "baseline" scenarios, which means that the current or future measures that limit GHG emissions (3) **are not to be rigidly defined**

Q5. **Absolute Pattern 2: Summary Question**
Summarizing a sentence or entire passage
Question Pattern: In the first paragraph (lines 1-6) the author defines **the magnitude and the rate of future climate** should be contingent on

A) divine will B) ocean sea level **C) various uncertain factors** D) the government policies E) acidity level in the oceans	The magnitude and rate of future climate change will primarily **depend on many uncertain factors**.

Q6. **Absolute Pattern 7: Understanding Attitude (Tone) Question**
Finding tone such as positive-negative, active-passive, mental-physical, subjective-objective
Question Pattern: The **author's primary tone in line 11-13 (Many greenhouse gases...hundreds years.)** is one of

A) pessimistic B) optimistic C) futuristic D) fantastic E) fascinated	even if emissions stopped increasing, atmospheric greenhouse gas concentrations would **continue to increase and remain elevated for hundreds of years.**

Q7. **Absolute Pattern 3: Inference Question** Finding an indirect suggestion (or guessing)
Question Pattern: It can be inferred that **if we stabilize and gradually reduce current greenhouse gas emission**, surface air temperatures will

A) soon cool down B) slowly cool down C) spike with great magnitude **D) continue to warm** E) not to be known at present	even if emissions stopped increasing, atmospheric greenhouse gas concentrations would **continue to increase and remain elevated for hundreds of years.**

Q8. **Absolute Pattern 5: Word-In-Context Question**
Finding a clue word and the keyword from the sentence in question
Question Pattern: The word "**comparable**" in line 10 most nearly means

A) applicable B) limited C) compatible D) available E) unavailable	the SRES scenarios are **widely** comparable in range. *"widely" implies B) should be the opposite case. C) is only the similar sound D) is too broad concept.

Q9. **Absolute Pattern 2: Summary Question**
Summarizing a sentence or entire passage
Question Pattern: According to the 3rd paragraph (lines 11-13), the main **cause for the unresponsive greenhouse gas** concentrations is due to

A) the characteristics of precipitation **B) the characteristics of oceans** C) the characteristics of earth D) the characteristics of human E) the characteristics of seasons	**This is because the oceans, which store heat, take many decades to fully respond** to higher greenhouse gas concentrations.

Questions 10-15 are based on the following passage.

Emma Woodhouse was the youngest of the two daughters. Her mother had died too long ago for her to have more than an indistinct remembrance of her caresses; and her place had been supplied by an excellent woman as governess, who had fallen little short of a mother in affection. Sixteen years had Miss Taylor been in Mr. Woodhouse's family, less as a governess than a friend. (10) **Between *them* it was more the intimacy of sisters.**

The real evils, indeed, of Emma's situation were the power of having rather (11) **too much her own way, and a disposition to think a little too well of herself; these were the disadvantages which threatened** alloy to her many enjoyments. (12) Sorrow came--a happy sorrow. Miss Taylor married. It was on the wedding-day of this beloved friend that Emma first sat in mournful thought of any continuance. The (13 &14) **want of Miss Taylor would be felt every hour of every day.** She recalled her past kindness--the kindness--how she had taught and how she had played with her from five years old—how she had devoted all her powers to attach and amuse her in health-and how nursed her through the various illnesses of childhood. A large debt of gratitude was owing here followed Isabella's marriage, on their being left to each other, (15) **was yet a dearer, tenderer recollection.**

Q10. Absolute Pattern 9: Relationships Question
Finding relations between the cause-effect, comparison-contrast, characters, and ideas
Question Pattern: The relationship between **Emma's family and Miss Taylor** can be best summarized as that

A) Miss Taylor had been in romantic relations with Emma's father B) Miss Taylor had a genuinely condescending view on Emma **C) Miss Taylor had a strong affinity to Emma** D) Miss Taylor had been a subservient governess E) Emma and Miss Taylor shared no same affection	Between *them* it was more the intimacy of sisters

Q11. Absolute Pattern 6: Analogy Question Finding a similar situation
Question Pattern: Which of the following examples is most analogous to Emma's character described in lines 5-7?

A) A girl bragging her cooking skills messes up the kitchen B) A pizza delivery man grateful for a big tip C) A store manager nonchalant about selling the goods D) A teacher elated about one student who excelled on the test E) A company president earning a huge salary and perk	**too much her own way, and a disposition to think a little too well of herself; these were the disadvantages** which threatened alloy to her many enjoyments.

Q12. Absolute Pattern 5: Word-In-Context Question
Finding a clue word and the keyword from the sentence in question
Question Pattern: Line 7 (**"happy sorrow"**) make use of which of the following literary devices?

A) Oxymoron B) Onomatopoeia C) Metaphor D) Literary allusion E) simile	An oxymoron is a rhetorical device that uses an ostensible self-contradiction to illustrate a rhetorical point or to reveal a paradox

Q13. Absolute Pattern 5: Word-In-Context Question
Question Pattern: In line 8 **"want"** most nearly means?

A) Wish **B) Lack** C) Sympathy D) Invoke E) Obsession	lack **(want)** of Miss Taylor would be felt every hour of every day

Q14. Absolute Pattern 10: Understanding the Structure of the Passage
Finding the structural organization of the passage or paragraph
Question Pattern: The author uses **parallel structures in lines 9-11 (how she...childhood)** as a part of larger attempt to

A) **convey the impact of separation** B) illustrate the advent of cheerful moments C) honor Miss Taylor's contribution D) describe she won't have the same experiences in the future E) confess the relations had been exploited	**want of Miss Taylor would be felt every hour of every day.** She recalled her past kindness--the kindness--how she had taught and how she had played with her from five years old—how she had devoted all her powers ... ***The answer for the example sentence (i.e., how she...) is usually located right before the question sentence.**

Q15. Absolute Pattern 7: Understanding Attitude (Tone) Question
Finding tone such as positive-negative, active-passive, mental-physical, subjective-objective
Question Pattern: After Isabella's marriage, both Emma and Miss Taylor realized

A) **a strengthened unity after feeling abandoned** B) they were not real sisters and had no tender relations C) a peculiar interest in marriage D) Isabella left a large debt under their names E) they should follow Isabella and soon to get married	Isabella's marriage, on their being left to each other, **was yet a dearer, tenderer recollection**

Questions 16-20 are based on the following passage.

Each year, CDER approves hundreds of new medications, most of which are variations of (16) **previously existing products**, such as (17) **new dosage** forms of **already-approved** products, or **cost-saving** generics. These new products contribute to quality of care, greater **access to medication**, more consumer choice that enhances affordability and **public health**.

However, products in a small subset of these new approvals, that we refer to as <u>novel drugs</u>, are among the more truly (19) **innovative products** that often help advance clinical care to another level. Every year, CDER summarizes these new products. <u>The annual summary</u> reports (18) the **quantity** of novel drugs that it approved.

However, it also focuses on the **high quality** of many of these new drugs, their contributions to enhanced patient care. This year, we approved many new drugs to treat various forms of cancer, including myeloma, lung, skin, breast. This year's field also includes new drugs to treat (21) **reversal agent** for a blood thinner.

For the first year, we approved more "<u>orphan</u>" drugs (20) for **rare diseases** than any previous year in our history.

Q16. Absolute Pattern 2: Summary Question
Summarizing a sentence or entire passage
Question Pattern: In the 1st paragraph, the author emphasizes **that new medications will enhance** all of the followings EXCEPT

A) **they will completely replace existing products** B) they will contribute to quality of care C) they will allow greater accessibility to mediation D) they will give more consumer choice E) they will give cost-saving alternatives	most of which are variations of (16) **previously existing products** The other choices are all written.

Q17. **Absolute Pattern 2: Summary Question**
Summarizing a sentence or entire passage
Question Pattern: According to the 1st paragraph, which of the following medications would **LEAST likely be approved by CDER?**

A) Pills already-approved with new dosage forms B) Cost-saving generic pills C) Pills that allow greater access to the patients D) Pills that enhance public health **E) Already-approved pills with more appealing name**	**new dosage** forms of **already-approved** products, or **cost-saving** generics. These new products contribute to quality of care, greater **access to medication**, more consumer choice that enhances affordability and **public health**.

Q18. **Absolute Pattern 6: Analogy Question** Finding a similar situation
Question Pattern: Which of the following analogies most **resembles the annual summary** in line 7?

A) A boy reads over dozens of comics to kill time. B) A respected physicist writes his autobiography **C) A chef buys over twenty boxes of only the highest quality tomatoes** D) A pianist renders music with a low quality piano E) A grandma buys a generic drug to save money	The annual summary reports the **quantity** of novel drugs that it approved. However, it also focuses on the **high quality** of many of these new drugs,

Q19. **Absolute Pattern 2: Summary Question**
Summarizing a sentence or entire passage
Question Pattern: Novel drug is characterized as the one with?

A) advanced and innovative drug B) less expensive C) more concerned with public health D) little known previously E) barely passed the regulations	we refer to as novel drugs, are among the more truly **innovative products**

Q20. **Absolute Pattern 5: Word-In-Context Question**
Finding a clue word and the keyword from the sentence in question
Question Pattern: In Line 11, **"orphan"** most nearly refers to

A) a drug for child without parent **B) a drug for rare diseases with a single purpose** C) illegal drug without name D) highly replicable and affordable drug E) a drug approved by the law enforcement	orphan" drugs (20) for **rare diseases**

Q21. **Absolute Pattern 2: Summary Question**
Summarizing a sentence or entire passage
Question Pattern: Paragraph 3 (lines 8—11) suggests that **CDER has approved the new drugs** available to the patients with or need of EXCEPT

A) multiple myeloma B) skin cancer C) lung cancer **D) a new blood thinner** E) breast cancer	new drugs to treat **reversal agent** for a blood thinner.

Questions 22-27 are based on the following passage.

The World Digital Library (WDL) is an international digital library operated by UNESCO. (22) Its mission is to **promote international and intercultural understanding, expand the volume** and variety of **cultural content** on the Internet and **build capacity in partner institutions** to **narrow the digital divide** within and among countries.

   The library intends to make available on the Internet, free of charge and in multilingual format, significant primary materials from cultures around the world, including manuscripts, maps, rare books, musical scores, recordings, (23) **films,** prints, photographs, drawings. After almost 20 years (24) **without participation,** the United States re-established its permanent delegation to the United Nations Educational, Scientific and Cultural Organization (UNESCO) in 2003. The WDL opened with 1,236 items. As of late 2015, (25) **it lists more than 12,000 items from nearly 200 countries,** dating back **to 8,000 BCE**. (26) **Foremost was the belief that the World Digital Library should engage partners** in planning the four main project areas: technical architecture, selection, governance, and garnering funding. (27) **This was achieved** in December 2006, that 45 national library directors and library technical directors from UNESCO met in Paris to discuss the development of the World Digital Library.

Q22. **Absolute Pattern 2: Summary Question**
Summarizing a sentence or entire passage
Question Pattern: The mission of the World Digital Library includes all of the following **EXCEPT**

A) **expand the volume of students participation** B) narrow the digital divide within countries C) build partner institutions' capacity D) expand volumes of the cultural content E) promote intercultural understanding	Its mission is to **promote international and intercultural understanding, expand the volume** and variety of **cultural content** on the Internet and **build capacity in partner institutions** to **narrow the digital divide** within and among countries.

Q23. **Absolute Pattern 2: Summary Question**
Question Pattern: Which of the following statements is true with "The library" in line 4?

A) it is accessible to mostly English language users B) hardcopies and physical library are also available C) free of charge policy with certain age limits D) primary cultural materials are accessible with scholar I.D. E) **films are available**	The library intends to make available on the Internet, free of charge and in multilingual format, significant primary materials from cultures around the world, including manuscripts, maps, rare books, musical scores, recordings, **films,** prints, photographs, drawings.

Q24. **Absolute Pattern 2: Summary Question**
Question Pattern: The role of the **United States to UNESCO in the past 20 years** can best be described as

A) **sporadic at best** B) permanent C) representative D) significant E) readily available	After almost 20 years **without participation,** the United States re-established its permanent delegation to the United Nations Educational

Q25. **Absolute Pattern 4: Example Question**
Finding the true purpose behind a specific name or idea within a sentence
Question Pattern: The author mentions **8,000 BCE** in line 9 in order to

A) impress the old history of the library B) **exemplify some of the materials readers can find** C) boast the rarity of the collection D) establish the link between WDL and a specific collection E) commend the superiority of the library collections	it lists more than 12,000 items from nearly 200 countries, dating back **to 8,000 BCE** *It's only a part of materials available.

Q26. Absolute Pattern 2: Summary Question
Summarizing a sentence or entire passage
Question Pattern: The passage mentions which of the following **groups would play the significant role** to advance the WDL?

A) the reader B) UNESCO Council C) U.S. President **D) partners** E) librarians	**Foremost** was the belief that the World Digital Library **should engage partners**

Q27. Absolute Pattern 8: Understanding True Purpose
Finding the true purpose of statement, sentences, or the entire paragraph
Question Pattern: The author mentions **December 2006 UNESCO meeting in Paris** primarily to

A) give an example of materialized goals of the WDL B) suggest contrasting views among countries C) suggest the significant role of the WDL in the world D) impress the reader that even Paris is working with WDL E) give an example of failed attempt of UNESCO	**This was achieved** in December 2006, that 45 national library directors and library technical directors from UNESCO met in Paris to discuss the development of the World Digital Library.

Questions 28-33 are based on the following passage.

In the mid 1800's, hydraulic power performed diverse mechanical works that replaced workers' arduous labor, dawning the Industrial Revolution. Contemporary historians naively believed the industrialization in workplaces revolutionized the deprived lives of city dwellers. During this time, observing girls and married women flowing into factories, Adam Togason, an English economist, cautioned that women without femininity would advent. politicians such as (28) Ruth Henry, or Smith Tyler, however, saw the phenomenon as an (32) **opportunity to liberate women** from the socioeconomic submission. **Sociologists, adamantly questioned the early observers' beliefs.**
Their reasoning behind this was that such dramatic mechanical developments as spinning jenny, washing machine (31) **have not endowed better lives to women**. Although women's participation in industry has changed a lot since the Industrial Revolution, (33) **glass ceiling by gender, low pay jobs that usually require rudimentary skills gave little chance to women to advance in society.** Historical investigation concerning the Industrial Revolution (30) **needs serious revision** in that Industrial Revolution did not necessarily revolutionize women's status in society. (29) **Rather, Industrial Revolution may even have failed** to secure women from their conventional roles.

Q28. Absolute Pattern 9: Relationships Question
Finding relations between the cause-effect, comparison-contrast, characters, and ideas
Question Pattern: Ruth Henry in line 5 would most likely respond to Sociologists in line 6 as they are

A) analytical B) realistic C) absolutely correct **D) misleading** E) amateurs	Ruth Henry, or Smith Tyler, however, saw the **phenomenon as an opportunity to liberate women** from the socioeconomic submission. **Sociologists, adamantly questioned the early observers' beliefs** *"questioned" means doubted or rejected. Therefore, Ruth might have said sociologists are misleading the situation.

Q29. Absolute Pattern 9: Relationships Question
Finding relations between the cause-effect, comparison-contrast, characters, and ideas
Question Pattern: The author would most likely respond to Ruth Henry, or Smith Tylerin in line 5 by

A) approving that industrialization would improve womanhood in American society B) approving that industrialization would liberate women from society C) approving that industrialization would degrade womanhood D) approving that women were primarily interested in industrialization **E) disapproving that industrialization would improve womanhood in American society**	The author wrote in the conclusion **"Rather, Industrial Revolution may even have failed** to secure women from their conventional roles" <u>Therefore, he would disapprove Ruth Henry's argument.</u> C) is opposite as are A), B) and D)

Q30. Absolute Pattern 9: Relationships Question
Question Pattern: In line 10, the author views historical investigation as

A) a poorly drafted reference B) a revolutionary scholarly work C) a quintessential guidebook for feminism study **D) an erroneous theory** E) a typical history book with conventional idea	<u>Historical investigation</u> concerning the Industrial Revolution (30) **needs serious revision** in that Industrial Revolution did not necessarily revolutionize women's status in society. A) is incorrect because it is more than a reference.

Q31. Absolute Pattern 8: Understanding True Purpose
Question Pattern: The description in line 7 (dramatic mechanical Developments) serves primarily to illustrate

A) that with the right equipment, women could enjoy good living **B) how women's livelihood was stagnant** C) many steps involving industrialization D) the importance of having good equipment for domestic work E) specific examples endowed by industrialization	<u>dramatic mechanical developments</u> as spinning jenny, washing machine (31) **have not endowed better lives to women**. *E) is repeating the question (the exact sentence) not the answer behind the sentence

Q32. Absolute Pattern 4: Example Question
Finding the true purpose behind a specific name or idea within a sentence
Question Pattern: Which of the following characteristics would LEAST likely be attributed to "phenomenon" mentioned in line 5?

A) The usage of spinning jenny and washing machine B) The employment of married women in industry C) Laboring fewer hours **D) Women living with the traditional pattern of female society** E) Girls flowing into factories	During this time, observing girls and married women flowing into factories, <u>Adam Togason</u>, an English economist, cautioned that women without femininity would advent. Some socialists such as <u>Ruth Henry, or Smith Tyler,</u> however, saw the <u>phenomenon</u> as an **opportunity** to liberate women from the socioeconomic submission.

Q33. Absolute Pattern 9: Relationships Question
Question Pattern: It can be inferred that women's feelings toward the Industrialization may eventually have changed to that of

A) contemporary historians in line 2 B) politicians in line 5 **C) Adam Togason in line 4** D) Ruth Henry in line 5 E) Smith Tyler in line 5	<u>Adam Togason</u>, an English economist, **cautioned that women without femininity would advent. ... Rather, Industrial Revolution may even have failed** to secure women from their conventional roles. (WOMEN) **glass ceiling by gender, low pay jobs that usually require rudimentary skills gave little chance to women to advance in society.**

Questions 34-36 are based on the following passage.

It would (34) **seem** that Cicero's love for literature was inherited from his father.
Cicero's first systematic lessons in philosophy were given him by the Epicurean Phaedrus, whose lectures he attended at a very early age. At this time Cicero also heard the lectures of Diodotus the Stoic the art of dialectic. This art, which Cicero deems so important to the (35) **orator** that he calls it "abbreviated eloquence," was then the (36) **monopoly of the Stoic school.**

Q34. Absolute Pattern 7: Understanding Attitude (Tone) Question
Finding tone such as positive-negative, active-passive, mental-physical, subjective-objective
Question Pattern: In line 1 ("It would...his father.") the author makes use of which of the following?

A) Speculation B) Allusion C) Analogy D) Confirmation E) Euphemism	It would **seem** that Cicero's love for literature was inherited from his father. *The author is using "it would seem." That is speculation.

Q35. Absolute Pattern 3: Inference Question Finding an indirect suggestion (or guessing)
Question Pattern: Who would be most likely to learn "the art of dialectic" mentioned in line 4?

A) Merchant B) Scientist C) Poet D) Farmer **E) Politician**	This art, which Cicero deems so important to the **Orator.** Good politicians are good orators.

Q36. Absolute Pattern 3: Inference Question Finding an indirect suggestion (or guessing)
Question Pattern: In line 5, "the monopoly of the Stoic school" implies that the education system then was

A) cooperative B) diversified **C) limited** D) expansive E) underdeveloped	This art, which Cicero deems so important to the orator that he calls it "abbreviated eloquence," was then the **monopoly** of the Stoic school. The word "monopoly" is exclusive privilege without competitors. Therefore, C) is the answer.

Questions 37-40 are based on the following passage.

Sand constitutes from 1/3 of the volume of concrete; when a large amount of concrete is to be made a contractor cannot, therefore, afford to guess at his source of sand supply. (39) **A long haul over poor roads** can easily make the **sand cost more than the stone** of concrete. Tests show conclusively that (40) **sand with rounded grains makes quite as strong** a mortar as does sand with angular grains. The admixture with sand of a considerable percentage of (37 & 38) **loam or clay is also not the unmixed evil**. These experiments demonstrate conclusively that loam and clay in sand to the amount of 10 to 15 per cent result in minimal material reduction in the strength of mortars made with this sand as compared with mortars made with the same sand after washing. There can be no doubt but that washing sand is an unnecessary one.

Q37. Absolute Pattern 2: Summary Question
Summarizing a sentence or entire passage
Question Pattern: According to the author, **using clay** as a concrete material is

A) still debatable **B) an alternative** C) superior to sand D) to be avoid E) more expensive	**loam or clay is also not the unmixed evil.** That is, it can be an alternative.

Q38. Absolute Pattern 5: Word-In-Context Question
Finding a clue word and the keyword from the sentence in question
Question Pattern: The term **"unmixed evil"** in line 6 mainly indicates

A) thoroughly washed sand B) concrete C) rounded sand D) sharp sand **E) loam**	**loam** or clay is also not the **unmixed evil.**

Q39. Absolute Pattern 2: Summary Question
Summarizing a sentence or entire passage
Question Pattern: The passage states that when builders **buy sand they should consider which of the following**

A) the quality of loam B) the quality of concrete **C) poor roads condition** D) the quality of clay E) the size of long haul	**A long haul over poor roads** can easily make the **sand cost more than the stone**

Q40. Absolute Pattern 2: Summary Question
Summarizing a sentence or entire passage
Question Pattern: Which of the following makes the **ideal concrete**?

A) 1/3 of the best quality cleaned and sharp sand **B) 1/3 of cheap rounded sand** C) thoroughly washed cheap sand D) 1/3 of clay E) 1/2 of loam	Tests show conclusively that **sand with rounded grains makes quite as strong** a mortar as does sand with angular grains. All mentioned are costs of sand, rounded sand is acceptable, and 1/3 of quantity of sand to concrete. A), C) are, according to the author, wasteful. D), E) are only 10%.

Test 2 Absolute Patterns for the Analogy Section

Absolute Pattern 3. Purpose (Tool) Pattern
Finding Relationships between the Purpose of Individual to Object, to its Function, its User, its Use, and its Association

Q31. C is the Best Answer. Pedal moves bike as (C) engine does to automobile.

Absolute Pattern 4. Characteristic Pattern
Finding Characteristic of Person, Place, Object, or Idea and its Associated Action

Q32. C is the Best Answer. Hieroglyph uses pictograph as English uses alphabet.

Absolute Pattern 8. Production Pattern
Finding Cause-and-Effect in Person, Concept, and Object

Q33. D is the Best Answer. Mistake causes failure. Virus causes disease.
(A) is incorrect because it doesn't follow the proper cause-effect sequence.

Absolute Pattern 8. Production Pattern
Finding Cause-and-Effect in Person, Concept, and Object

Q34. D is the Best Answer. Factory makes product as business makes money.

Absolute Pattern 1. Category Pattern
Finding Part/Whole, Same Type/Kind, Association

Q35. A is the Best Answer. Mercury, Saturn, Jupiter, and (A) Venus are all planets in the solar system.

Absolute Pattern 1. Category Pattern
Finding Part/Whole, Same Type/Kind, Association

Q36. A is the Best Answer. Painting (whole) is to Modernism (part) as (A) music (whole) is to Baroque (part), parts in here indicate a certain era in art. (C) too broad to define. (D) and (E) are not responding to the question.

Absolute Pattern 2. Synonym/Antonym
Finding a similar or an opposite meaning between words

Q37. C is the Best Answer. Abstract is conceptually abstruse. (C) belief is steadfast in attitude.
All the other choices are antonym pattern.

Absolute Pattern 2. Synonym/Antonym
Finding a similar or an opposite meaning between words

Q38. A is the Best Answer. Allusion and hint are synonym. (A) reference and inference are synonym.
(B) is unrelated words. (D) fancy is real or imaginable beauty. Fantasy is completely out of imagination.

Absolute Pattern 1. Category Pattern
Finding Part/Whole, Same Type/Kind, Association

Q39. B is the Best Answer. Elephant is herbivore and cheetah is carnivore. (E) is flipped over.

Absolute Pattern 1. Category Pattern
Finding Part/Whole, Same Type/Kind, Association

Q40. B is the Best Answer. People invest in Industry as they deposit in (B) savings account. They are both money category. (A) is a part-whole pattern. (C), (E) are not related with the question. (D) is purpose pattern.

Absolute Pattern 5. Degree Pattern
Finding a Degree and a Shape in person, place, thing, and emotion

Q41. C is the Best Answer. Love is greater degree of feeling than sympathy so as (C) overjoy is to tolerable. They are both related with our emotion. (E) is flipped. Is (A) emotion?

Absolute Pattern 3. Purpose (Tool) Pattern
Finding Relationships between the Purpose of Individual to Object, to its Function, its User, its Use, and its Association

Q42. A is the Best Answer. Trap catches for hunting as copyright catches for (A) plagiarism. The other choices are synonym pattern to copyright.

Absolute Pattern 1. Category Pattern
Finding Part/Whole, Same Type/Kind, Association

Q43. D is the Best Answer. Infrastructure sustains the entire society. (D) ecosystem sustains the entire nature. (A) is too abstract concept.

Absolute Pattern 4. Characteristic Pattern
Finding Characteristic of Person, Place, Object, or Idea and its Associated Action

Q44. B is the Best Answer. Spring rejuvenates everything as Winter contracts everything. (D) does not answer the question "rejuvenate. "

Absolute Pattern 4. Characteristic Pattern
Finding Characteristic of Person, Place, Object, or Idea and its Associated Action

Q45. A is the Best Answer. Guerrilla is atypical (untraditional) fighters. Military is typical (traditional) army.

Absolute Pattern 1. Category Pattern
Finding Part/Whole, Same Type/Kind, Association

Q46. E is the Best Answer. Laundry produces scent, a pleasant smell. We should find the same sensory type, which is (E).

Absolute Pattern 1. Category Pattern
Finding Part/Whole, Same Type/Kind, Association

Q47. A is the Best Answer. Step 1: find the same sport category: (A) and (E). Step 2: consider similarity: Baseball and soccer are team sports, a ball playing vs. taekwondo and boxing are individual sports.

Absolute Pattern 5. Degree Pattern
Finding a Degree and a Shape in person, place, thing, and emotion

Q48. B is the Best Answer. Hunch is smaller degree than conviction as is (B) intuition than faith. All these four words are synonyms to each other. All other choices are synonyms but have no degree.

Absolute Pattern 5. Degree Pattern
Finding a Degree and a Shape in person, place, thing, and emotion

Q49. A is the Best Answer. Career is considered primary as hobby is secondary.

Absolute Pattern 5. Degree Pattern
Finding a Degree and a Shape in person, place, thing, and emotion

Q50. D is the Best Answer.
Candle and spear are stick shape as (D) T.V. monitor and chopping board are square shape.

Absolute Pattern 6. Definition Pattern
Finding Definition/Concept of person, place, thing, and emotion

Q51. A is the Best Answer. Book requires proofreading as (A) symptom requires diagnose (B) sketchy is a preparation before painting. (E) is flipped over.

Absolute Pattern 6. Definition Pattern
Finding Definition/Concept of person, place, thing, and emotion

Q52. D is the Best Answer. Protest is to overthrow the status quo as (D) debate is to put forward status quo. (A), (E) are opposite. (C) is synonym

Absolute Pattern 6. Definition Pattern
Finding Definition/Concept of person, place, thing, and emotion

Q53. B is the Best Answer. Manner defines good expression as privacy defines out of the sight.

Absolute Pattern 8. Production Pattern
Finding Cause-and-Effect in Person, Concept, and Object

Q54. B is the Best Answer. Olympic produces medal as (B) athlete scorecard produces point (A) winter produces snow, but not associated with the question.

Absolute Pattern 2. Synonym/Antonym
Finding a similar or an opposite meaning between words

Q55. C is the Best Answer. Diversity is a synonym to flexibility as (C) uniformity is a synonym to agreement

UNAUTHORIZED COPYING OR REUSE OF ANY PART OF THIS PAGE IS ILLEGAL

Absolute Pattern 8. Production Pattern
Finding Cause-and-Effect in Person, Concept, and Object

Q56. A is the Best Answer. Baby produces noise as (A) accident produces injury.
(C), (D), and (E) are working opposite way.

Absolute Pattern 6. Definition Pattern
Finding Definition/Concept of person, place, thing, and emotion

Q57. E is the Best Answer. Music gives relaxation as (E) movie gives entertainment—the same category.

Absolute Pattern 6. Definition Pattern
Finding Definition/Concept of person, place, thing, and emotion

Q58. B is the Best Answer. Travel gives memory as (B) itinerary gives schedule. These four words are related with the travel category. (D) and (E) aren't related with the question.

Absolute Pattern 11. Subjective-Objective Pattern
Finding Quality-Quantity, Tangible-Intangible Association

Q59. C is the Best Answer. 150 pound and (C) double-digit are numeric quantifier with objective view.
(E) 100° F is to 37° C has no objective view.

Absolute Pattern 4. Characteristic Pattern
Finding Characteristic of Person, Place, Object, or Idea and its Associated Action

Q60. D is the Best Answer. Shark is characteristically aggressive and sloth is characteristically passive. Only (D) pit bull is to panda meets this criterion.

Chapter 2 Summary

The Chapter Summary contains equal portions of

12 Absolute Patterns for Analogy Section and

10 Absolute Patterns for Reading Section.

You may study all at once to significantly

improve your understanding and your scores.

Chapter 2

How SSAT Analogy Section is Created

Jimin: So, does each Analogy question ask one analogy at a time?

San: Each question is made of one Analogy-stem example and five choices. These five choices usually contain different analogies. Therefore, each question may have more than one Analogy.

San: The most critical part is to understand the question (the Analogy-stem example), based upon which we can find similar Analogy from the five choices.

Thus, identifying the Analogy-stem is our first task!

Now, let's combine all the analogies from Elementary level to Middle and Upper Level, and then further simplify all these analogy concepts by grouping them into the similar categories.

Fundamental Analogy Concept (Elementary/Middle/Upper Level Combined)

1. Synonyms/Antonyms

2. Part/Whole & Whole/Part

3. Characteristic/Type/Kind/ Category/Association

4. Degree

5. Product to Producer/ Individual to Object/Defining relationships

6. Purpose/Cause-Effect/ Function

7. Homonyms

8. Noun/Verb

9. Word

Jimin: They're Easier and simpler. That's all?

San: Official SSAT guys hate to be called they are easy. They were born to make our lives difficult just like theirs. So I added a couple of integral concepts in the following chapter.

SSAT ABSOLUTE PATTERNS

Chapter 2

How SSAT Analogy Section is Created

San: In the last chapter we simplified the entire SSAT Analogy Concept into nine fundamental categories.

In this chapter we will review these categories using the actual questions, and create the Analogy Patterns, so that we can solve the questions swimming through the Patterns.

*The pattern number is aligned with the level of importance and frequency in the actual test.

Chapter 2

12 Absolute Patterns for the Analogy Section

Absolute Pattern 1. Category Pattern
Finding Part/Whole, Same Type/Kind, Association

Q1.Smell is to pungent as

A) sight is to strong

B) hear is to Mozart

C) touch is to fire

D) taste is to sweet

E) sense is to anger

San: This Pattern is the Category Pattern.
You should find a part from the whole, a same type or kind, or an associated category with the question.

The correct answer is D

San: The question focuses on our five sensory devices (touch, smell, hearing, sight, taste).

     The pungent smell is a strong smell. It is very strong smell like you fart after eating a lot of onions because they're cheap.

     Pungent is associated with a smell as sweet is associated with a taste.

     You can also say like pungent is a part of or a type of smell.

     A) strong, B) Mozart, and C) fire and E) anger are all unrelated words.

Jimin: But I didn't know what pungent was.

San: If the question contains a word that you don't know, look for the most meaningful pair from the five choices.

Jimin: For me, Mozart in B) is more meaningful though.

San: "pungent"—even though you don't know its meaning—is adjective. You can tell that much, can't you?

     You should find the same adjective from the five choices.

     B) and C) are nouns and A) doesn't make sense.

Jimin: What is this pungent smell! Did you eat onions?

The Absolute Patterns for Analogy summary continues in the following chapters.

Chapter 2

10 Absolute Patterns for the Reading Section

Absolute Pattern 4: Example Question

Jimin : I think I can give a real shot for this kind of question. I love reading example sentences.

San: Because it's easy!
The example sentence is almost certainly identifiable through a specific name or idea used within a sentence. However...

...However, the example sentence itself rarely contains the answer in it.
It merely supports the main idea.

The example sentence supports the main argument by merely illustrating the event or idea. Sometimes, it uses historical figures or authorities' quotation, or analogy, or a mom's speech, etc. Since the example sentence is easier to understand than the main argument, folks like you try to find the answer by focusing on the example, but fail to get the answer.

When a question points at some obviously easy-to-read example sentences, it doesn't necessarily mean the answer should automatically be found in the example sentence.

Instead, the answer should mostly be located right above or right below the example sentence. That's where the topic or the concluding sentences are.

Sometimes, the last sentence in a paragraph can be the example sentence.
In that case, the topic sentence in the following paragraph can produce the answer because that's where the main idea starts—although many students overlook this fact.

Chapter 2

10 Absolute Patterns for the Reading Section

Pattern 5: Word-in-Context Question

Jimin : Do I need to memorize tons of uninspiring vocabularies?

San: Yes. You should because the Word-in-Context Pattern asks two types of questions: (1) Finding the precise meaning of the word—normally high-level vocabulary. (2) Identifying the word usage in passage—normally figurative or metaphorical meaning that carries several precise meanings in the choices as a bait.

San: I made those uninspiring vocabularies into pretty sexy ones. If you need them, let me know. Here's my email: satvancouver@gmail.com

(1) When the question asks the literal meaning of a difficult vocabulary, consider only the very first definition from the dictionary, not the second or third one.

(2) When the word-in-context question asks the meaning of a seemingly easy vocabulary, Never rely on your memory. I guarantee that you will miss this question if you do not read the passage and rely on your memory. For the figurative word, you must find a clue word (s) from the sentence. The passage should provide the clue word (s). Never skip this process and rely on your memory. The Word-in-Context question is not a piece-of-cake because it's a short question.

  Most importantly, you must distinguish between the clue word and the keyword in the multiple choices. Be careful though. A clue word can be a flamboyant adjective or adverb, sitting pretty next to the answer that can be as simple as "it" (the singular pronoun). Your job is to find the keyword for the answer," not the pretty clue word.

San: Look! What would you just choose between (A) foreboding relationship (B) it. In Any circumstance whatsoever.?

Jimin: (A)!?

Chapter 2

10 Absolute Patterns for the Reading Section

Absolute Pattern 8: Understanding the True Purpose

> Jimin : I wouldn't be here without understanding the purpose of understanding True Purpose pattern!

> San: To understand the true purpose of the statement, isolating the example sentence or concessional phrase (i.e., although…., while…,) is the key point.

> San: in other words, distinguishing the primary information from the secondary.

For instance, the author of the passage uses a single line expression or quotation made by some authority or a character within a passage.

However, the true purpose behind the quotation needs to be interpreted based on the main idea of the passage (the author or the narrator).

The trickiest part of this pattern is that it does not give you the clear keywords, just like from the inference question or analogy question.

Paradoxically, the exactly written statement in the passage can be an incorrect option because that won't be the true purpose.

For example, if you are so hungry that you need to go home, your primary purpose is not going home or reminding yourself that you are hungry.

These true premises, albeit true, but by this very fact, should definitely be the incorrect options.

Chapter 2

10 Absolute Patterns for the Reading Section

Absolute Pattern 9: Relationship Question

Jimin : Wow! I thought I was on the sideline. We are indeed building a Relationship that is in question.

San: This pattern asks many different types of relations within the passage.

(1) The relationships between the cause-effect situation. Pay Attention to subordinating conjunctions such as "because, since, for, as…" (or similar word).

(2) The relationships within comparison-contrast, flagged by "more", "better", "never", often" ,"if."

(3) The relationships between historical or certain events

(4) The relationships between characters, ideas, and arguments.

Common mistakes in this pattern!

When question asks

"compared to the paragraph 1, paragraph 2…is?"

A very effective way is to crossing out irrelevant information using your pencil.

(e.g., "compared to the paragraph 1, paragraph 2…is?" .)

The keywords in the passage should be located at/near the:

√ coordinating conjunction "but (or similar perception),

√ correlative conjunction such as "more ~ than"

√ transition words/phrase for supporting detail, contrast, consequence such as "on the other hand", "in fact,", "Consequently".

The Absolute Patterns for Reading summary continues in the following chapters.

SSAT UPPER LEVEL 7 PRACTICE TESTS WITH THE ABSOLUTE PATTERNS

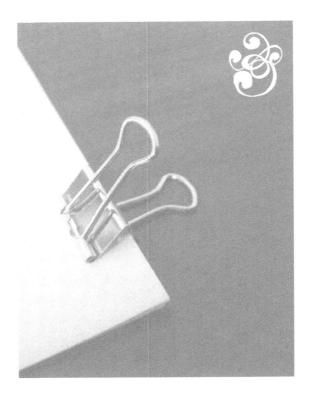

Chapter 3

1. TEST 3

2. ANSWER EXPLANATIONS for TEST 3

3. CHAPTER SUMMARY

SSAT
Reading & Verbal
Test 3

This chapter starts with Test 3.

Your goal is not getting good enough scores, but 100%.

It's your book

It's up to you to practice the Answer Explanation first.

UNAUTHORIZED COPYING OR REUSE OF ANY PART OF THIS PAGE IS ILLEGAL

Test 3 Reading Section
Time: 40 Minutes, 40 Questions

Directions: Each reading passage is followed by questions about it. Answer the questions that follow a passage on the basis of what is stated or implied in that passage.

Questions 1-6 are based on the following passage.

Line

Mr. Collins's triumph was complete. The power of displaying the grandeur of his patroness to his wondering visitors, and of letting them see her civility towards himself and his wife, was exactly what he had wished for.

"I should not have been at all surprised by her ladyship's asking us on Sunday to drink tea. Who could have foreseen such an attention as this?"

5 As the weather was fine, they had a pleasant walk. Every park has its beauty and its prospects, though she could not be in such raptures as Mr. Collins expected.

Lady Catherine was a tall woman. Her air was not conciliating, nor was her manner of receiving them such as to make her visitors forget their inferior rank. She was formidable by silence and was in authoritative tone.

1

According to the first paragraph, Mr. Collins invited his visitors to Lady Catherine mainly to

A) build a new constructive relations with the visitors

B) let the visitors observe Lady Catherine's hospitality towards him

C) reconcile the visitors with Lady Catherine

D) find an opportunity to amass wealth

E) work as a Lady Catherine's messenger

2

According to the first paragraph, Mr. Collins' persona can be described as

A) cheerful

B) condescending

C) humble

D) showy

E) irate

3

The description in lines 5-6 (Every park has... Mr. Collins expected) suggests that 'she' in line 5

A) was resentful to the other characters

B) distasted about the surroundings

C) was in such great rapture

D) was not in such a joyful mood

E) was greatly inspired by the surroundings

4

Which of the following analogies would be most in keeping with the main character trait of Mr. Collins?

A) Susan often uses an assumed name similar to that of rich people to impress others

B) Max morally opposes rich people's wrongdoings

C) Daniel lives in constant fear of running out of money and relies on rich people

D) Cathy finds condescending gesture of rich people and advises her friends to ignore it

E) San always maintains humility to both the rich and the poor

5

Lady Catherine's role with Mr. Collins is of

A) an aunt

B) an old friend

C) an abiding beneficiary

D) a condescending benefactor

E) a benign neighbor

6

In lines 7-8, the narrator observes that Lady Catherine as

A) realistic and truly respectful person

B) young and handsome person

C) a person hiding a slightly inferiority

D) a person creating superiority by lowering others

E) a talkative person

Questions 7-11 are based on the following passage.

Line | Quantum mechanics is a fundamental branch of physics.
Important applications of quantum theory include <u>superconducting magnets, laser transistor, and semiconductors</u> <u>such as the computer microprocessor</u> to understand many biological and physical phenomena.
   When quantum mechanics was originally formulated, it was applied to models that do not correspond to
5 relativistic classical mechanics. Early attempts to merge quantum mechanics <u>for special relativity has involved</u> the replacement of the Schrödinger equation with a covariant equation. These theories were successful in explaining <u>many experimental results</u>, although they had certain unsatisfactory qualities stemming from their neglect of the relativistic creation and annihilation of particles.
   A fully relativistic quantum theory required the development of quantum field theory, which applies
10 quantization to a field less than a fixed set of particles.

7

The author uses the example in lines 2-3 (superconducting magnets…physical phenomena) to

A) describe practicality of Quantum mechanics
B) list currently unavailable technologies
C) introduce a fundamental concept of Quantum mechanics
D) emphasize how scientific theory can impact our lives
E) list obsolete technology in the past

8

The second paragraph (lines 4-8) presents the relationship between Quantum mechanics and classical mechanics were originally

A) limited
B) insignificant
C) beneficial
D) problematic
E) compatible

9

When the author mentions "many experimental results" (line 7), his tone mainly suggests

A) complete satisfaction
B) pessimism
C) stimulation
D) criticism
E) limited appreciation

10

The author implies that in order to gain satisfactory qualities in experimental results (line 7), which areas should be further studied?

A) classic mechanics
B) theory of relativity
C) particles
D) mathematics
E) classic physics

11

It can be inferred from the passage that the main reason for the development of quantum field theory was to gain more knowledge about

A) annihilation of particles
B) physics
C) overall quantum theory applications in our lives
D) superconducting magnets
E) laser transistor

Questions 12-17 are based on the following passage.

Line

   Airbnb is an online marketplace that enables people to list, browse a place to stay temporarily, and rent vacation homes. It now has over 1,500,000 listings in 191 countries. Founded in 2008 in San Francisco, California, the company is privately owned.

5   Shortly after moving to San Francisco, roommates Chesky and Gebbia could not afford the rent for their loft in San Francisco. They made their living room into a bed and breakfast, accommodating three guests on air mattresses and providing homemade breakfast. In 2008, the founders focused on high-profile events where alternative lodging was————[QUESTION 14]

   To help fund the site, the founders created special edition breakfast cereals, with presidential candidates Barack Obama and John McCain, which generated more than $30,000 for the company's incubation.
10 $30,000 was not enough for the hotel business. [QUESTION 15]

   In the past, businesses in New York were regulated by zoning laws, but Mayor Steven Fulop thought that the city does not have enough inspectors to deal the number of local units being rented, and that rapid-evolving technology such as Airbnb made doing so impossible. Under the new legislation, Airbnb started to pay the city 6 percent hotel tax on the residential properties for temporary living space.

12

The first paragraph (lines 1-3) is constructed based on which of the following sequences?
A) the definition is made, current operating size is presented, and the company history is introduced
B) the company history is introduced, the definition is made, and current operating size is presented
C) the company history is introduced, current operating size is presented, and the definition is made
D) the definition is made, the company history is introduced, and current operating size is presented
E) current operating size is presented, the definition is made, and the company history is introduced

13

The purpose of the second paragraph (lines 4-7) is to
A) show the close tie between two friends
B) illustrate how the founders were inspired by the idea before established the company
C) announce any room can be rented out
D) show the humility of the company founders
E) illustrate chronic housing issues in San Francisco

14

Based on the information in the passage, which of the following words would most likely be used in the underlined portion in line 7?
A) plenty
B) affordable
C) easily accessible
D) scarce
E) vacant

15

Which choice best replaces the underlined sentence (line 10) to connect with the following sentenes?
A) NO CHANGE
B) Obama became the 44th President
C) Many hotels also provide cereal as breakfast
D) Airbnb soon started cereal business
E) They used the fund to fly to New York to promote.

16

The way Mayor Steven Fulop deals with Airbnb in line 11 can be seen as
A) practical
B) ideal
C) outmoded
D) authoritative
E) aggressive

17

The author mentions the new legislation in line 13 in order to
A) demonstrate every city is governed by legislation
B) reveal many hotels are operated illegally
C) emphasize Mayor Steven Fulop's achievement
D) describe the company's initial stage in New York
E) show the company's affinity to New York

Questions 18-23 are based on the following passage.

Line   I speak tonight for the dignity of man and the destiny of democracy. <u>I urge every member of both parties, Americans of all religions and of all colors, from every section of this country, to join me in that cause.</u> At times history and fate meet at <u>a single time in a single place</u> to shape a turning point in man's unending search for freedom. <u>So it was at Lexington and Concord. So it was a century ago at</u>
5   <u>Appomattox. So it was last week in Selma, Alabama.</u> Our lives have been marked with debate about <u>great issues;</u> issues of war and peace, issues of prosperity and depression. But rarely in any time does an issue lay bare <u>the secret heart of America</u> itself. Rarely are we met with a challenge, not to our growth or abundance, our welfare or our security, but rather to the values and the purposes and the meaning of our beloved Nation. <u>The issue of equal rights</u> for American Negroes is such an issue.
10   <u>There is no Negro problem. There is no Southern problem. There is no Northern problem. There is only an American problem.</u> The great phrases of that purpose till sound in every American heart.

18

The speaker's main concern when he addresses "I urge every member…that cause" (lines 1-3) is to

A) encourage the united participation
B) reveal the intensity of the problem
C) present the enjoyment of working together
D) urge the emotional responses
E) show the pleasure of better society

19

The phrase "a single time in a single place" in line 3 most directly implies the author's assumption that

A) a time to change has finally arrived
B) every American is anxious about unequal rights
C) man's unending search for freedom requires
    more time and place
D) there's a growing concern about equalization of
    men and women
E) the dignity of man hasn't been fully recognized yet

20

The speaker uses parallelism (There is no…American problem.) in lines 10-11 in order to

A) compare between actual problem and the secret
    heart of America
B) argue that there is no negro problem
C) list the least important problem to most important
    problem
D) generalize the issue as a single concern in society at
    large
E) devalue remaining problems from America

21

The speaker suggests that the cities mentioned in lines 4-5 were most strongly influenced by

A) the biased control from the law enforcement
B) the lack of pacifists' efforts
C) their own desire for freedom
D) the speaker's speech
E) economic and social problems

22

"The secret heart of America" in line 7 can most accurately be referred to as

A) the welfare of the public
B) the security of the public
C) the pursuit of abundance
D) the redistribution of wealth
E) the equal rights among races

23

Compared to the equal rights in line 9, the speaker's assumption of a great issue in line 6, was

A) easier to unite people
B) more openly debated
C) less significant
D) more urgent
E) less mentioned

Questions 24-29 are based on the following passage.

Line

What Drives Consumer Spending? First and foremost, income drives consumer spending. Recall that January's outsized gain was driven immediately by the lower tax withholdings called for by the Middle Class Tax Relief Act of 2010 (I certainly noticed a difference in my paycheck, and my local restaurants and bakeries were the primary beneficiaries). Another factor in consumers' spending decisions is how wealthy they are.

5 When consumers become wealthier, their spending goes up.

Why is the stock market up, especially given the tumultuous events in North Africa, the Middle East, and Japan? Good question but no data. A factor with no good data being one of the primary culprits, I'd like to think it's because folks have developed a more positive outlook on the U.S. economy, and indeed economic forecasts for growth in the U.S. have been revised upward since November of last year.

10 The Theory of Economics is not difficult in the sense in which mathematical and scientific techniques are difficult; but the fact that its modes of expression are much less precise than these, renders decidedly difficult the task of conveying it correctly to the minds of learners.

24

The author responds to the question in line 1, (what drive...spending?) with

A) emphatic confirmation

B) limited consent

C) scholastic curiosity

D) ambivalence

E) analytical speculation

25

The author mentions his local restaurant and bakeries in line 3 in order to introduce

A) some major beneficiaries of Tax Relief Act

B) some people unaffected by Tax Relief Act

C) the middle class consumer's spending habits

D) alternative explanation for consumer spending habit

E) humble neighbors he is living with

26

The author explains that consumer spending is primarily driven by

A) the periodic income increase alone

B) the periodic spending habit alone

C) the government policy such as Tax Relief Act of 2010

D) the periodic income increase and individual's wealth

E) stock market

27

The author implies that mathematical technique in line 10 is

A) highly developed than the Theory of Economics

B) concerned more with the minds of learners

C) easier than the Theory of Economics

D) less accurate than the Theory of Economics

E) more precise in its modes of expression

28

When the author says "expression are much less precise" (line 11), he implies that the economics is

A) inferior subject than math

B) not precisely developed subject

C) more conceptual subject than math

D) more advanced subject than math

E) less expressive subject than math

29

The author seems to find the economic forecasts for growth in line 9 from

A) tumultuous events in North Africa

B) the folks' more positive outlook on U.S. economy

C) the fact that the stock market went up

D) the direct impact of the Tax Relief Act of 2010

E) a factor with good data

Questions 30-35 are based on the following passage.

Line
Internet utopia begot carcinogenic diseases: cyberbullying. Some people see cyber-bullying as a form of cyberstalking, which involves more strategic and provoking intention than Internet trolling. A cyberbully may be anonymous and may solicit involvement of other people online who do not know the target. This is known as a "digital pile-on." Cyberbullying has been defined as "when the Internet, cell phones or other devices are
5 used to send or post text or images intended to hurt or embarrass another person." Cyberstalking has increased exponentially. Even police and prosecutors find themselves at risk, as gang members find out where they live — often to intimidate them into dropping a case." The FBI released the study "Stalking Victimization," which showed that one in four stalking victims had been cyberstalked as well. The Rape, Abuse and Incest National Network has released statistics that there are 3.4 million stalking victims each year. Of those, one in four
10 reported experiencing cyberstalking. According to Robin M. Kowalski, a social psychologist at Clemson University, cyberbullying has been shown to cause higher levels of anxiety for victims than normal bullying. Kowalksi states that this stems from the anonymity of the perpetrators, a common feature of cyberstalking.

30

In describing cyberstalking in line 1-2, the author sees that
A) it usually glosses itself over with Internet utopia
B) it can cause carcinogenic diseases to its victims
C) it is usually associated with physical attack
D) it has no strategy and attacks victims randomly
E) it has provocative strategy than Internet trolling

31

Which of the following statements would LEAST likely support the cyberbullying in the passage?
A) sending an anonymous message to intimidate victims
B) fabricating a story and posting it on Facebook
C) repeatedly sending defaming text messages
D) repeatedly damaging the internet cable of the target
E) solicit the involvement of other people

32

Which statement resembles most the pattern of "digital pile-on" mentioned in line 4?
A) An illegal drug dealer hires innocent followers, who do not know they are committing a crime
B) A corrupted politician works with his staff silently to defame other candidates
C) An unknown high school student sends multiple text messages to a victim to spread rumors
D) An older brother suggests his sibling to post a classmate's family matter on Facebook
E) A stalker uses a pile of emails to his victims

33

In lines 6-7, the reference to "police and prosecutors" is used mainly to suggest
A) even law enforcement are using cyberbullying
B) the countermeasure is not very effective
C) some police are conniving with organized criminals
D) cyberstalking is pervasive crime
E) police and prosecutors are hidden victims

34

"one in four" in lines 8 and 9 show the relations between stalking and cyberstalking victims are
A) exactly identical victims
B) possible representative of general pattern
C) difficult to verify
D) indicating the decline of cyberstalking victims
E) negligible because 75% of stalking victims are not cyberstalking victims

35

According to Robin M. Kowalski in line 10, cyberbullying is different from normal bullying primarily in that normal bullying
A) is more pervasive in society
B) is committed by anticipated perpetrators
C) causes no challenging mental pains
D) causes more anxiety and depression to victims
E) is mainly committed by family or close relatives

UNAUTHORIZED COPYING OR REUSE OF ANY PART OF THIS PAGE IS ILLEGAL

Questions 36-40 are based on the following passage.

Line
The natural position of woman is clearly a subordinate one. Such it has always been throughout the world, in all ages, and in many widely different conditions of society.

FIRST. Woman in natural physical strength is so greatly inferior to man that she is entirely in his power, quite incapable of self-defense, trusting to his generosity for protection.

5 This difference in physical strength must, in itself, always prevent such perfect equality.

Woman is also inferior to man in intellect. The difference in this particular may very probably be only a consequence of greater physical strength, giving greater power of endurance and increase of force to the intellectual faculty. connected with it. In many cases, as between the best individual minds of both sexes, the difference is no doubt very slight.

36

The primary purpose of the passage is to

A) advance one-sided opinion

B) question the common belief

C) change one's prejudice

D) predict the future condition of men

E) support generally accepted principle

37

Male chauvinist would most likely disagree with which assertion from the passage?

A) Man has greater endurance than woman

B) Woman won't change her subordinate position

C) The difference is no doubt very slight among the best individual minds of both sexes

D) Woman is intellectually inferior to man

E) Woman is physically inferior to man

*Male chauvinist = a male sexist

38

Which woman would generally agree with the author's belief in the passage?

A) female soldier

B) female university professor

C) female truck driver

D) female taekwondo master

E) the author's wife

39

The author believes that woman's subordinate position

A) will remain unchanged

B) is predicted to get worse in the future

C) depends on geographic constraints

D) has improved greatly

E) is limited to women's certain age group

40

The main difference between the second and third paragraph is that the second paragraph presents

A) the author's view; the third, public view

B) woman's intellectual; the third, that of man

C) woman's physical inferiority; the third, woman's intellectual inferiority

D) widely accepted view; the third, the author's

E) man's intellectual inferiority; the third, women's Intellectual inferiority

Test 3 Verbal Section   30 MINUTES, 60 QUESTIONS

Directions: the synonym questions ask you to find the most appropriate synonym to the question.

The analogy questions ask you to find the most appropriate analogy to the question.
Select the answer that best matches to the question.

Synonym Sample Question:

Q: SUPERIOR

   A higher rank

   B inferior

   C considerable

   D supermarket

   E supper

A) is the best answer because the synonym for superior is higher rank.

B) is incorrect because it applies the 'opposite concept.

C) and E) are irrelevant words.

D) is incorrect because it applies physical concept to mental concept

Test 3 Synonym questions 1 to 30

1. MODIFY
(A) model
(B) copy
(C) adhere
(D) alter
(E) mobilize

2. IMPLICATE
(A) divide
(B) disconnect
(C) imply
(D) conflict
(E) duplicate

3. ITEMIZE
(A) enumerate
(B) article
(C) lining
(D) confine
(E) idiomatic

4. VACILLATE
(A) vary
(B) unmoving
(C) value
(D) vocal
(E) fluctuate

5. REVITALIZE
(A) healthy
(B) bring back to life
(C) living
(D) release
(E) render

6. VERIFY

(A) authenticate

(B) veracity

(C) heartfelt

(D) sound

(E) obtain

7. RUMINATE

(A) forget

(B) ponder

(C) illuminate

(D) light

(E) roomy

8. ALLUSION

(A) direct

(B) reference

(C) avoid

(D) distance

(E) condone

9. ALTRUISM

(A) generosity

(B) alternation

(C) change

(D) truthfulness

(E) alter ego

10. AMBIENCE

(A) mood

(B) unpleasantness

(C) ambulance

(D) noise

(E) emergency

11. SLUGGISH

(A) agile

(B) slow

(C) independent

(D) clear

(E) steadfast

12. GLEE

(A) happiness

(B) sadness

(C) benevolence

(D) syndication

(E) mood

13. SCURRY

(A) stew

(B) funny

(C) tempt

(D) inactive

(E) rush

14. COWER

(A) cow like

(B) diffident

(C) obey

(D) stupid

(E) endanger

15. HOSTILE

(A) hospitalize

(B) heal

(C) aggressive

(D) medical

(E) lenient

16. EXTENSION

(A) delay

(B) cut short

(C) vast

(D) immaculate

(E) stipple

17. ROYAL

(A) regal

(B) declare

(C) creep

(D) invite

(E) name

18. LUNGE

(A) clear

(B) move briskly

(C) organ

(D) lung

(E) thrust

19. UNCLEAR

(A) ambiguous

(B) stalemate

(C) prosaic

(D) dormant

(E) patrician

20. IMPROVE

(A) recalcitrant

(B) ameliorate

(C) inadvertent

(D) proxy

(E) auspicious

21. BIG

(A) austere

(B) augment

(C) frugal

(D) fraternal

(E) gesticulate

22. TALKATIVE

(A) furtive

(B) gregarious

(C) genteel

(D) fraternal

(E) garrulous

23. INTIMATE

(A) lovely

(B) pacify

(C) friendly

(D) threaten

(E) interval

24. FROWN

(A) fish

(B) shrimp

(C) disapproval

(D) approval

(E) fame

25. CONCEITED

(A) nebulous

(B) lionize

(C) proud

(D) hidden

(E) centered

26. DECIDE

(A) tactic

(B) resolve

(C) rash

(D) meeting

(E) reconciliation

27. COMPREHENSIVE

(A) understanding

(B) covering everything

(C) proposal

(D) polite

(E) refined

28. PERSISTENT

(A) tenacious

(B) obedient

(C) clumsy

(D) strong

(E) ample

29. DIDACTIC

(A) teach

(B) dialect

(C) divisive

(D) intended to learn

(E) propel

30. FOOLISH

(A) imprudent

(B) glut

(C) grandiloquent

(D) free

(E) unjustified

Analogy Sample Question:

Q: River is to Ocean as:

A better is to good

B rain is to cloud

C father is to mother

D city is to country

E fork is to spoon

D is the correct answer. Just as the river is smaller than the Ocean, the city is smaller than the country. The pattern applied in this question is the Degree Pattern (small to big)

A) is incorrect because the word order is flipped over.

B) is incorrect because it applies the production pattern (cloud produces rain) C),

E) are incorrect because they apply the Antonym patterns.

Test 3 Analogy questions 31 to 60

31. Stamp is to letter as

(A) receipt is to credit card

(B) email is to internet

(C) song is to copyright

(D) ticket is movie

(E) post office is to postman

32. Hen is to rooster as
(A) horse is to race
(B) chicken is to KFC
(C) lion is to cat
(D) dragon is to myth
(E) lizard is to tail

33. Inflation is to price as bank loan is to
(A) interest
(B) mortgage
(C) credit card
(D) money
(E) borrowing

34. School year is to term as
(A) kitten is to puppy
(B) refrigerator is to kitchen
(C) tire is to vehicle
(D) poison is to ivy
(E) lollipop is to sugar

35. Lid is to trousers as
(A) coffee is to zipper
(B) shirt is to coat
(C) sleeve is to collar
(D) button is to clasp
(E) cuff is to bend

36. All-round entertainer is to entertainment as
(A) panacea is to medicine
(B) singer is to musician
(C) talent is to practice
(D) square is to strict
(E) dance is to performance

37. Abysmal is to bottomless as
(A) bottle is to neck
(B) malice is to bliss
(C) infinite is to endless
(D) fast is to slow
(E) humble is to meek

38. Ambiguous is to unclear as
(A) dubious is to doubtful
(B) ambience is to unpleasant mood
(C) ambivalent is to decided
(D) cleanse is to purification
(E) decisive is to quandary

39. Restriction is to freedom as
(A) circumvent is to direct
(B) enemy is to friend
(C) heterogeneous is to homogeneous
(D) skillful is to clumsy
(E) limitation is to liberty

40. Analyst is to data as
(A) mathematician is to teaching
(B) musician is to mp3
(C) teacher is to chalk
(D) biologist is to biology
(E) historian is to record

41. Authorize is to endorse as
(A) copy is to imitate
(B) borrow is to steal
(C) certify is to agree
(D) forgive is to excuse
(E) official is to formal

42. Unicorn is to myth as

(A) horse is to mammal

(B) myth is to fabrication

(C) Hercules is to legend

(D) Zeus is to god

(E) art is to tradition

43. Citation is to reference as advice is to

(A) expectation

(B) protection

(C) opinion

(D) announcement

(E) Implication

44. Country is to sovereignty as individual is to

(A) dependency

(B) independency

(C) veracity

(D) fidelity

(E) democracy

45. Farm is to muscle as

(A) laboratory is to brain

(B) ranch is to cattle

(C) garden is to flower

(D) school is to exam

(E) river is to boat

46. Magician is to illusion

(A) church is to holiness

(B) refrigerator is to preservation

(C) music is to lyric

(D) school is to report card

(E) company is to employee

47. Golden is to money as time is

(A) valuable

(B) silence

(C) patience

(D) mineral

(E) precious

48. Sometimes is to always as

(A) no one is to everyone

(B) rarely is to always

(C) often is to frequently

(D) seldom is to never

(E) little is to belittle

49. Needle is to spear as

(A) electric pole is to shield

(B) protect is to attack

(C) stitch is to fix

(D) decoration is to weapon

(E) armament is to knitting tool

50. Torch is to cigarette

(A) lamp is to health

(B) habit is to hazard

(C) beacon is to safety

(D) electric pole is to needle

(E) lighter is to extinguisher

51. Legacy is to birthright as

(A) alimony is to compensation

(B) tradition is to legend

(C) estate is to division

(D) endowment is to share

(E) heir is to ancestor

52. Conference room is to keynote speaker as

(A) zoo is to endangered animal

(B) boarder security guard is to border

(C) astronomy is to scientist

(D) physics is to logic

(E) movie is to hero

53. Cancer is to latent as

(A) economy is to stagnation

(B) economy is to inflation

(C) economy is to deflation

(D) finance is to default

(E) finance is to money

54. Vehicle is to insurance as

(A) egg is to shell

(B) shopping center is to mall

(C) chicken is to chick

(D) bus is to car

(E) bathroom is to shower curtain

55. Homebuilder is to house as

(A) coach is to strategy

(B) teacher is to grade

(C) governor is to mayor

(D) child is to play

(E) plumber is to repair

56. Wood is to chair as

(A) tank is to metal

(B) tire is to rubber

(C) strawberry is to jam

(D) wall is to brick

(E) gold is to mineral

57. Obesity is to heart attack as

(A) company is to work

(B) magazine is to issue

(C) autobiography is to life story

(D) virus is to flu

(E) lamp is to light

58. Star is to fan as

(A) politician is to voter

(B) teacher is to student

(C) director is to staff

(D) employer is to employee

(E) mom is to child

59. 180cm is to tall as

(A) 2am is to early

(B) 14hours is to 2pm

(C) sandwich is to two dollars

(D) population is to three million

(E) one gallon is to 3.7liters

60. Anger is to concern as

(A) despair is to dissatisfaction

(B) doubt is to suspect

(C) hope is to wish

(D) like is to hate

(E) antipathy is to apathy

Test 3

Answer Explanations

&

The Pattern Analyses

If your Test 3 scores are unsatisfactory,

Please Practice the Answer Explanations and then

solve the Actual Test 3 again.

ALL THE LOGIC AND RULES BEHIND EVERY
SINGLE SSAT QUESTION

TEST 3
READING SECTION

Please refer to the Reading Section Absolute Pattern Analyses

THE SYNONYM QUESTIONS	THE ANALOGY QUESTIONS
TEST 3 NO.1 ~ 60	TEST 3 NO. 31 ~ 60

Please refer to the Analogy Section Absolute Pattern Analyses

1	D	16	A
2	C	17	A
3	A	18	E
4	E	19	A
5	B	20	B
6	A	21	B
7	B	22	E
8	B	23	C
9	A	24	C
10	A	25	C
11	B	26	B
12	A	27	B
13	E	28	A
14	E	29	A
15	C	30	A

Questions 1-6 are based on the following passage.

Mr. Collins's triumph was complete. (1 & 2 & 3) **The power of displaying the grandeur of his patroness to his wondering visitors, (4) and of letting them see her civility towards himself** and his wife, was exactly what he had wished for.

"I should not have been at all surprised by her ladyship's asking us on Sunday to drink tea. Who could have foreseen such an attention as this?"

As the weather was fine, they had a pleasant walk. Every park has its beauty and its prospects, (3) **though she could not be in such raptures** as Mr. Collins expected.

Lady Catherine was a tall woman. (6) **Her air was not conciliating, nor was her manner of receiving them such as to make her visitors forget their inferior rank.** She was formidable by silence and was in authoritative tone.

Q1. Absolute Pattern 8: Understanding True Purpose
Question Pattern: According to the first paragraph, **Mr. Collins invited his visitors to Lady Catherine** mainly to

A) build a new constructive relations with the visitors **B) let the visitors observe Lady Catherine's hospitality towards him** C) reconcile the visitors with Lady Catherine D) find an opportunity to amass wealth E) work as a Lady Catherine's messenger	The power of displaying the grandeur of his patroness to his wondering visitors, and of letting them see her civility towards himself

---

Q2. Absolute Pattern 7: Understanding Attitude (Tone) Question
Question Pattern: According to the first paragraph, Mr. **Collins' persona** can be described as

A) cheerful B) condescending C) humble **D) showy** E) irate	**The power of displaying** the grandeur of his patroness to his wondering visitors, and of letting them see her civility towards himself

---

Q3. Absolute Pattern 3: Inference Question Finding an indirect suggestion (or guessing)
Question Pattern: The description in lines 5-6 (**Every park has... Mr. Collins expected**) **suggests that** 'she' in line 5

A) was resentful to the other characters B) distasted about the surroundings C) was in such great rapture **D) was not in such a joyful mood** E) was greatly inspired by the surroundings	Every park has its beauty and its prospects, (3) **though she could not be in such raptures** as Mr. Collins expected.

Q4. Absolute Pattern 6: Analogy Question Finding a similar situation
Question Pattern: Which of the following **analogies would be most in keeping with the main character trait of Mr. Collins?**

A) Susan often uses an assumed name similar to that of rich people to impress others B) Max morally opposes rich people's wrongdoings C) Daniel lives in constant fear of running out of money and relies on rich people D) Cathy finds condescending gesture of rich people and advises her friends to ignore it E) San always maintains humility to both the rich and the poor	The power of displaying the grandeur of his patroness to his wondering visitors, and of letting them see her civility towards himself..

Q5. **Absolute Pattern 9: Relationships Question**
Question Pattern: Lady Catherine's role with Mr. Collins is of

A) an aunt B) an old friend C) an abiding beneficiary **D) a condescending benefactor** E) a benign neighbor	The power of displaying the grandeur of **his patroness** to his wondering visitors, and of letting them see her civility towards himself

Q6. **Absolute Pattern 7: Understanding Attitude (Tone) Question**
Question Pattern: In lines 7-8, The narrator **observes that Lady Catherine** as

A) realistic and truly respectful person B) young and handsome person C) a person hiding a slightly inferiority **D) a person creating superiority by lowering others** E) a talkative person	Her air was not conciliating, nor was her manner of receiving them such as to make her visitors forget their inferior rank

Questions 7-11 are based on the following passage.

Quantum mechanics is a fundamental branch of physics. Important applications of quantum theory include <u>superconducting magnets, laser transistor, and semiconductors</u> such as (7) **the computer microprocessor** to understand many biological and physical phenomena.

When quantum mechanics was originally formulated, it was applied to models that (8) **do not correspond to relativistic classical mechanics.** Early attempts to merge quantum mechanics <u>for special relativity has involved</u> the replacement of the Schrödinger equation with a covariant equation. These theories were successful in explaining many <u>experimental results</u>, (9) **although they had certain unsatisfactory qualities** stemming from (10 & 11) **their neglect of the relativistic creation and annihilation of particles**.

A fully relativistic quantum theory required the development of quantum field theory, which applies quantization to a field less than a fixed set of particles.

Q7. **Absolute Pattern 4: Example Question**
Question Pattern: The author uses the example in lines 2-3 (**superconducting magnets…physical phenomena**) to

A) **describe practicality of Quantum mechanics** B) list currently unavailable technologies C) introduce a fundamental concept of Quantum mechanics D) emphasize how scientific theory can impact our lives E) list obsolete technology in the past	Important applications of quantum theory include superconducting magnets, laser transistor,and semiconductors such as (7) **the computer microprocessor** to understand many biological and physical phenomena

Q8. **Absolute Pattern 9: Relationships Question**
Question Pattern: The second paragraph (lines 4-8) presents the **relationship between Quantum mechanics and classical mechanics were originally**

A) **limited** B) insignificant C) beneficial D) problematic E) compatible	was applied to models that **do not correspond to relativistic classical mechanics.**

UNAUTHORIZED COPYING OR REUSE OF ANY PART OF THIS PAGE IS ILLEGAL

Q9. Absolute Pattern 7: Understanding Attitude (Tone) Question
Finding tone such as positive-negative, active-passive, mental-physical, subjective-objective
Question Pattern: When the author mentions "**many experimental results**" **(line 7), his tone** mainly suggests

A) complete satisfaction B) pessimism C) stimulation D) criticism **E) limited appreciation**	These theories were **successful in explaining many experimental results, although they had certain unsatisfactory qualities** stemming from their neglect of the relativistic creation and annihilation of particles.

Q10. Absolute Pattern 3: Inference Question Finding an indirect suggestion (or guessing)
Question Pattern: The author implies that in order **to gain satisfactory qualities in experimental** results (line 7), which areas should be further studied?

A) classic mechanics B) theory of relativity **C) particles** D) mathematics E) classic physics	although they had certain unsatisfactory qualities stemming from **their neglect of the relativistic creation and annihilation of particles.**

Q11. Inference Question Finding an indirect suggestion (or guessing)
Question Pattern: It can be inferred from the passage that the main reason **for the development of quantum field** theory was to gain more knowledge about

A) annihilation of particles B) physics C) overall quantum theory applications in our lives D) superconducting magnets E) laser transistor	although they had certain unsatisfactory qualities stemming from their **neglect of the relativistic creation and annihilation of particles.**

Questions 12-17 are based on the following passage.

(12) **Airbnb is an online marketplace** that enables people to list, browse a place to stay temporarily, and rent vacation homes. **It now has over 1,500,000 listings** in 191 countries. **Founded in 2008** in San Francisco, California, the company is privately owned.

Shortly after moving to San Francisco, roommates Chesky and Gebbia could not afford the rent for their loft in San Francisco. (13) **They made their living room into a bed and breakfast, accommodating three guests on air mattresses and providing homemade breakfast.** In 2008, the founders focused on high-profile events where (14) **alternative lodging was————[QUESTION 14]**

To help fund the site, the founders created special edition breakfast cereals, with presidential candidates Barack Obama and John McCain, which generated more than $30,000 for the company's incubation. $30,000 was not enough for the hotel business. [QUESTION 15]

(15) In the past, businesses in New York were regulated by zoning laws, but Mayor Steven Fulop thought that (16) **the city does not have enough inspectors to deal the number of local units being rented, and that rapid-evolving technology such as Airbnb made doing so impossible.** Under (17) the new legislation, **Airbnb started** to pay the city 6 percent hotel tax on the residential properties for temporary living space.

Q12. Absolute Pattern 10: Understanding the Structure of the Passage
Question Pattern: The first paragraph (lines 1-3) is constructed based on which of the following sequences?

A) **the definition is made, current operating size is presented, and the company history is introduced** B) the company history is introduced, the definition is made, and current operating size is presented C) the company history is introduced, current operating size is presented, and the definition is made D) the definition is made, the company history is introduced, and current operating size is presented E) current operating size is presented, the definition is made, and the company history is introduced	**Airbnb is an online marketplace** that enables people to list, browse a place to stay temporarily, and rent vacation homes. **It now has over 1,500,000 listings** in 191 countries. **Founded in 2008** in San Francisco, California, the company is privately owned.

Q13. Absolute Pattern 1: Main Idea Question
Question Pattern: The purpose of the second paragraph (lines 4-7) is to

A) show the close tie between two friends B) **illustrate how the founders were inspired by the idea before established the company** C) announce any room can be rented out D) show the humility of the company founders E) illustrate chronic housing issues in San Francisco	They made their living room into a bed and breakfast, accommodating three guests on air mattresses and providing homemade breakfast.

Q14. Absolute Pattern 5: Word-In-Context Question
Question Pattern: Based on the information in the passage, which of the following words would most likely be used in the underlined portion in line 7?

A) plenty B) affordable C) easily accessible D) **scarce** E) vacant	In 2008, the founders focused on high-profile events where (14) **alternative lodging was scarce.** *The remaining choices are all opposite.

UNAUTHORIZED COPYING OR REUSE OF ANY PART OF THIS PAGE IS ILLEGAL

Q15. Absolute Pattern 10: Understanding the Structure of the Passage
Finding the structural organization of the passage or paragraph
Question Pattern: Which choice best replaces the **underlined sentence (line 10) to connect with the following sentences?**

A) NO CHANGE B) Obama became the 44th President C) Many hotels also provide cereal as breakfast D) Airbnb soon started cereal business **E) They used the fund to fly to New York to promote**	Only (E) connects the previous sentence and the following one: "In the past, businesses **in New York** were regulated by zoning laws,"

Q16. Absolute Pattern 7: Understanding Attitude (Tone) Question
Finding tone such as positive-negative, active-passive, mental-physical, subjective-objective
Question Pattern: The way **Mayor Steven Fulop deals with Airbnb** in line 11 can be seen as

A) practical B) ideal C) outmoded D) authoritative E) aggressive	but Mayor Steven Fulop thought that **the city does not have enough inspectors to deal the number of local units being rented, and that rapid-evolving technology such as Airbnb made doing so impossible.**

Q17. Absolute Pattern 10: Understanding the Structure of the Passage
Question Pattern: The author mentions the **new legislation** in line 13 in order to

A) demonstrate every city is governed by legislation B) reveal many hotels are operated illegally C) emphasize Mayor Steven Fulop's achievement **D) describe the company's initial stage in New York** E) show the company's affinity to New York	**the new legislation,** Airbnb started to pay the city 6 percent hotel tax on the residential properties for temporary living space. * The main focus of the passage is on Airbnb. All the rest choices deviate from the main focus.

Questions 18-23 are based on the following passage.

I speak tonight for the dignity of man and the destiny of democracy. (18) **I urge every member of both parties**, Americans of all religions and of all colors, from every section of this country, **to join me** in that cause. At times history and fate meet at a single time in a single place (19) **to shape a turning point** in man's unending (21) **search for freedom. So it was** at Lexington and Concord. So it was a century ago at Appomattox. So it was last week in Selma, Alabama. Our lives have been marked with debate about great issues; issues of war and peace, issues of prosperity and depression. (23) **But rarely in any time does an issue lay bare** the secret heart of America itself. Rarely are we met with a challenge, not to our growth or abundance, our welfare or our security, but rather to the values and the purposes and the meaning of our beloved Nation. (22) The issue of equal rights for American Negroes **is is such an issue**.

There is no Negro problem. There is no Southern problem. There is no Northern problem. (20) **There is only an American problem**. The great phrases of that purpose till sound in every American heart.

Q18. Absolute Pattern 3: Inference Question Finding an indirect suggestion (or guessing)
Question Pattern: The speaker's main concern when he addresses "**I urge every member...that cause**" (lines 1-3) is to

| A) encourage the united participation
B) reveal the intensity of the problem
C) present the enjoyment of working together
D) urge the emotional responses
E) show the pleasure of better society | **I urge every member of both parties**, Americans of all religions and of **all colors**, from every section of this country, to **join me** |

Q19. Absolute Pattern 3: Inference Question Finding an indirect suggestion (or guessing)
Question Pattern: The phrase "**a single time, in single place**" in line 3 most directly implies the author's assumption that

| A) a time to change has finally arrived
B) every American is anxious about unequal rights
C) man's unending search for freedom requires more time
D) there's a growing concern about equalization of men and women
E) the dignity of man hasn't been fully recognized yet | At times history and fate meet at a single time in a single place to shape a turning point in man's unending search for freedom.
E) is too abstract |

Q20. Absolute Pattern 10: Understanding the Structure of the Passage
Question Pattern: The speaker uses **parallelism (There is no...American problem.)** in lines 10-11 in order to

| A) compare between actual problem and the secret heart of America
B) argue that there is no negro problem
C) list the least important problem to most important problem
D) generalize the issue as a single concern in society at large
E) devalue remaining problems from America | **There is only an American problem** |

Q21. Absolute Pattern 8: Understanding True Purpose
Question Pattern: The speaker suggests that the **cities mentioned in lines 4-5** were most strongly influenced by

| A) the biased control from the law enforcement
B) the lack of pacifists' efforts
C) their own desire for freedom
D) the speaker's speech
E) economic and social problems | **search for freedom. So it was** at Lexington and Concord. So it was a century ago at Appomattox. So it was last week in Selma, Alabama. |

Q22. Absolute Pattern 3: Inference Question Finding an indirect suggestion (or guessing)
Question Pattern: "**The secret heart of America**" in line 7 can most accurately be referred to as

A) the welfare of the public B) the security of the public C) the pursuit of abundance D) the redistribution of wealth **E) the equal rights among races**	The issue of equal rights for American Negroes **is such an issue**.

Q23. Absolute Pattern 9: Relationships Question
Question Pattern: Compared to the equal rights in line 9, the speaker's assumption of a **great issue in line 6**, was

A) easier to unite people **B) more openly debated** C) less significant D) more urgent E) less mentioned	But rarely in any time does an issue lay bare the secret heart of America itself. *The question asks the opposite situation.

Questions 24-29 are based on the following passage.

What Drives Consumer Spending? (24) **First and foremost**, income drives consumer spending. Recall that January's outsized gain was driven immediately by the lower tax withholdings called for by the Middle Class Tax Relief Act of 2010 (I certainly noticed a difference in my paycheck, and my local restaurants and bakeries were the (25) **primary beneficiaries**). (26) **Another factor in consumers' spending decisions is how wealthy** they are. When consumers become wealthier, their spending goes up.

Why is the stock market up, especially given the tumultuous events in North Africa, the Middle East, and Japan? Good question but no data. A factor with no good data being one of the primary culprits, (29) I'd like to think it's because folks have developed **a more positive outlook** on the U.S. economy, and indeed economic forecasts for growth in the U.S. have been revised upward since November of last year. The Theory of Economics is not difficult in the sense in which mathematical and scientific techniques are difficult; but the fact that its modes of (27 & 28) **expression are much less precise** than these, renders decidedly difficult the task of conveying it correctly to the minds of learners.

Q24. Absolute Pattern 7: Understanding Attitude (Tone) Question
Finding tone such as positive-negative, active-passive, mental-physical, subjective-objective
Question Pattern: The author **responds to the question in line 1, (what drive...spending?)** with

A) emphatic confirmation B) limited consent C) scholastic curiosity D) ambivalence E) analytical speculation	**First and foremost**, income drives consumer spending

Q25. Absolute Pattern 4: Example Question
Finding the true purpose behind a specific name or idea within a sente
Question Pattern: The author mentions his **local restaurant and bakeries** in line 3 in order to introduce

A) some major beneficiaries of Tax Relief Act B) some people unaffected by Tax Relief Act C) the middle class consumer's spending habits D) alternative explanation for consumer spending habit E) humble neighbors he is living with	(I certainly noticed a difference in my paycheck, and my local restaurants and bakeries were the **primary beneficiaries**).

Q26. Absolute Pattern 2: Summary Question
Summarizing a sentence or entire passage
Question Pattern: The author explains that **consumer spending is primarily driven** by

A) the periodic income increase alone B) the periodic spending habit alone C) the government policy such as Tax Relief Act of 2010 **D) the periodic income increase and individual's wealth** E) stock market	First and foremost, **income drives consumer spending.** **...Another factor in consumers'** **spending decisions is how wealthy** they are. *****When two things (i.e., comparison, contrast, list)** **are presented, ALWAYS rely on the SECOND thing.**

Q27. Absolute Pattern 9: Relationships Question
Finding relations between the cause-effect, comparison-contrast, characters, and ideas
Question Pattern: The author implies that **mathematical technique** in line 10 is

A) highly developed than the Theory of Economics B) concerned more with the minds of learners C) easier than the Theory of Economics D) less accurate than the Theory of Economics **E) more precise in its modes of expression**	The Theory of Economics is not difficult in the sense in which mathematical and scientific techniques are difficult; but the fact that its modes of **expression are much** **less precise**

Q28. Absolute Pattern 9: Relationships Question
Finding relations between the cause-effect, comparison-contrast, characters, and ideas
Question Pattern: When the author says **"expression are much less precise"** (line 11), he implies that the
economics is

A) inferior subject than math B) not precisely developed subject **C) more conceptual subject than math** D) more advanced subject than math E) less expressive subject than math	its modes of **expression are much less precise.** * All the other choices are opposite in one way or another. Mode of expression can be understood as "conceptual."

Q29. Absolute Pattern 3: Inference Question Finding an indirect suggestion (or guessing)
Question Pattern: The author seems to find the **economic forecasts for growth in line 9** from

A) tumultuous events in North Africa **B) the folks' more positive outlook on U.S. economy** C) the fact that the stock market went up D) the direct impact of the Tax Relief Act of 2010 E) a factor with good data	I'd like to think it's because folks have developed **a more** **positive outlook**

Questions 30-35 are based on the following passage.

Internet utopia begot carcinogenic diseases: cyberbullying. Some people see cyber-bullying as a form of cyberstalking, which involves (30) **more strategic and provoking intention than Internet trolling**. (31) **A cyberbully may be anonymous and may solicit involvement of other people online (32) who do not know the target**. This is known as a "digital pile-on." Cyberbullying has been defined as "when the Internet, cell phones or other devices are used to send or post text or images intended to hurt or embarrass another person."
(33) **Cyberstalking has increased exponentially**. Even police and prosecutors find themselves at risk, as gang members find out where they live — often to intimidate them into dropping a case." The FBI released the study "Stalking Victimization," which showed that (34) one in four stalking victims had been cyberstalked as well. The Rape, Abuse and Incest National Network has released statistics that there are 3.4 million stalking victims each year. Of those, one in four reported experiencing cyberstalking. According to Robin M. Kowalski, a social psychologist at Clemson University, cyberbullying has been shown to cause higher levels of anxiety for victims than normal bullying. Kowalksi states that this (35) **stems from the anonymity** of the perpetrators, a common feature of cyberstalking.

Q30. Absolute Pattern 9: Relationships Question
Finding relations between the cause-effect, comparison-contrast, characters, and ideas
Question Pattern: In describing **cyberstalking in line 1-2**, the author sees that

A) it usually glosses itself over with Internet utopia B) it can cause carcinogenic diseases to its victims C) it is usually associated with physical attack D) it has no strategy and attacks victims randomly **E) it has provocative strategy than Internet trolling**	cyberstalking, which involves **more strategic and provoking intention than Internet trolling**

Q31. Absolute Pattern 2: Summary Question   Summarizing a sentence or entire passage
Question Pattern: Which of the following statements would **LEAST likely support the cyberbullying** in the passage?

A) sending an anonymous message to intimidate victims B) fabricating a story and posting it on Facebook C) repeatedly sending defaming text messages **D) repeatedly damaging the internet cable of the target** E) solicit the involvement of other people	A cyberbully may be anonymous and may solicit involvement of other people online who do not know the target D) is physical.

Q32. Absolute Pattern 6: Analogy Question Finding a similar situation
Question Pattern: Which statement resembles most the pattern of "**digital pile-on**" mentioned in line 4?

A) An illegal drug dealer hires innocent followers, who do not know they are committing a crime B) A corrupted politician works with his staff silently to defame other candidates C) An unknown high school student sends multiple text messages to a victim to spread rumors D) An older brother suggests his sibling to post a classmate's family matter on Facebook E) A stalker uses a pile of emails to his victims	**who do not know the target**. **This is** known as a "digital pile-on." *"**This**" is called the amplifier in technical term. Amplifier plays a key role in finding the main issue.

Q33. Absolute Pattern 4: Example Question
Finding the true purpose behind a specific name or idea within a sentence
Question Pattern: In lines 6-7, the reference to **"police and prosecutors"** is used mainly to suggest

A) even law enforcement are using cyberbullying B) the countermeasure is not very effective C) some police are conniving with organized criminals **D) cyberstalking is pervasive crime** E) police and prosecutors are hidden victims	**Cyberstalking has increased exponentially**. Even police and prosecutors find themselves at risk,

Q34. Absolute Pattern 3: Inference Question Finding an indirect suggestion (or guessing)
Question Pattern: "one in four" in lines 8 and 9 show the relations between stalking and cyberstalking victims are

A) exactly identical victims **B) possible representative of general pattern** C) difficult to verify D) indicating the decline of cyberstalking victims E) negligible because 75% of stalking victims are not cyberstalking victims	<u>one in four</u> stalking victims had been cyberstalked. <u>one in four</u> reported experiencing cyberstalking. "One in four" or 25% illustrates a possible representative of general pattern.

Q35. Absolute Pattern 9: Relationships Question
Finding relations between the cause-effect, comparison-contrast, characters, and ideas
Question Pattern: According to **Robin M. Kowalski** in line 10, cyberbullying is different from normal bullying primarily in that **normal bullying**

A) is more pervasive in society **B) is committed by anticipated perpetrators** C) causes no challenging mental pains D) causes more anxiety and depression to victims E) is mainly committed by family or close relatives	cyberbullying has been shown to cause higher levels of anxiety for victims than normal bullying. Kowalksi states that this **stems from the anonymity** of the perpetrators. *The opposite of anonymity should be "anticipated".

UNAUTHORIZED COPYING OR REUSE OF ANY PART OF THIS PAGE IS ILLEGAL

Questions 36-40 are based on the following passage.

> (Q36.A) **The natural position of woman is clearly a subordinate one.** (Q39.A) **Such it has always been through-out the world, in all ages**, and in many widely different conditions of society.
>
> FIRST. (Q40.C) **Woman in natural physical strength is so greatly inferior** to man that she is entirely in his power, quite incapable of self-defense, trusting to his generosity for protection. This difference in physical strength must, in itself, always prevent such perfect equality.
>
> Woman is also inferior to man in intellect. The difference in this particular may very probably be only a consequence of greater physical strength, **giving greater power of endurance** and increase of force to the intellectual faculty. connected with it. In many cases, as between the best individual minds of both sexes, (Q37.C) **the difference is no doubt very slight.**

Q36. Absolute Pattern 1: Main Idea Question
Finding the main idea of the entire passage, a specific paragraph, or sentences
Question Pattern: The primary purpose of the passage is to

A) advance one-sided opinion B) question the common belief C) change one's prejudice D) predict the future condition of men E) support generally accepted principle	The natural position of woman is clearly, to a limited degree, a subordinate one. *The author does not compare others' view. Therefore, it is one-sided opinion

Q37. Absolute Pattern 3: Inference Question Finding an indirect suggestion (or guessing)
Question Pattern: Male chauvinist would most likely <u>disagree</u> with which assertion from the passage?

A) Man has greater endurance than woman B) Woman won't change her subordinate position **C) The difference is no doubt very slight among the best individual minds of both sexes** D) Woman is intellectually inferior to man E) Woman is physically inferior to man *Male chauvinist = a male sexist	There have been women of a very high order of genius; there have been very many women of great talent *male chauvinist =a person who is excessively prejudiced to male dominance. Male chauvinist will disagree with the statement (C) "the difference is no doubt very slight."

Q38. Absolute Pattern 3: Inference Question Finding an indirect suggestion (or guessing)
Question Pattern: Which woman would generally agree with the author's belief in the passage?

A) female soldier B) female university professor C) female truck driver D) female taekwondo master **E) the author's wife**	The author views women are innately inferior to men both physically and mentally, for which only his wife may agree. The rest choices are those who won't accept the author's view on physical and mental inferiority.

Q39. Absolute Pattern 7: Understanding Attitude (Tone) Question
Finding tone such as positive-negative, active-passive, mental-physical, subjective-objective
Question Pattern: The author believes that woman's subordinate position

A) will remain unchanged B) is predicted to get worse in the future C) depends on geographic constraints D) has improved greatly E) is limited to women's certain age group	The author believes that woman's subordinate position will remain unchanged

Q40. **Absolute Pattern 10: Understanding the Structure of the Passage**
Finding the structural organization of the passage or paragraph
Question Pattern: The main difference between the **second and third paragraph** is that the second paragraph presents

A) the author's view; the third, public view
B) woman's intellectual; the third, that of man
C) woman's physical inferiority;
   the third, woman's intellectual inferiority
D) widely accepted view; the third, the author's
E) man's intellectual inferiority;
   the third, women's Intellectual inferiority
	The second paragraph presents a woman's physical inferiority, whereas the third one presents intellectual inferiority.
	When two things (i.e., two paragraphs, characters, sentences, theories, ideas, numbers) are being compared in a question, focus on the SECOND THING. This will clarify the most opaque two choices.
	
	A) There's no public view B), E) Main issue should be women's inferiority, not men's. D) there's no widely accepted view

Test 3 Absolute Patterns for the Analogy Section

Absolute Pattern 3. Purpose (Tool) Pattern
Finding Relationships between the Purpose of Individual to Object, to its Function, its User, its Use, and its Association

Q31. D is the Best Answer.   Letter needs Stamp as (D) (watching) movie needs a ticket, a sort of approval for using the service. (A) is incorrect because receipt is used after, not before the service.

Absolute Pattern 1. Category Pattern
Finding Part/Whole, Same Type/Kind, Association

Q32. C is the Best Answer. Hen and rooster are chicken category. (C) lion and cat are feline category.

Absolute Pattern 1. Category Pattern
Finding Part/Whole, Same Type/Kind, Association

Q33. A is the Best Answer. Inflation is measured by price index as bank loan is measured by interest rate.

Absolute Pattern 1. Category Pattern
Finding Part/Whole, Same Type/Kind, Association

Q34. E is the Best Answer.   Term is part of School year as sugar is a part of lollipop (whole).
(B), (C), and (D) are flipped over.

Absolute Pattern 3. Purpose (Tool) Pattern
Finding Relationships between the Purpose of Individual to Object, to its Function, its User, its Use, and its Association

Q35. A is the Best Answer. Lid prevents coffee from spill as does zipper to trousers.

Absolute Pattern 4. Characteristic Pattern
Finding Characteristic of Person, Place, Object, or Idea and its Associated Action

Q36. A is the Best Answer.   All-round entertainer performs every field of entertainment as (A) panacea does to illness.

Absolute Pattern 2. Synonym/Antonym
Finding a similar or an opposite meaning between words

Q37. C is the Best Answer.   Abysmal is a synonym to bottomless as (C) infinite is a synonym to endless. (B) malice is to bliss, (D) fast is to slow are antonym.

(E) humble is a synonym to meek. The problem is that it doesn't correspond to the question category.

Absolute Pattern 2. Synonym/Antonym
Finding a similar or an opposite meaning between words

Q38. A is the Best Answer. Ambiguous is a synonym to unclear as (A) dubious is a synonym to doubtful. (B), (C), and (E) are all antonym. (D) cleanse is a synonym to purification. The problem is that the words are positive while the question and (A) are negative—different category.

Absolute Pattern 2. Synonym/Antonym
Finding a similar or an opposite meaning between words

Q39. E is the Best Answer. Restriction is an antonym to freedom as (E) limitation is an antonym to liberty. All four words are related to each other .

Absolute Pattern 3. Purpose (Tool) Pattern
Finding Relationships between the Purpose of Individual to Object, to its Function, its User,
its Use, and its Association

Q40. E is the Best Answer. Analyst uses data as (E) historian uses record. Both data and record are synonym.

Absolute Pattern 12. Human-Nonhuman Pattern
Finding Active-Passive/Human-Nonhuman Association

Q41. C is the Best Answer. Authorize and endorse and (C) certify and agree are all synonym.

Absolute Pattern 1. Category Pattern
Finding Part/Whole, Same Type/Kind, Association

Q42. C is the Best Answer. Unicorn is myth as (C) Hercules is to legend. Myth and legend are synonym and the same category. (D) is only two examples that has no bigger category like legend and myth.

Absolute Pattern 2. Synonym/Antonym
Finding a similar or an opposite meaning between words

Q43. C is the Best Answer. Citation is a synonym to reference as advice is a synonym to (C) opinion

6. Definition Pattern
Finding Definition/Concept of person, place, thing, and emotion

Q44 B is the Best Answer. Country has sovereignty as individual has (B) independency. They are synonym.

6. Definition Pattern
Finding Definition/Concept of person, place, thing, and emotion

Q45. A is the Best Answer. This question asks aboutsymbolic meaning behind the word.

Farm uses muscle as (A) laboratory uses intellect. Both muscle and brain are symbolic words rather than literal word. All the remaining choices use literal words.

UNAUTHORIZED COPYING OR REUSE OF ANY PART OF THIS PAGE IS ILLEGAL

Absolute Pattern 7. Mental (Emotion) Pattern
Finding Feeling/Mental Concept and its Emotion

Q46. A is the Best Answer. Magician uses illusion as (A) church uses holiness. These are our emotion or mental concept. The other choices use physically verifiable words.

6. Definition Pattern
Finding Definition/Concept of person, place, thing, and emotion

Q47 B is the Best Answer. Silence is Golden. Time is money. Both refers to the proverb.

Absolute Pattern 5. Degree Pattern
Finding a Degree and a Shape in person, place, thing, and emotion

Q48 D is the Best Answer.
Sometimes and seldom are synonymous adverb in opposite way as are always and never.

Absolute Pattern 1. Category Pattern
Finding Part/Whole, Same Type/Kind, Association   Absolute Pattern

Q49 E is the Best Answer. It appears Shape pattern in the beginning. So we searched something looks similar to twig. No luck. The answer is: (E) armament (spear) is to knitting tool (needle).

Absolute Pattern 5. Degree Pattern
Finding a Degree and a Shape in person, place, thing, and emotion

Q50 D is the Best Answer. "Torch and cigarette" has the same shape as is (D) electric pole is to needle

6. Definition Pattern
Finding Definition/Concept of person, place, thing, and emotion

Q51 A is the Best Answer. Legacy is given by birthright as (A) alimony is given by compensation.

Absolute Pattern 1. Category Pattern
Finding Part/Whole, Same Type/Kind, Association   Absolute Pattern

Q52. E is the Best Answer. Conference room hosts a keynote speaker as the main figure. Movie has the main figure, usually a hero.

6. Definition Pattern
Finding Definition/Concept of person, place, thing, and emotion

Q53. A is the Best Answer. Cancer is to latent means that cancer is inside of our body but not yet detected. Stagnation in economy acts in the same way.

Absolute Pattern 3. Purpose (Tool) Pattern
Finding Relationships between the Purpose of Individual to Object, to its Function, its User, its Use, and its Association

Q54. A is the Best Answer. Vehicle is protected by insurance as is (A) egg.to shell

Absolute Pattern 3. Purpose (Tool) Pattern
Finding Relationships between the Purpose of Individual to Object, to its Function, its User, its Use, and its Association

Q55. A is the Best Answer. Homebuilder creates house as (A) coach creates strategy.

Absolute Pattern 3. Purpose (Tool) Pattern
Finding Relationships between the Purpose of Individual to Object, to its Function, its User, its Use, and its Association

Q56. C is the Best Answer. Chair is made of wood as jam is made of strawberry. (A), (B), and (D) are flipped over. (E) is part/whole pattern.

Absolute Pattern 8. Production Pattern
Finding Cause-and-Effect in Person, Concept, and Object

Q57. D is the Best Answer. This question asks about what causes what plus the same category with the question: Obesity causes heart attack as (D) virus is to flu.

Absolute Pattern 8. Production Pattern
Finding Cause-and-Effect in Person, Concept, and Object

Q58. A is the Best Answer. Star needs Fans as politician needs voters.
Such a voluntarily supporting relation doesn't exist in any other choices.

Absolute Pattern 11. Subjective-Objective Pattern
Finding Quality-Quantity, Tangible-Intangible Association

Q59. A is the Best Answer. Both "tall" and "early" are subjective view. All the remaining choices use numeric quantifiers that can be measured objectively.

Absolute Pattern 5. Degree Pattern
Finding a Degree and a Shape in person, place, thing, and emotion

Q60. A is the Best Answer. Anger is greater degree than concern as (A) despair is to dissatisfaction.

(B) doubt is to suspect is synonym; (C) hope is to wish is synonym;

(D) like is to hate is antonym; (E) antipathy is to apathy has a degree but not as clear as (A).

Chapter 3 Summary

The Chapter Summary contains equal portions of

12 Absolute Patterns for Analogy Section and

10 Absolute Patterns for Reading Section.

You may study all at once to significantly

improve your understanding and your scores.

Chapter 3

12 Absolute Patterns for the Analogy Section

Absolute Pattern 2. Synonym/Antonym
Finding similar or opposite meaning between words

Q2-1 Chronicle is to history as	Q2-2. Antipathy is to sympathy as love is to
A) epoch is to era	A) abhor
B) businessman is to entrepreneur	B) dislike
C) dancer is to choreography	C) friendship
D) ending is to beginning	D) illusion
E) inform is to reform	E) magic

(Q2-1) The correct answer is A

San: Chronicle is a synonym to history as epoch is a synonym to era.

Jimin: Isn't an entrepreneur a fancy word for a businessman?

San: Make sure your choice belongs to the same category with the question: chronicle, history, epoch, and era are all history related words—the same category.

B) is wrong for two reasons: first, non-category. Second, B) is human. The question is a non-human concept. So, it's a different category.

For choice C, Dancer is human, while choreography is a synonym to dance (concept).

The choreography is the act performed by a dancer.

Jimin How about D)?

San Choice D is Antonym Pattern. Choice E is assonance or Homophony that we will be discussed later.

San Q2-2: Antipathy is antonym for sympathy; Love is antonym for (A) abhor.

Jimin I didn't know what the "abhor" was, so I chose B. why not B, San?

San If you had no idea what the "ABHOR" was, don't worry. Just divide it into meaningful fractions like ab/hor. (Oh! Horror) So, next time, when you spot some difficult, never-heard-of word, don't be shy, just divide it and get some clue out of it. You can at least see if the meaning is a negative type or a positive type.

Choice B is wrong because "love" is not the antonym for "dislike." "like" is its antonym.

Chapter 3

12 Absolute Patterns for the Analogy Section

Absolute Pattern 3. Purpose (Tool) Pattern
Finding Relationships between the Purpose of Individual to Object, to Its Function, Its User, Its Use, and Its Association

Q3 Stopwatch is to timing as

    A) oxygen tank is to breathe

    B) swim fins is to fast

    C) swim vest is to heavy

    D) beach is to vacation

    E) security guard is to safeguard

The correct answer is A

San   The purpose of stopwatch is to measure timing as the purpose of oxygen tank is to breathe in the water.

Jimin: Still don't get it. For B) the purpose of swim fins is to swim fast.

Jimin: For C) when we use swim vest, we feel heavy.

Jimin: For D) the purpose of going to beach is for vacation

Jimin: Finally For E) the purpose of security guard is for safeguarding the area.
Then, no choices are less qualified than the answer I think.

San   First, stopwatch is a tool to check the time. You must follow the same paradigm.

What I mean is that you should look for a pair of words that shows similar functions or purposes.

For B) the purpose of swim fins is to SWIMMING fast, not fast. Fast is only a degree, not what it does.

For C) the purpose of swim vest is to floating. "Heavy," again, is a degree just as fast is in B).

For D) beach is location not a tool like a stopwatch in the question.

For E) it is correct to say the purpose of security guard is to safeguarding. And also security guard can be found on the beach. In that sense, it is highly likely to be associated with the question.

However, most importantly, it is human. That is, a different category with the question, the tool.

Stopwatch and oxygen tank are more closely associated with each other than human.

Chapter 3

12 Absolute Patterns for the Analogy Section

Absolute Pattern 4. Characteristic Pattern
Finding a Characteristic of Person, Place, Object, or Idea and its Associated Action

Q4 Embarrassment is to time as

    A) gift is to cake

    B) conceal is to fleeting

    C) arrow is to mistake

    D) permanent is to happiness

    E) birthday is to celebration

The correct answer is B

San   We tend to conceal Embarrassment as time tends to fleeting.

    The other choices are not associated with each other and with the question-stem.

Jimin: so Embarrassment goes straight down to "conceal" and time goes straight down to "fleeting." For this question, the answer itself wasn't difficult to understand, once we know it. But the question was quite out of place.

Jimin: that wasted me a lot of time to figure out what it meant to each choice. I chose C) thinking that mistake causes embarrassment and time is as fast as arrow

San: "arrow" is a thing. "Embarrassment," "time," "conceal," and "fleeting" are all mental concept.

Jimin: How each choice is created, San? It's all confusing because they are all related words with the question.

You mean how SSAT guys create the questions like these? Do you know the game called "Word Relay?"

San: To confuse students, they tag or relay the question words like mother to father or forward to backward.

San: and also, they use different patterns from the question-stem. We will learn a great deal as we practice the real questions in the following chapters.

Chapter 3

12 Absolute Patterns for the Analogy Section

Absolute Pattern 5. Degree Pattern
Finding Degree and Shape in person, place, thing, and emotion

Q5-1. Dime is to cent as	Q5-2. Round is to bottle as
A) yard is to area	A) bottle is to glass
B) meter is to centimeter	B) indication is to sign
C) sea is to sky	C) coffee is to caffeine
D) phone is to communication	D) monitor is to square
E) big is to great	E) monitor is to flat

(Q5-1) The correct answer is B

San: Dime is bigger than cent, and meter is bigger than centimeter.
The degree is shrinking. Therefore, you should select the one that has a degree concept, with shrinking pattern.

Jimin How about A)?

San   Yard is used to measure an area. It's the Tool or Association pattern that has no degree in it.
Bye the way, did you notice E) has also the degree pattern but moves backward from small to big?

San   Q5-2 Round is a shape of a bottle, so is a monitor to square.   Therefore, the answer is D).
The Shape Pattern quite often comes along with the Degree Pattern because it visualizes the degree of person, things, emotion, and place.

Jimin How about Choice E)?

San   It's wrong because the compatible shape for "round" is 'square,' not 'flat'

The Absolute Patterns for Analogy summary continues in the following chapters.

Chapter 3

10 Absolute Patterns for the Reading Section

Category B: Technique Question has five patterns:

San: Metaphorically speaking, if Category A: Content Question is about asking the interior of the building,

Category B: Technique Question is about understanding the foundation and the skeletons of the building.

Category B: Technique Question has five patterns:

> ▶ **Absolute Pattern 1: Main Idea Question**
> Finding the main idea of the entire passage, a specific paragraph, or sentences
>
> ▶ **Absolute Pattern 3: Inference Question**
> Finding an indirect suggestion (or guessing)
>
> ▶ **Absolute Pattern 6: Analogy Question**
> Finding a similar situation
>
> ▶ **Absolute Pattern 7: Understanding Attitude (Tone) Question**
> Finding tone such as positive-negative, active-passive, mental-physical, subject-objective
>
> ▶ **Absolute Pattern 10: Understanding the Structure of the Passage**
> Finding the formal intention of the entire passage or relations between the paragraphs or sentences

Chapter 3

10 Absolute Patterns for the Reading Section

Absolute Pattern 1: Main Idea Question

San: The main idea question asks either from the entire passage or from the specific paragraph or a couple of sentences within a paragraph.

When the question asks about the main idea of the entire passage, the answer is highly likely to be located in the concluding paragraph.—if not the last sentence.

The best way is to skip and save it for last until you have solved all the other questions because you might need a holistic approach (knowing the general idea of the entire passage).

For instance, if you found option (A) from the middle of the second paragraph while option (B) from the concluding paragraph (e.g., the fifth paragraph), the answer will be more likely (B) than (A) due to the unique characteristic of this question.

And also, the frequency does matter in the main idea question.

As an example, if option (A) has the keywords that appeared three times throughout the passage while option (B) five times, then (B) has the greater chance to be the answer because (B) appeared nearly twice more.

Finally, there's a technique called "amplifier."
The amplifier is located right after the sentence in question. The amplifier starts with a pronoun, such as "It" or "This"
The amplifier sentence often emphasizes—or de-emphasizes—the sentence in question, hence the answer. Also, pay special attention to the contrasting transitional conjunctions, transitional words or a phrase such as "because", "but", "however", "with all due respect", etc.

Chapter 3

10 Absolute Patterns for the Reading Section

Absolute Pattern 3: Inference Question

San: Suppose you're a 2-year-old kid and extremely hungry (your mom is lazy and doesn't bother feeding you).

When you saw the McDonald's sign and pointing at it to your mom, what do you mean?

(A) I want to have that McDonald's signage (B) I want to have a hamburger.

That's the inference. Finding an indirect suggestion (or guessing)

The inference question usually sends us a signal in the question. It normally starts with "refers to...," "suggests..."   "may think..." "implies..." etc.

   The inference question seeks an indirect suggestion (not the McDonald's signage, but hamburger) behind the reading passage. Therefore, whatever directly copied from the reading passage should never be the answer because the incorrect choice that you may choose—whether it is true statement or not—should belong to the description type question, not inference.

   For the inference question, you need to take a guess—an educated guess, NOT a wild guess, based on the cause-and-effect reasoning.

As an example, let's suppose that you need a hammer to nail something.
If a question asked "Based on the passage, we use a hammer to secure something" what the hammer suggests?"

The answer should never be "(A) to nail and secure something."
Instead, you should pick the choice that implies, such as the solidity of hammer or our feeling of hammer, etc.

Please refer to the following inference questions related with a hammer.
- It can be reasonably inferred from the hammer that it...
- The author suggests hammer is...
-The literary device applied in the word hammer is...
-The author tells that from the view of the reader hammer can be...
-The author does all the followings when referring to hammer EXCEPT

Chapter 3

10 Absolute Patterns for the Reading Section

Absolute Pattern 6: Analogy Question

San: Analogy question is pretty much similar to the verbal section analogy questions. Although it may appear to be finding a situational statement, the analogy question in reading section contains very well organized logic and premises.

In analogy question,—unlike other questions—you may not find the same wording from the multiple choices. Instead, you should focus on the logical relation between the reading passage and the multiple choices, such as the positive vs. negative value / active vs. passive value / physical vs. mental value / quantity-quality / a single individual vs. two individuals.

So, don't be shocked when all the statements in the multiple choices are totally different information from the reading passage.

The Absolute Patterns for Reading summary continues in the following chapters.

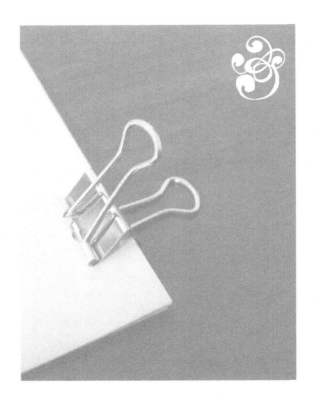

Chapter 4

1. TEST 4

2. ANSWER EXPLANATIONS for TEST 4

3. CHAPTER SUMMARY

SSAT
Reading & Verbal
Test 4

This chapter starts with the Actual Test 4.

Your goal is not getting good enough scores, but 100%.

It's your book

It's up to you to practice the Answer Explanation first.

UNAUTHORIZED COPYING OR REUSE OF ANY PART OF THIS PAGE IS ILLEGAL

Test 4 Reading Section
Time: 40 Minutes, 40 Questions

Directions: Each reading passage is followed by questions about it. Answer the questions that follow a passage on the basis of what is stated or implied in that passage.

Questions 1-6 are based on the following passage.

Line

    German Editor, Gunter Schiller having written to me for an account of the development of my mind and character with some sketch of my autobiography, I have thought the attempt and found no difficulty for life is nearly over with me. I have taken no pains about my style of writing.

    I was born at Shrewsbury on February 12th, 1809. I must have been a very simple little fellow when I first
5 went to the school. A boy the name of Garnett took me into a cake shop one day, and bought some cakes for which he did not pay, as the shop man trusted him. When we came out I asked him why he did not pay for them, and he instantly answered, "Why, do you not know that my uncle left a great sum of money to the town on condition that every tradesman should give whatever was wanted without payment to anyone who wore his old hat and moved it in a particular manner?" and he then showed me how it was moved. He then went into
10 another shop where he was trusted, and asked for some small article, moving his hat in the proper manner, _____[QUESTION 6]
When we came out he said, "Now if you like to go by yourself into that cake-shop (how well I remember its exact position) I will lend you my hat.   —— from the autobiography of Charles Darwin

---

1

It can be inferred that the proposal for writing the autobiography could have been turned down if

A) Darwin hadn't known Gunter Schiller's plan

B) Darwin had been young

C) Gunter's plan didn't amuse Darwin

D) Darwin had been nearly dying

E) Darwin had taken an issue with his style of writing

2

"as the shop man trusted him" in line 6 implies that

A) the shop man didn't see the boy shoplifting

B) the shop man trusted Garnett's uncle

C) young Darwin trusted the shop man

D) the uncle would pay later for what Garnett owed

E) the shop man was such a trustworthy person

3

The boy name Garnett's true intention for using "his old hat" (line 9) is to

A) impress tradesman

B) honor his uncle

C) deceive young Darwin

D) persuade tradesman

E) deceive tradesman

4

Young Charles Darwin's remarks in line 6 "When we came out...for them" suggests his

A) naivety

B) stupidity

C) witty

D) zealotry

E) pessimism

5

The parenthesis (how well..exact position) emphasizes

A) Young Charles Darwin's innate accuracy for species

B) Young Charles Darwin's significant personal flaws

C) Young Charles Darwin's humorous character

D) Young Charles Darwin's deceptive nature

E) Young Charles Darwin's unspoiled nature

6

Which statement most closely concludes the previous portion of the sentence in line 11?

A) so that the tradesman could remember the remarks from the boy's uncle.

B) and Garnett took it without payment.

C) and mentioned about his uncle to the tradesman

D) and Garnett made a payment for the article.

E) and the tradesman mentioned about his uncle.

Questions 7-12 are based on the following passage.

Line

I cannot tell my story without reaching a long way back. Novelists when they write novels tend to take an almost godlike attitude toward their subject, pretending to a total comprehension of the story, which they can therefore recount as God Himself might. I am as little able to do this as the novelist is, even though my story is more important to me than any novelist's is to him--for this is my story; it is the story of a man, not

5 of an invented, or possible, or idealized. If we were not something more than unique human beings, if each one of us could really be done away with once and for all by a single bullet, storytelling would lose all purpose. My story is not a pleasant one as invented stories are.

No man has ever been entirely and completely himself. Some never become human, remaining frog. We all share the same origin, our mothers; all of us come in at the same door.

10 Two Realms I shall begin my story with an experience I had when I was ten and attended our small town's Latin school. The realms of day and night, two different worlds coming from two opposite poles, mingled during this time. The sweetness of many things from that time still stirs and touches me with melancholy: rooms rich and comfortable, warm and relaxed. Everything bears the scent of warm intimacy. This was the world in which morning hymns were sung and Christmas celebrated.

7

According to the first paragraph (line 1-7), the thematic focus of the author's story will be

A) gaining a total comprehension of his subject

B) finding an alter ego in a unique circumstance

C) finding ultimate meaning in every detail

D) recounting man's life from God's view

E) illustrating the author's future self

8

In the first paragraph (lines 1-7), the author likens his story

A) with a unique writing skill

B) without fabrication

C) as any other novelist's writing

D) with a man with clairvoyance

E) with someone between God and human

9

In the first paragraph (lines 1-7), the author mentions about other novelists' story as it

A) has to go a long way back in memories

B) is more like a single bullet storytelling

C) is not of an idealized one

D) is about a man as a unique human being

E) is not so pleasant as it is invented

10

In line 7 (My story is...stories are), the author's description of his book conveys a sense of

A) adventure

B) relief

C) melancholy

D) true-to-life

E) invention

11

"frogs" in line 8 and "mothers" in line 9 probably imply between

A) qualification and generalization

B) stupid and smart

C) amphibian and mammal

D) cause and effect

E) luck and fate

12

Compared to the description of one realm in lines 10-14, which of the following situations would most probably portray the other Realm?

A) A world where murderer, ghost, and all the wild things happen

B) A father's room with full of books

C) An alcove in a house where two siblings play

D) A mother reading Bible for her child

E) A Christmas evening and carol singing

Questions 13-18 are based on the following passage.

Line

Solar panel refers to a panel designed to absorb the sun's rays as a source of energy for generating electricity or heating. <u>Photovoltaic modules</u> generates and supplies solar electricity in commercial and residential applications. The majority of modules use wafer-based crystalline silicon or thin-film cells. Most modules are rigid, but semi-flexible ones are available. The conducting wires that take the current off the modules may

5   contain silver, copper or other non-magnetic conductive. Hence, much of the incident sunlight energy is wasted by solar modules, and they can give far higher efficiencies if illuminated with mono-chromatic light. Scientists from Spectrolab have reported development of multi-junction solar cells with an efficiency of more than 40%. The Spectrolab scientists also predict that concentrator solar cells could achieve efficiencies of more than 45% or even 50% in the future. Currently the best achieved sunlight conversion rate (solar module

10 efficiency) is around 21.5%. Research by Imperial College, London has shown that the efficiency of a solar panel can be improved by
the light-receiving semiconductor surface with aluminum nanocylinders similar to the ridges on <u>Lego blocks</u>. This could bring down the cost significantly as aluminum is more

13

The primary purpose of the passage is to
A) explore needs to change energy source from fossil fuel to solar energy
B) explain currently renewable energy sources
C) establish a brief introduction about solar panel
D) emphasize the cost-effectiveness of all the renewable energy
E) illustrate pros and cons of solar panel

14

Which of the following description is true with photovoltaic modules (line2)?
A) commercial modules will soon be available
B) modules must be flexible
C) Modules are often characteristically rigid
D) aesthetic approach is also important consideration
E) the thicker the film cell is, the better efficiency can be achieved

15

It can be inferred from the passage that the advanced solar panel in the future would most likely include
A) commercial modules
B) mononchromatic light splitter
C) thick-film cells
D) aluminum nanocylinders
E) wafer-based crystalline silicon cells

16

Which of the following best resembles the most ideal solar panel in its energy efficiency?
A) modules available for both commercial and residential purpose
B) modules that use wafer-based crystalline silicon
C) modules as cheap as possible per sq. meter
D) modules made of gold
E) modules with mono-chromatic light

17

By comparing the research result with Lego blocks, Imperial College researchers in line 12 primarily show
A) the efficiency of a solar panel
B) the flexibility of a solar panel
C) relatively convenient assembly method
D) ideal mass production method of solar panel
E) cost-effective manufacturing approach

18

According to the last sentence, which of the following factors can expand the solar-generated electricity in the future?
A) Using aluminum
B) Achieving up to 21% of sunlight conversion rate
C) Public go-green campaign
D) Application of gold at the optimum level
E) Using Lego blocks

Questions 19-24 are based on the following passage.

Line

In 2005 Brad Neuberg organized a co-working site originally called the "Hat Factory" or "9 to 5 group" in San Francisco, a live-work loft that was home to three technology workers. Now, co-working places exist worldwide, with over 700 locations in the United States alone.

San Francisco continues to have a large presence in the co-working community. The New York co-working
5 community has also been evolving rapidly in places like Regus and Rockefeller Center.

The demand for co-working in Brooklyn neighborhoods is almost never ending. Despite of the rise in the Millennial workforce, nearly one in 10 workers in the Gowanus area work from home that adds the reason for high demand. The industrial area of Gowanus, Brooklyn is seeing a surge in new startups like Co-workers, which are redesigning old buildings into new co-working spaces. Some co-working places were developed by
10 nomadic Internet entrepreneurs lured by an enormous financial interest. A 2007 survey showed that many employees worry about feeling isolated and losing human interaction as telecommuters working at home.

19

In line 1, the quotation marks around the word "Hat Factory" or "9 to 5 group" mainly serves to

A) emphasize strict punctuality

B) criticize employers exploiting their workers

C) celebrate the founder of the organization

D) demonstrate the author's support for the organization

E) add the initial name dubbed by its founder

20

The author develops the second paragraph (lines 4-5) by presenting

A) different opinions concerning the single issue

B) specific illustrations of the main idea

C) the author's personal analyses for the issue

D) a number of possible improvements

E) potential criticism

21

Which of the following assertions corresponds LEAST from the positive outlook of co-working community described in the passage?

A) Many telecommuters are single mom with baby

B) Most co-working places prioritize professional human interaction

C) Many co-working communities provide working space at very affordable rates

D) Most co-working communities provide low-rate work assistance programs

E) Most Internet entrepreneurs using co-working communities do not need a huge investment

22

The reference to nomadic Internet entrepreneurs in line 10 extends the author's idea that

A) enormous financial rewards was realized by co-working community

B) mobility in co-working community is important consideration to all telecommuters

C) co-working community works better to Internet entrepreneurs than to other professions

D) traditional office does not fit to Internet entrepreneurs

E) co-working community can provide a mobile work environment

23

The reference to telecommuters in line 11 presents the operation of co-working community focuses on

A) human interaction

B) millennial workforce

C) financial gains for the telecommuters

D) redesigning old buildings

E) industrial area

24

In the last paragraph (lines 6-11), the author finds the popularity of co-working community from

A) technological advancement

B) 9 to 5 punctuality

C) high demand by work-from-home workforce

D) the rise in the Millennial workforce

E) unique regional characteristics

Questions 25-30 are based on the following passage.

Line   Coffee is universal in its appeal. All nations do it homage. It has become recognized as a human necessity. It is a favorite beverage of the men and women who do the world's work.
   No "food drink" has ever encountered. so much opposition as coffee. Given to the world by the church and dignified by the medical profession, nevertheless it has had to suffer from religious superstition and medical
5   prejudice. During the thousand years of its development it has experienced fierce political opposition.
   Like all good things in life, the drinking of coffee may be abused. Indeed, those having an idiosyncratic susceptibility to alkaloids should be temperate in the use of tea, coffee, or cocoa. Some people cannot eat strawberries; but that would not be a valid reason for a general condemnation of strawberries.
   One may be poisoned, says Thomas A. Edison, from too much food. Horace Fletcher was certain that over-feeding causes all our ills. Over-indulgence in meat is likely to spell trouble for the strongest of us.
10   Trading upon the credulity of the hypochondriac and the caffeine-sensitive, in recent years there has appeared in America and abroad a curious collection of so-called coffee substitutes. They are "neither fish nor flesh." Sodas and substitutes have been shown by official government analyses to be sadly deficient in food value--their only alleged virtue.

25

The author mentions "men and women" in line 2 mainly to
A) pay the homage to those who do the world's work
B) celebrate coffee's commercial success as a drink
C) show people's indulgence on coffee
D) emphasize coffee's delightful taste
E) illustrate some of the human necessities

26

Which of the following person would most likely disagree with the author's view on coffee
A) men and women (line 2)
B) the medical profession (line 4)
C) those having a idiosyncratic susceptibility (line 6)
D) Horace Fletcher (line 8)
E) Thomas A. Edison (line 8)

27

In line 8, the reference to Thomas A. Edison and Horace Fletcher is used to emphasize the
A) pervasive historical evidence against coffee
B) argument that coffee is harmful
C) beneficial effect of coffee
D) certain individual characteristics
E) authoritative tone against coffee

28

The analogy "neither fish nor flesh" in lines 11 serves to underscore the
A) unlikelihood that substitutes would replace coffee
B) increasing homogenization of coffee substitutes
C) universal availability of coffee substitutes
D) substitutes have their own merits
E) coffee are truly treated as both fish and flesh

29

The author's tone concerning coffee substitute in line 11 is
A) hopelessness
B) qualified approval
C) mild skepticism
D) celebration
E) ambivalence

30

The relationship between the first and second paragraph (lines 1~ 5) is that paragraph 1?
A) offers an anecdote that the paragraph 2 confirms
B) justifies the necessity of coffee, while paragraph 2 limits its justification
C) elaborates a one-sided opinion, while paragraph 2 describes a popular misconception
D) constitutes the history of coffee, while paragraph 2 shows what makes coffee unique
E) offers pros, while the paragraph 2 offers cons

Questions 31-36 are based on the following passage.

Line
Dichlorodiphenyltrichloroethane (DDT) is a colorless, tasteless, and odorless organochlorine known for its insecticidal properties. DDT has been formulated in multiple forms including smoke candles and lotions.
First synthesized in 1874, DDT was used as an agricultural insecticide. DDT is a persistent organic pollutant that is readily adsorbed to soils. Depending on conditions, its soil half-life can range from 22 days to
5   30 years. Due to hydrophobic properties, in aquatic ecosystems DDT and its metabolites are absorbed by aquatic organisms, leaving little DDT dissolved in the water. Its breakdown products and metabolites, DDE and DDD, are also persistent. DDT and its breakdown products are transported from warmer areas to the Arctic by the phenomenon of global distillation, where they then accumulate in the region's food web.
Because of its lipophilic properties, DDT can bio accumulate, especially in predatory birds. DDT, DDE and
10   DDD magnify through the food chain, with apex predators such as raptor birds concentrating more chemicals than other animals in the same environment. They are stored mainly in body fat.

31

The primary focus of the first sentence (lines 1-2) is on

A) scientific theories related with DDT

B) a brief overview of DDT's beneficial application

C) some characteristics of DDT and as a product

D) why DDT is not beneficial?

E) DDT to the environment

32

Which of the following statements about DDT is true?

A) Once exposed, soil's half-life of DDT may persist for over a quarter century

B) Depending on types of agricultural products, DDT may not cause damage to the produce

C) DDT, with conscionable application, may not affect human health

D) DDT's chemical property is observable

E) DDT property may dissolve before it reaches to sea animals

33

According to the passage, if 10 grams of DDT insecticide absorbed in soil have undergone half-life, the original amount of DDT applied must have been

A) 20 grams applied 11 days ago

B) 10 grams applied 22 days ago

C) 14 grams applied 22 years ago

D) 20 grams applied 30 years ago

E) 20 grams applied 100 years ago

34

As used in line 5, "hydrophobic" most nearly means

A) suffering from an aquatic organism

B) repellant to water from mixing

C) easily combined with non-aquatic organisms

D) incapable of working with fishery

E) susceptible to liquid

35

In the second paragraph (lines 3-8), the author suggests that the studies attempting to understand the impact of DDT on environment will produce the evidence of

A) relatively large amount of DDT residues in the contaminated water

B) DDT affected aquatic organisms in warmer areas but not in the Arctic.

C) higher than average DDT metabolites, but no DDE and DDD.

D) DDT affected aquatic organisms in the Artic, but not in warmer area.

E) almost no DDT residue in the water

36

Which of the following statements is true about DDT?

A) DDT is toxic substance but DDE, and DDD are not

B) DDT was once used for people's skin care product

C) DDT, due to its strong toxic property, only raptor birds can be immune to the chemical

D) DDT residue inside the aquatic organisms is reduced through metabolism

E) DDT is relatively recent chemical compounds made for insecticide

Questions 37-40 are based on the following passage.

Line

The medical profession is justly conservative. Conservatism, however, is too often a welcome excuse for lazy minds, loath to adapt themselves to fast changing conditions. Remember the scornful reception which first was accorded to Freud's discoveries in the domain of the unconscious. When after years of patient observations, he finally decided to appear before medical bodies to tell them modestly of some facts which always recurred in

5 his dream and the patients' dreams. He was first laughed at and then avoided as a crank. Some of them, like Professor Boris Sidis, reach at times conclusions which are strangely similar to Freud's, but in their ignorance of psychoanalytic literature, they fail to credit Freud antedating theirs.

37

"The medical profession" in line 1 may have seen the research of Professor Boris Sidis in line 6 with
A) curiosity
B) acceptance
C) ambivalence
D) skepticism
E) indifference

38

The author thinks Professor Boris Sidis' research is
A) a valuable theory
B) a central example of psychoanalytic literature
C) an example of unfair treatment to Freud's thesis
D) as equally problematic as Freud's thesis
E) better than Freud's thesis

39

"psychoanalytic literature" in line 7 is mentioned because it is
A) the major backbone of all conservatism
B) the brainchild of Professor Boris Sidis
C) impractical theory
D) inferior literature than classic novel
E) the representation of medical profession's ignorance back then

40

The author characterizes that the "conservatism" in line 1 is
A) too difficult
B) harmful
C) used as an excuse
D) the standard to follow
E) irrelevant to practice

Test 4 Verbal Section   30 MINUTES, 60 QUESTIONS

Directions: the synonym questions ask you to find the most appropriate synonym to the question.

The analogy questions ask you to find the most appropriate analogy to the question.
Select the answer that best matches to the question.

Synonym Sample Question:

Q: SUPERIOR

A higher rank

B inferior

C considerable

D supermarket

E supper

A) is the best answer because the synonym for superior is higher rank.

B) is incorrect because it applies the 'opposite concept.

C) and E) are irrelevant words.

D) is incorrect because it applies physical concept to mental concept

---

Test 4 Synonym questions 1 to 30

1. CONGENIAL
(A) generational
(B) pleasant
(C) congratulation
(D) conventional
(E) hostile

2. CONJECTURE
(A) evidence
(B) summon
(C) expertise
(D) guess
(E) taste

3. CONSECRATE
(A) disloyal
(B) holy
(C) secretive
(D) consensus
(E) respite

4. VENERABLE
(A) respect
(B) aged
(C) dignity
(D) benevolent
(E) benign

5. PUERILE
(A) pure
(B) foolish
(C) child
(D) intelligent
(E) estimable

6. LEVITY

(A) tender

(B) improper gaiety

(C) overly excited

(D) heavenly

(E) grave

7. FRUGAL

(A) husbandry

(B) wasteful

(C) fruitful

(D) attributive

(E) serious

8. AVOCATION

(A) vacation

(B) side job

(C) love to enjoy nature

(D) trip

(E) profession

9. CHARLATAN

(A) imposter

(B) unreal

(C) fake

(D) character

(E) Christian

10. ELUCIDATE

(A) dirty

(B) clear

(C) elusive

(D) hard to understand

(E) election

11. INDOLENT

(A) diligent

(B) Indonesian

(C) lazy

(D) cute

(E) indulgent

12. LUDICROUS

(A) serious

(B) ridiculous

(C) dictionary

(D) shiny

(E) ratio

13. CALLOW

(A) low in value

(B) expert

(C) shallow

(D) immature

(E) cow like

14. BLITHE

(A) literal in meaning

(B) bless

(C) two liters

(D) gloomy

(E) cheerful

15. MALIGN

(A) mad

(B) mail delivery

(C) slander

(D) praise

(E) linger

16. POSTHUMOUS

(A) after death

(B) finally humorous

(C) delivery

(D) before death

(E) person's literary work

17. HEINOUS

(A) histrionic

(B) heroic

(C) hairy

(D) generous

(E) wicked

18. REFUTE

(A) futuristic

(B) repeating

(C) disapprove

(D) approve

(E) past

19. CURSORY

(A) hasty

(B) cautious

(C) curbing

(D) mouse

(E) deep apology

20. RETICENT

(A) money

(B) clothe

(C) un-talkative

(D) talkative

(E) very cheap

21. OPULENCE

(A) abundance

(B) lack

(C) opportunity

(D) flowing

(E) opposite

22. ARDUOUS

(A) door

(B) dangerous

(C) difficult

(D) duet

(E) easy

23. PALTRY

(A) serious

(B) trifling

(C) try out

(D) palpitate

(E) paypal

24. ABDUCT

(A) channel

(B) bring forth

(C) kidnap

(D) aqueduct

(E) homicide

25. TRACTABLE

(A) stubborn

(B) tractor related

(C) long road

(D) onerous

(E) easily controlled

26. OBLITERATE

(A) obedience

(B) literal

(C) obligation

(D) destroy

(E) revamp

27. PRODIGIOUS

(A) enormous

(B) tiny

(C) professional

(D) amateur

(E) digital

28. HAUGHTY

(A) humble

(B) contempt

(C) height

(D) hauling

(E) mighty

29. EXACERBATE

(A) good

(B) bad

(C) worse

(D) better

(E) best

30. INCREDULOUS

(A) sincere

(B) skeptical

(C) incredible

(D) credit

(E) edible

Analogy Sample Question:

Q: River is to Ocean as:

A better is to good

B rain is to cloud

C father is to mother

D city is to country

E fork is to spoon

D is the correct answer. Just as the river is smaller than the Ocean, the city is smaller than the country. The pattern applied in this question is the Degree Pattern (small to big)

A) is incorrect because the word order is flipped over.

B) is incorrect because it applies the production pattern (cloud produces rain)

C), E) are incorrect because they apply the Antonym patterns.

Test 4 Analogy questions 31 to 60

31. Rehearsal is to play as boxing is to

(A) championship

(B) sports

(C) gloves

(D) sparring

(E) fight

32. Stress is to exam as horror movie is to
(A) uncertainty
(B) anticipation
(C) suspense
(D) excitement
(E) worry

33. A double-edge sward is to proverb as theory is to
(A) hypothesis
(B) paper
(C) doctors
(D) university
(E) difficult

34. Buffet is to variety as song is to
(A) pitch
(B) performer
(C) voice
(D) chorus
(E) solo

35. Receipt is to report card as
(A) recipe is to instruction
(B) school is to restaurant
(C) money is to honor
(D) certificate is to proof
(E) tip is to service

36. Peril is to storm as
(A) brace is necklace
(B) science fiction is to fantasy
(C) romance is to love
(D) wave is to surfing
(E) supernatural is to aliens

37. Acerbic is to sour as
(A) saccharine is sweet
(B) sentimental is to emotion
(C) shine is to dazzle
(D) cold is to freezing
(E) noise is to blast

38. Capricious is to unpredictable as
(A) change is to volatile
(B) precious is to expensive
(C) predictability is to all-knowing
(D) priceless is to preemptive
(E) cautious is to careful

39. Coalesce is to fragment as
(A) support is to betrayal
(B) mining is to coal
(C) fragrance is to smell
(D) unification is to faction
(E) synchronization is to cooperation

40. Company is to spokesman as fiction is to
(A) editor
(B) writer
(C) publisher
(D) narrator
(E) reader

41. Optional is to requirement as
(A) diminishing is to extinct
(B) compatible is to essential
(C) gap is to chasm
(D) part is to whole
(E) critical is to important

UNAUTHORIZED COPYING OR REUSE OF ANY PART OF THIS PAGE IS ILLEGAL

42. Community center is to tax as company is to

(A) private restroom

(B) profit

(C) rack center

(D) staff

(E) politeness

43. Animal trait is to civilization as evolution is to

(A) nature

(B) extinction

(C) survival

(D) artificial

(E) humanity

44. Church minister is to doctrine as

(A) singer is to strategy

(B) scientist is to data

(C) president is to talent

(D) coach is to instinct

(E) fortune teller is to leadership

45. Earing is to decoration as

(A) underwear is to indication

(B) uniform is to fashion

(C) socks is to attachment

(D) gloves is to protection

(E) shoes is to run

46. Basement is to damp as

(A) penthouse is to spectacle

(B) God is to holy

(C) parliament is to humble

(D) urban is to rustic

(E) mendicant is to arrogant

47. Korean is to Asian as

(A) flower is to plant

(B) snail is to ant

(C) insecticide is to pesticide

(D) valley is to meadow

(E) African is to European

48. Discontent is to animosity as

(A) humility is to bragging

(B) error is to mistake

(C) revelation is to exposure

(D) urge is to censure

(E) exaggeration is to depreciation

49. Sun is to orange as

(A) earth is to crystal ball

(B) solar is to lunar

(C) heat is to cool

(D) planet is to universe

(E) warmth is to fresh

50. Solder is to army as

(A) enemy is to hostility

(B) battle is to war

(C) soccer is to sports

(D) seat is to stadium

(E) striker is to soccer team

51. Committee is to decision as

(A) government is to control

(B) school is to competition

(C) research is to database

(D) analysis is to denial

(E) book is to justification

52. Vow is to respect as

(A) leadership is to safety

(B) terrorism is to forgiveness

(C) competition is to passion

(D) finger is to obey

(E) nod is to remorse

53. Bait is to captivate

(A) practice is to training

(B) trap is to attract

(C) money is to rich

(D) investment is to lucrative

(E) disease is to degenerative

54. Farmers is to sweat as

(A) labor is to hard work

(B) corn is to cornfield

(C) cry is to tears

(D) lover is to heat

(E) coal is to pollution

55. Fisherman is to fish as

(A) fish is to egg

(B) pope is to holy

(C) supervisor is to oversee

(D) accident is to injury

(E) coal is to minor

56. Rough is to specific as

(A) nature is to wildlife

(B) shelter is to protection

(C) crude is to delicate

(D) city is to rural

(E) battle is to peace

57. The homeless is to sympathy as

(A) hyena is to horror

(B) soil is to harvest

(C) Christmas is to gift

(D) New year celebration is to fireworks

(E) actor is to feeling

58. 250 dollars is expensive as

(A) steel is to 10 pounds

(B) feather is to 1 gram

(C) 100 pound is to 45kg

(D) twofold decrease is fast

(E) 10 mistakes is to B-

59. Interested is to thrilled as

(A) nice is to excellent

(B) hurt is to lonely

(C) amused is to delighted

(D) stunned is to shocked

(E) disturbed is to confused

60. Optional is to crucial as

(A) relax is to rest

(B) curious is to fervent

(C) weary is to concern

(D) hopeless is sorrow

(E) horrified is to terrified

Test 4

Answer Explanations

&

The Pattern Analyses

If your Test 4 scores are unsatisfactory,

Please practice the Answer Explanations and then

solve the Actual Test 4 again.

ALL THE LOGIC AND RULES BEHIND EVERY

SINGLE SSAT QUESTION

TEST 4
READING SECTION

Please refer to the Reading Section Absolute Pattern Analyses

| THE SYNONYM QUESTIONS | | THE ANALOGY QUESTIONS | |
| TEST 4 NO.1 ~ 30 | | TEST 4 NO. 31 ~ 60 | |

Please refer to the Analogy Section Absolute Pattern Analyses

1	B	16	A
2	D	17	E
3	B	18	C
4	A	19	A
5	B	20	C
6	B	21	A
7	A	22	C
8	B	23	B
9	A	24	C
10	B	25	E
11	C	26	D
12	B	27	A
13	D	28	B
14	E	29	C
15	C	30	B

Questions 1-6 are based on the following passage.

German Editor, Gunter Schiller having written to me for an account of the development of my mind and character with some sketch of my autobiography, I have thought the attempt and (1) **found no difficulty for life is nearly over with me**. I have taken no pains about my style of writing.

I was born at Shrewsbury on February 12th, 1809. I must have been a very simple little fellow when I first went to the school. A boy the name of Garnett took me into a cake shop one day, and bought some cakes for (2) **which he did not pay**, as the shop man trusted him. When we came out I asked him why he did not pay for them, and he instantly answered, "Why, do you not know that my uncle left a great sum of money to the town on condition that every tradesman should give whatever was wanted without payment to anyone who wore his old hat and moved it in a particular manner?" and he then showed me how it was moved. He then went into another shop where he was trusted, and asked for some small article, moving his hat in the proper manner, _____ [QUESTION 6]

When we came out he said, (3) **"Now if you like to go by yourself into that cake-shop** (4) (how well I remember its exact position) **I will lend you my hat.** —- from the autobiography of Charles Darwin

---

Q1. Absolute Pattern 3: Inference Question Finding an indirect suggestion (or guessing)
Question Pattern: It can be inferred that the **proposal for writing the autobiography could have been turned down if**

A) Darwin hadn't known Gunter Schiller's plan **B) Darwin had been young** C) Gunter's plan didn't amuse Darwin D) Darwin had been nearly dying E) Darwin had taken an issue with his style of writing	I have thought the attempt and **found no difficulty for life is nearly over with me**

Q2. Absolute Pattern 3: Inference Question Finding an indirect suggestion (or guessing)
Question Pattern: "**as the shop man trusted him**" in line 6 implies that

A) the shop man didn't see the boy shoplifting B) the shop man trusted Garnett's uncle C) young Darwin trusted the shop man D) the uncle would pay later for what Garnett owed E) the shop man was such a trustworthy person	which he did not pay, as the shop man trusted him

---

Q3. Absolute Pattern 8: Understanding True Purpose
Question Pattern: The boy name Garnett's true intention for using "**his old hat**" (line 9) is to

A) impress tradesman B) honor his uncle **C) deceive young Darwin** D) persuade tradesman E) deceive tradesman	**Now if you like to go by yourself into that cake-shop** I will lend you my hat.

Q4. Absolute Pattern 5: Word-In-Context Question
Question Pattern: Young Charles Darwin's remarks in line 6 "**When we came out...for them**" suggests his

A) naivety B) stupidity C) witty D) zealotry E) pessimism	(how well I remember its exact position) I will lend you my hat.

Q5. Absolute Pattern 8: Understanding True Purpose
Finding the true purpose of statement, sentences, or the entire paragraph
Question Pattern: The parenthesis (**how well..exact position**) emphasizes

A) Young Charles Darwin's innate accuracy for species B) Young Charles Darwin's significant personal flaws C) Young Charles Darwin's humorous character D) Young Charles Darwin's deceptive nature **E) Young Charles Darwin's unspoiled nature**	(how well I remember its exact position)

Q6. Absolute Pattern 2: Summary Question
Summarizing a sentence or entire passage
Question Pattern: Which statement most **closely concludes the previous portion** of the sentence in line 11?

A) so that the tradesman could remember the remarks from the boy's uncle. **B) and Garnett took it without payment.** C) and mentioned about his uncle to the tradesman D) and Garnett made a payment for the article. E) and the tradesman mentioned about his uncle.	He then went into another shop where he was trusted, and asked for some small article, moving his hat in the proper manner, **B) and Garnett took it without payment.**

Questions 7-12 are based on the following passage.

  I cannot tell my story without reaching a long way back. Novelists when they write novels tend to take an almost godlike attitude toward their subject, pretending to a total comprehension of the story, which they can therefore recount as God Himself might. I am as little able to do this as the novelist is, even though my story is more important to me than any novelist's is to him--(7) **for this is my story**; it is the story of a man, (8) **not of an invented, or possible, or idealized.** If we were not something more than unique human beings, if each one of us could really be done away with once and for (9) **all by a single bullet, storytelling would lose all purpose.** My story is (10) **not a pleasant one as invented stories are**.
  No man has ever been entirely and completely himself. (11) **Some never become human, remaining frog**.
We all share the same origin, our <u>mothers</u>; all of us come in at the same door.
  Two Realms I shall begin my story with an experience I had when I was ten and attended our small town's Latin school. The realms of day and night, (12) **two different worlds coming from two opposite poles,** mingled during this time. The sweetness of many things from that time still stirs and touches me with melancholy: rooms rich and comfortable, warm and relaxed. Everything bears the scent of warm intimacy. This was the world in which morning hymns were sung and Christmas celebrated.

Q7. Absolute Pattern 2: Summary Question
Summarizing a sentence or entire passage
Question Pattern: According to the first paragraph (line 1-7), the **thematic focus of the author's story** will be

A) gaining a total comprehension of his subject **B) finding an alter ego in unique circumstance** C) finding ultimate meaning in every detail D) recounting man's life from God's view E) illustrating the author's future self	**for this is my story**; it is the story of a man, not of an invented, or possible, or idealized

Q8. Absolute Pattern 2: Summary Question
Summarizing a sentence or entire passage
Question Pattern: In the first paragraph (lines 1-7), **the author likens his story**

A) with a unique writing skill **B) without fabrication** C) as any other novelist's writing D) with a man with clairvoyance E) with someone between God and human	it is the story of a man **not of an invented, or possible, or idealized.**

Q9. Absolute Pattern 7: Understanding Attitude (Tone) Question
Finding tone such as positive-negative, active-passive, mental-physical, subjective-objective
Question Pattern: In the first paragraph (lines 1-7), the author mentions about **other novelists' story** as it

A) has to go a long way back in memories **B) is more like a single bullet storytelling** C) is not of an idealized one D) is about a man as a unique human being E) is not so pleasant as it is invented	if each one of us could really be done away with once and for **all by a single bullet, storytelling would lose all purpose.** All the other choices are the narrator's writing.

Q10. Absolute Pattern 2: Summary Question
Summarizing a sentence or entire passage
Question Pattern: In line 7 (**My story is...stories are**), the author's description of his book conveys a sense of

A) adventure B) relief C) melancholy **D) true-to-life** E) invention	My story is **not a pleasant one as invented stories are.**

Q11. Absolute Pattern 9: Relationships Question
Finding relations between the cause-effect, comparison-contrast, characters, and ideas
Question Pattern: **"frogs" in line 8 and "mothers" in line 9** probably imply between

A) qualification and generalization B) stupid and smart C) amphibian and mammal D) cause and effect E) luck and fate	Some never become human, remaining frog (limitation or qualification). We all share (generalization) the same origin, our mothers

Q12. Absolute Pattern 9: Relationships Question
Finding relations between the cause-effect, comparison-contrast, characters, and ideas
Question Pattern: Compared to the description of one realm in lines 10-14, which of the following situations would most probably portray **the other Realm**?

A) A world where murderer, ghost, and all the wild things happen B) A father's room with full of books C) An alcove in a house where two siblings play D) A mother reading Bible for her child E) A Christmas evening and carol singing	**two different worlds coming from two opposite poles**, mingled during this time

Questions 13-18 are based on the following passage.

(13) **Solar panel** refers to a panel designed to absorb the sun's rays as a source of energy for generating electricity or heating. Photovoltaic modules generates and supplies solar electricity in commercial and residential applications. The majority of modules use wafer-based crystalline silicon or thin-film cells. (14) **Most modules are rigid**, but semi-flexible ones are available. The conducting wires that take the current off the modules may contain silver, copper or other non-magnetic conductive. Hence, much of the incident sunlight energy is wasted by solar modules, and (16) they can give far higher efficiencies if illuminated **with mono-chromatic light**. Scientists from Spectrolab have reported development of multi-junction solar cells with an efficiency of more than 40%. The Spectrolab scientists also predict that concentrator solar cells could achieve efficiencies of more than 45% or even 50% in the future. Currently the best achieved sunlight conversion rate (solar module efficiency) is around 21.5%. Research by Imperial College, London has shown that the (15 & 17) **efficiency of a solar panel can be improved** by studying the light-receiving semiconductor surface **with aluminum nanocylinders similar to the ridges on** <u>Lego blocks</u>. (18) This could bring down the **cost significantly as aluminum is more abundant** and less costly than gold. In 2013 the solar-generated less than 1% of the world's total grid electricity.

Q13. Absolute Pattern 1: Main Idea Question
Question Pattern: The primary purpose of the passage is to

A) explore needs to change energy source from fossil fuel to solar energy B) explain currently renewable energy sources **C) establish a brief introduction about solar panel** D) emphasize the cost-effectiveness of all the renewable energy E) illustrate pros and cons of solar panel	**Solar panel** refers to….

Q14. Absolute Pattern 2: Summary Question
Question Pattern: Which of the following description is true with **photovoltaic modules** (line2)?

A) commercial modules will soon be available B) modules must be flexible **C) Modules are often characteristically rigid** D) aesthetic approach is also important consideration E) the thicker the film cell is, the better efficiency can be achieved	**Most modules are rigid**

Q15. Absolute Pattern 3: Inference Question Finding an indirect suggestion (or guessing)
Question Pattern: It can be inferred from the passage that the **advanced solar panel in the future** would most likely include

A) commercial modules B) monochromatic light splitter C) thick-film cells **D) aluminum nanocylinders** E) wafer-based crystalline silicon cells	efficiency of a solar panel can be improved by studying the light-receiving semiconductor surface **with aluminum nanocylinders** B) is opposite. Monochromatic light should not be splintered.

Q16. Absolute Pattern 3: Inference Question Finding an indirect suggestion (or guessing)
Question Pattern: Which of the following best **resembles the most ideal solar panel** in its energy efficiency?

A) modules available for both commercial and residential purpose B) modules that use wafer-based crystalline silicon C) modules as cheap as possible per sq. meter D) modules made of gold **E) modules with mono-chromatic light**	they can give far higher efficiencies if illuminated **with mono-chromatic light**

Q17. **Absolute Pattern 8: Understanding True Purpose**
Finding the true purpose of statement, sentences, or the entire paragraph
Question Pattern: By comparing the research result with **Lego blocks**, Imperial College researchers in line 12 primarily show

A) the efficiency of a solar panel B) the flexibility of a solar panel C) relatively convenient assembly method D) ideal mass production method of solar panel E) cost-effective manufacturing approach	**efficiency of a solar panel can be improved** by studying the light-receiving semiconductor surface w**ith aluminum nanocylinders similar to the ridges on Lego blocks**

Q18. **Absolute Pattern 2: Summary Question**
Summarizing a sentence or entire passage
Question Pattern: According to the last sentence, which of the following factors can **expand the the solar-generated electricity in the future?**

A) Using aluminum B) Achieving up to 21% of sunlight conversion rate C) Public go-green campaign D) Application of gold at the optimum level E) Using Lego blocks	This could bring down the **cost significantly as aluminum is more abundant** and less costly than gold. B) is the current ratio. D) is opposite

Questions 19-24 are based on the following passage.

In 2005 Brad Neuberg organized a co-working site (19) **originally called the "Hat Factory" or "9 to 5 group"** in San Francisco, a live-work loft that was home to three technology workers. Now, co-working places exist worldwide, with over 700 locations in the United States alone.

(20) **San Francisco** continues to have a large presence in the co-working community. The New York co-working community has also been evolving rapidly in places like Regus and Rockefeller Center.

The demand for co-working in Brooklyn neighborhoods is almost never ending. Despite of the rise in the Millennial workforce, nearly (24) one in 10 **workers in the Gowanus area work from home that adds the reason for high demand.** The industrial area of Gowanus, Brooklyn is seeing a surge in new startups like Co-workers, which are redesigning old buildings into new co-working spaces. Some co-working places were developed by (22) **nomadic Internet entrepreneurs** lured by an enormous financial interest. A 2007 survey showed that many employees worry about (23) **feeling isolated and losing human interaction** as telecommuters (21) **working at home**.

Q19. **Absolute Pattern 2: Summary Question**
Summarizing a sentence or entire passage
Question Pattern: In line 1, the quotation marks around the word **"Hat Factory" or "9 to 5 group"** mainly serves to

A) emphasize strict punctuality B) criticize employers exploiting their workers C) celebrate the founder of the organization D) demonstrate the author's support for the organization **E) add the initial name dubbed by its founder**	originally called the "Hat Factory" or "9 to 5 group"

Q20. Absolute Pattern 10: Understanding the Structure of the Passage
Finding the structural organization of the passage or paragraph
Question Pattern: The author develops the **second paragraph** (lines 4-5) by presenting

A) different opinions concerning the single issue **B) specific illustrations of the main idea** C) the author's personal analyses for the issue D) a number of possible improvements E) potential criticism	**San Francisco** continues to have a large presence in the co-working community. **The New York** co-working community has also been evolving rapidly in places like **Regus and Rockefeller Center.** * specific illustrations develop with the specific names.

Q21. Absolute Pattern 2: Summary Question
Summarizing a sentence or entire passage
Question Pattern: Which of the following assertions **corresponds LEAST from the positive outlook of co-working** community described in the passage?

A) Many telecommuters are single mom with baby B) Most co-working places prioritize professional human interaction C) Many co-working communities provide working space at very affordable rates D) Most co-working communities provide low-rate work assistance programs E) Most Internet entrepreneurs using co-working communities do not need a huge investment	human interaction as <u>telecommuters</u> **working at home.** *For single mom or dad with baby, working at home alone is not an option or something to complain about, especially for the lack of human interaction.

Q22. Absolute Pattern 3: Inference Question Finding an indirect suggestion (or guessing)
Question Pattern: The reference to **nomadic Internet entrepreneurs** in line 10 extends the author's idea that

A) enormous financial rewards was realized by co-working community B) mobility in co-working community is important consideration to all telecommuters C) co-working community works better to Internet entrepreneurs than to other professions D) traditional office does not fit to Internet entrepreneurs **E) co-working community can provide a mobile work environment**	**nomadic** Internet. *nomadic, meaning moving from place to place, explains the needs of the entrepreneurs. B) contains absolutism "all telecommuters." Absolutism

Q23. Absolute Pattern 2: Summary Question
Summarizing a sentence or entire passage
Question Pattern: The reference to telecommuters in line 11 presents the **operation of co-working community** focuses on

A) human interaction B) millennial workforce C) financial gains for the telecommuters D) redesigning old buildings E) industrial area	that many employees worry about **feeling isolated and losing human interaction**

Q24 **Absolute Pattern 2: Summary Question**
Summarizing a sentence or entire passage
Question Pattern: In the last paragraph (lines 6-11), the author finds the **popularity of co-working community** from

A) technological advancement B) 9 to 5 punctuality **C) high demand by work-from-home workforce** D) the rise in the Millennial workforce E) unique regional characteristics	workers in the Gowanus area work from home that adds the reason for high demand.

Questions 25-30 are based on the following passage.

(30) **Coffee is universal** in its appeal. All nations do it homage. It has become recognized as a human necessity. (25) **It is a favorite beverage** of the men and women who do the world's work.

No "food drink" has ever encountered. so much opposition as coffee. Given to the world by the church and dignified by the medical profession, nevertheless it has had to suffer from religious superstition and medical prejudice. During the thousand years of its development it has experienced fierce political opposition.

Like all good things in life, the drinking of coffee may be abused. Indeed, those having an (26) **idiosyncratic susceptibility** to alkaloids should be temperate in the use of tea, coffee, or cocoa. Some people cannot eat strawberries; but that would not be a valid reason for a general condemnation of strawberries. (27) **One may be poisoned**, says Thomas A. Edison, **from too much food.** Horace Fletcher was certain that over-feeding causes all our ills. Over-indulgence in meat is likely to spell trouble for the strongest of us.

Trading upon the credulity of the hypochondriac and the caffeine-sensitive, in recent years there has appeared in America and abroad a curious collection of so-called coffee substitutes. They are (28 & 29) **"neither fish nor flesh."** Sodas and substitutes have been shown by official government analyses to be sadly deficient in food value--their only alleged virtue.

Q25. **Absolute Pattern 4: Example Question**
Finding the true purpose behind a specific name or idea within a sentence
Question Pattern: The author mentions "**men and women**" in line 2 mainly to

A) pay the homage to those who do the world's work B) celebrate coffee's commercial success as a drink **C) show people's indulgence on coffee** D) emphasize coffee's delightful taste E) illustrate some of the human necessities	**It is a favorite beverage** of the men and women

---

Q26. **Absolute Pattern 9: Relationships Question**
Finding relations between the cause-effect, comparison-contrast, characters, and ideas
Question Pattern: Which of the following person would most likely **disagree with the author's view on coffee**

A) men and women (line 2) B) the medical profession (line 4) **C) those having a idiosyncratic susceptibility (line 6)** D) Horace Fletcher (line 8) E) Thomas A. Edison (line 8)	**idiosyncratic susceptibility** to alkaloids should be temperate in the use of tea, coffee, * Idiosyncratic, meaning abnormal, expands the author's claim for those who can't drink coffee.

Q27. Absolute Pattern 8: Understanding True Purpose
Finding the true purpose of statement, sentences, or the entire paragraph
Question Pattern: In line 8, the reference to **Thomas A. Edison and Horace Fletcher** is used to emphasize the

A) pervasive historical evidence against coffee **B) argument that coffee is harmful** C) beneficial effect of coffee D) certain individual characteristics E) authoritative tone against coffee	**One may be poisoned**, says <u>Thomas A. Edison</u>, **from too much food.** C) is opposite. Thomas A. Edison didn't say coffee is beneficial. Rather, he is more adamant in rejecting the idea that coffee is harmful.

Q28. Absolute Pattern 7: Understanding Attitude (Tone) Question
Finding tone such as positive-negative, active-passive, mental-physical, subjective-objective
Question Pattern: The **analogy "neither fish nor flesh"** in lines 11 serves to underscore the

A) unlikelihood that substitutes would replace coffee B) increasing homogenization of coffee substitutes C) universal availability of coffee substitutes D) substitutes have their own merits E) coffee are truly treated as both fish and flesh	"neither fish nor flesh." alludes that substitutes would not replace coffee.

Q29. Absolute Pattern 7: Understanding Attitude (Tone) Question
Finding tone such as positive-negative, active-passive, mental-physical, subjective-objective
Question Pattern: The **author's tone concerning coffee substitute** in line 11 is

A) hopelessness B) qualified approval C) mild skepticism D) celebration E) ambivalence	"neither fish nor flesh." alludes that substitutes would not replace coffee. C) is incorrect because of the word "mild."

Q30. Absolute Pattern 10: Understanding the Structure of the Passage
Finding the structural organization of the passage or paragraph
Question Pattern: The relationship between the **first and second paragraph** (lines 1~ 5) is that paragraph 1?

A) offers an anecdote that the paragraph 2 confirms
B) justifies the necessity of coffee, while
    paragraph 2 limits its justification
**C) elaborates a one-sided opinion, while paragraph
    2 describes a popular misconception**
D) constitutes the history of coffee, while paragraph
    2 shows what makes coffee unique
E) offers pros, while the paragraph 2 offers cons
	Coffee is universal (elaborates a one-sided opinion,) in its appeal. All nations do it homage. It has become recognized as a human necessity.
	No "food drink" has ever encountered….(popular misconception)
	
	*When two things are compared, always focus on the SECOND one.

Questions 31-36 are based on the following passage.

Dichlorodiphenyltrichloroethane (DDT) is a colorless, tasteless, and odorless organochlorine known for its insecticidal properties. DDT has been formulated in multiple forms (31 &36) **including smoke candles and lotions.**
First synthesized in 1874, DDT was used as an agricultural insecticide. DDT is a persistent organic pollutant that is readily adsorbed to soils. Depending on conditions, its soil half-life can range from 22 days to (32 & 33) **30 years**. Due to hydrophobic properties, in aquatic ecosystems DDT and its metabolites are absorbed by aquatic organisms, (34 & 35) **leaving little DDT dissolved in the water**. Its breakdown products and metabolites, DDE and DDD, are also persistent. DDT and its breakdown products are transported from warmer areas to the Arctic by the phenomenon of global distillation, where they then accumulate in the region's food web. Because of its lipophilic properties, DDT can bio accumulate, especially in predatory birds. DDT, DDE and DDD magnify through the food chain, with apex predators such as raptor birds concentrating more chemicals than other animals in the same environment. They are stored mainly in body fat.

Q31. Absolute Pattern 2: Summary Question
Summarizing a sentence or entire passage
Question Pattern: The **primary focus of the first sentence** (lines 1-2) is on

A) scientific theories related with DDT B) a brief overview of DDT's beneficial application **C) some characteristics of DDT and as a product** D) why DDT is not beneficial? E) DDT to the environment	including smoke candles and lotions.

Q32. Absolute Pattern 2: Summary Question
Question Pattern: Which of the following statements about **DDT is true?**

A) Once exposed, soil's half-life of DDT may persist for over a quarter century B) Depending on types of agricultural products, DDT may not cause damage to the produce C) DDT, with conscionable application, may not affect human health D) DDT's chemical property is observable E) DDT property may dissolve before it reaches to sea animals	, its soil half-life can range from 22 days to **30 years**

Q33. Absolute Pattern 3: Inference Question Finding an indirect suggestion (or guessing)
Question Pattern: According to the passage, **if 10 grams of DDT insecticide absorbed in soil have undergone half-life, the original amount of DDT applied must have been**

A) 20 grams applied 11 days ago B) 10 grams applied 22 days ago C) 14 grams applied 22 years ago **D) 20 grams applied 30 years ago** E) 20 grams applied 100 years ago	, its soil half-life can range from 22 days to **30 years**

Q34. Absolute Pattern 5: Word-In-Context Question
Question Pattern: As used in line 5, "**hydrophobic**" most nearly means

A) suffering from an aquatic organism **B) repellant to water from mixing** C) easily combined with non-aquatic organisms D) incapable of working with fishery E) susceptible to liquid	Due to hydrophobic properties, in aquatic ecosystems DDT and its metabolites are absorbed by aquatic organisms, **leaving little DDT dissolved in the water**

Q35. **Absolute Pattern 3: Inference Question** Finding an indirect suggestion (or guessing)
Question Pattern: In the second paragraph (lines 3-8), the author suggests that the studies attempting to understand the **impact of DDT on environment will produce the evidence** of

A) relatively large amount of DDT residues in the contaminated water B) DDT affected aquatic organisms in warmer areas but not in the Arctic. C) higher than average DDT metabolites, but no DDE and DDD. D) DDT affected aquatic organisms in the Artic, but not in warmer area. **E) almost no DDT residue in the water**	Due to <u>hydrophobic</u> properties, in aquatic ecosystems DDT and its metabolites are absorbed by aquatic organisms, **leaving little DDT dissolved in the water**

Q36. **Absolute Pattern 2: Summary Question**
Summarizing a sentence or entire passage
Question Pattern: Which of the following statements is **true about DDT?**

A) DDT is toxic substance but DDE, and DDD are not
B) DDT was once used for people's skin care product
C) DDT, due to its strong toxic property, only raptor
    birds can be immune to the chemical
D) DDT residue inside the aquatic organisms is
    reduced through metabolism
E) DDT is relatively recent chemical compounds made for insecticide
	including smoke candles and lotions

Questions 37-40 are based on the following passage.

The **medical profession** is justly conservative. **Conservatism**, however, is too often a welcome (Q40) **excuse for lazy minds**, loath to adapt themselves to fast changing conditions. Remember the scornful reception which first was accorded to Freud's discoveries in the domain of the unconscious. When after years of patient observations, he finally decided to appear before medical bodies to tell them modestly of some facts which always recurred in his dream and the patients' dreams. He was first laughed at and then avoided as a crank. Some of them, like Professor **Boris Sidis**, reach at times conclusions which are (Q37 & Q38) **strangely similar to Freud's**, but in (Q39) **their ignorance** of psychoanalytic literature, **they fail to credit Freud antedating theirs.**

Q37. **Absolute Pattern 7: Understanding Attitude (Tone) Question**
Finding tone such as positive-negative, active-passive, mental-physical, subjective-objective
Question Pattern: "The medical profession" in line 1 may have seen the research of **Professor Boris Sidis** in line 5 with

A) curiosity **B) acceptance** C) ambivalence D) skepticism E) indifference	Some of them**,** <u>like professor Boris Sidis</u>, reach at times conclusions which are strangely similar to Freud's, but in **their** <u>ignorance of psychoanalytic literature, they fail to credit Freud</u> for observations antedating theirs. The underlined portions state that Freud, unlike Boris Sidis, was not well received even though their conclusions were similar to each other. This proves that Boris Sides earned acceptance C) ambivalence = undecided

Q38. Absolute Pattern 4: Example Question
Finding the true purpose behind a specific name or idea within a sentence
Question Pattern: The author thinks Professor **Boris Sidis' research** is

A) a valuable theory B) a central example of psychoanalytic literature **C) an example of unfair treatment to Freud's thesis** D) as equally problematic as Freud's thesis E) better than Freud's thesis	Some of them, <u>like professor Boris Sidis</u>, reach at times conclusions which are strangely similar to Freud's, but in <u>their</u> ignorance of psychoanalytic literature, they fail to credit Freud for observations antedating theirs. The example of Boris shows the discriminatory treatment to Freud.

Q39. Absolute Pattern 4: Example Question
Finding the true purpose behind a specific name or idea within a sentence.
Question Pattern: "**psychoanalytic literature**" in line 8 is mentioned because it is

A) the major backbone of all conservatism B) the brainchild of Professor Boris Sidis C) impractical theory D) inferior literature than classic novel **E) the representation of medical profession's ignorance back then**	but in their <u>ignorance of psychoanalytic literature</u>, they fail to credit Freud for observations antedating theirs.

Q40. Absolute Pattern 7: Understanding Attitude (Tone) Question
Finding tone such as positive-negative, active-passive, mental-physical, subjective-objective.
Question Pattern: The author characterizes that the "**conservatism**" in line 1 is

A) too difficult B) harmful **C) used as an excuse** D) the standard to follow E) irrelevant to practice	Conservatism, however, is too often a welcome excuse for lazy minds," B), E) are too extreme A) is not mentioned. D) is opposite

Test 4 Absolute Patterns for the Analogy Section

Absolute Pattern 3. Purpose (Tool) Pattern
Finding Relationships between the Purpose of Individual to Object, to its Function, its User,
its Use, and its Association

Q31. D is the Best Answer.

Rehearsal is a final practice before the play as (D) sparring is a final practice before the boxing match.

Absolute Pattern 7. Mental (Emotion) Pattern
Finding Feeling/Mental Concept and its Emotion

Q32. C is the Best Answer. Exam gives stress as horror movie gives suspense, emotional intensity.

Absolute Pattern 1. Category Pattern
Finding Part/Whole, Same Type/Kind, Association   Absolute Pattern

Q33. A is the Best Answer. A double-edge sward is proverb as hypothesis is a part of theory

Absolute Pattern 4. Characteristic Pattern
Finding Characteristic of Person, Place, Object, or Idea and its Associated Action

Q34. D is the Best Answer. The question is seeking a synonym to variety from song, (D) chorus.

Absolute Pattern 1. Category Pattern
Finding Part/Whole, Same Type/Kind, Association   Absolute Pattern

Q35. B is the Best Answer. Restaurant gives receipt as school gives report card.

6Absolute Pattern 7. Mental (Emotion) Pattern
Finding Feeling/Mental Concept and its Emotion

Q36. C is the Best Answer. This question asks aboutwhat we feel about something.

We feel peril from the storm as we feel romance from love. (B) is flipped over.

Absolute Pattern 5. Degree Pattern
Finding a Degree and a Shape in person, place, thing, and emotion

Q37. A is the Best Answer. This question asks aboutsensory category: acerbic, sour and (A) saccharine and

sweet are all taste category. (B) is not in our five senses. (C) is sight category. (D) touch category.

(E) is hearing category.

UNAUTHORIZED COPYING OR REUSE OF ANY PART OF THIS PAGE IS ILLEGAL

Absolute Pattern 2. Synonym/Antonym
Finding a similar or an opposite meaning between words

Q38 A is the Best Answer. Capricious, unpredictable and (A) change, volatile are all synonym.

Absolute Pattern 2. Synonym/Antonym
Finding a similar or an opposite meaning between words

Q39 D is the Best Answer. Coalesce is an antonym to fragment as (D) unification is an antonym to faction. All of them have the synonymic relations to each other.

Absolute Pattern 3. Purpose (Tool) Pattern
Finding Relationships between the Purpose of Individual to Object, to its Function, its User, its Use, and its Association

Q40. E is the Best Answer. Spokesman represents the voice of the company as does narrator of the fiction.

Absolute Pattern 5. Degree Pattern
Finding a Degree and a Shape in person, place, thing, and emotion

Q41. B is the Best Answer. Optional and compatible are synonym; requirement and essential are synonym.

Absolute Pattern 1. Category Pattern
Finding Part/Whole, Same Type/Kind, Association   Absolute Pattern

Q42. B is the Best Answer. Community center is operated by tax (money). Company, by (B) profit (money)

Absolute Pattern 2. Synonym/Antonym
Finding a similar or an opposite meaning between words

Q43. E is the Best Answer. Animal trait develops through evolution as (E) humanity, through civilization.

Absolute Pattern 4. Characteristic Pattern
Finding Characteristic of Person, Place, Object, or Idea and its Associated Action

Q44. B is the Best Answer. Church minister gives doctrine (principle) as (B) scientist gives data.
(A) singer is NOT to strategy, but talent. (C) president is NOT to talent, but leadership
(D) coach is NO to instinct, but strategy. (E) fortune teller is NOT to leadership, but instinct

Absolute Pattern 3. Purpose (Tool) Pattern
Finding Relationships between the Purpose of Individual to Object, to its Function, its User, its Use, and its Association

Q45. D is the Best Answer. Earing is for decoration as (D) gloves is for protection

Absolute Pattern 4. Characteristic Pattern
Finding Characteristic of Person, Place, Object, or Idea and its Associated Action

Q46. A is the Best Answer. Basement is to damp is how we feel about basement so as (A) penthouse is to

Absolute Pattern 1. Category Pattern
Finding Part/Whole, Same Type/Kind, Association   Absolute Pattern

Q47. A is the Best Answer. Korean belongs to Asian as (A) flower belongs to plant

Absolute Pattern 5. Degree Pattern
Finding a Degree and a Shape in person, place, thing, and emotion

Q48. D is the Best Answer. Discontent less degree than animosity as (D) urge is to censure
(A), (E) are antonym: (B), (C) are synonym

Absolute Pattern 5. Degree Pattern
Finding a Degree and a Shape in person, place, thing, and emotion

Q49. A is the Best Answer. Sun, orange, earth and crystal ball are all round shape.

Absolute Pattern 1. Category Pattern
Finding Part/Whole, Same Type/Kind, Association   Absolute Pattern

Q50. B is the Best Answer. Solder (part) is to army (whole) as (B) battle (part) is to war (whole). They are all war category.

Absolute Pattern 3. Purpose (Tool) Pattern
Finding Relationships between the Purpose of Individual to Object, to its Function, its User, its Use, and its Association

Q51. A is the Best Answer. The purpose of Committee is to make a decision as (A) government is to control.

Absolute Pattern 4. Characteristic Pattern
Finding Characteristic of Person, Place, Object, or Idea and its Associated Action

Q52. E is the Best Answer. Vow is to show respect as (E) nod indicates remorse.

6. Definition Pattern
Finding Definition/Concept of person, place, thing, and emotion

Q53. B is the Best Answer. Bait and trap are synonym. Captivate and attract are synonym.

Absolute Pattern 7. Mental (Emotion) Pattern
Finding Feeling/Mental Concept and its Emotion

Q54. D is the Best Answer. Sweat symbolizes farmer's labor as (D) heat symbolizes lover's passion.
All the other choices have no symbolic meanings.

Absolute Pattern 3. Purpose (Tool) Pattern
Finding Relationships between the Purpose of Individual to Object, to its Function, its User, its Use, and its Association

Q55. C is the Best Answer. Fisherman catches fish as (C) supervisor oversees others. (E) is flipped over.

UNAUTHORIZED COPYING OR REUSE OF ANY PART OF THIS PAGE IS ILLEGAL

Absolute Pattern 5. Degree Pattern
Finding a Degree and a Shape in person, place, thing, and emotion

Q56. C is the Best Answer. Rough greater degree than specific as is (C) crude to delicate.

Absolute Pattern 7. Mental (Emotion) Pattern
Finding Feeling/Mental Concept and its Emotion

Q57 A is the Best Answer. Homeless creates sympathy as (A) hyena creates horror.

(E) feeling is irrelevant word. It should be more specific like fantasy.

Absolute Pattern 11. Subjective-Objective Pattern
Finding Quality-Quantity, Tangible-Intangible Association

Q58. D is the Best Answer. This question asks aboutsubjective view: "expensive" and "fast."

All the remaining choices have quantifiers, therefore, no subjective view.

Absolute Pattern 5. Degree Pattern
Finding a Degree and a Shape in person, place, thing, and emotion

Q59. A is the Best Answer. Interested is less degree than thrilled as (A) nice is to excellent

Absolute Pattern 5. Degree Pattern
Finding a Degree and a Shape in person, place, thing, and emotion

Q60. B is the Best Answer. Optional is less degree than crucial as (B) curious is to fervent.

Chapter 4 Summary

The Chapter Summary contains equal portions of

12 Absolute Patterns for Analogy Section and

10 Absolute Patterns for Reading Section.

You may study all at once to significantly

improve your understanding and your scores.

Chapter 4

12 Absolute Patterns for the Analogy Section

Absolute Pattern 6. Definition Pattern
Finding Definition/Concept of person, place, thing, and emotion

Q6. Love is to confession as

    A) declaration is to independence

    B) announcement is to news

    C) rude is to apology

    D) phone is to communication

    E) error is to mistake

The correct answer is C

San: We express confession for love, and express apology for rudeness.

    Keep in mind though that the Definition Pattern does not simply represent the literal definition for a certain word.

    It can also include the imaginative representation of a certain word.

    For example, mother conjures up an image of love, although love is not actually the definition of mother.

Jimin   How about A) and B)?

    We declare independence and announce news. That's a good definition. I think!

San   You're right only up to that point! But Love acts like a noun and confession acts like a verb as if to say "I confess love."

    So we must find the same Noun-Verb category: we declare independence or we announce news, not the other way around. It is a common flipping technique that switches the word order.

Jimin   Then, how about D)?

    We communicate through the phone. It's the same word order as in the question-stem.

San   Not quite. Love, Independence, News are all conceptual words, meaning that they are all idea.

    Love has no shape, color, volume, smell, or nothing. It's just concept.

    Love and Rude are the same conceptual category, while phone is a tangible object.

Chapter 4

12 Absolute Patterns for the Analogy Section

Absolute Pattern 7. Mental (Emotion) Pattern
Finding Feeling/Mental Concept and its Emotion

Q7. Veneration is to Queen as

   A) prince is to royal family

   B) princess is to elegance

   C) apple is to poison

   D) weakness is to old lady

   E) king is to kingdom

San: The key point here in this question-stem is that we see a mental concept from the word "veneration (respect)." You must develop skills to sort it out fast from the choices.

The correct answer is D

San: this question asks us how we feel about a certain word.
To queen we feel veneration as we feel weakness from an old lady.

Jimin: How about B)?
We feel elegance to princess in fairytale.

San: Again! It's flipped.

Jimin: Is poison a concept or thing?

San: Your poisonous pungent fart?
A "thing" definitely.

Chapter 4

12 Absolute Patterns for the Analogy Section

Absolute Pattern 8. Production Pattern
Finding Cause-and-Effect in Person, Concept, and Object

Q8. Fire is to heat as

   A) job is to money

   B) waiter is to restaurant

   C) lamp is to bulb

   D) shower is to bathroom

   E) meal is to chef

The correct answer is A

San: Fire produces heat as job produces money. No other choices meet this pattern

Jimin   What about E? Chef produces meal, doesn't he?

San   I know. There's always a catch, right?
        Patterns can be shown in the opposite order that can make your decision even harder.
        But you should know that choice A) follows the same order as shown in the question.
        You can't pick E), which is flipped over and say A) is wrong.
        Besides, the question and A) are nonhuman concept, while E) "chef" is human.

Jimin   Then, if the words are flipped over, would that choice always be wrong?

San   Yes and No. In this question, yes because Choice E can't beat Choice A.
        If choice A were not there in this question, which one would you choose?

Jimin   E.

San   That's right. you should Inevitably choose E because there's no other alternative, but to choose E.

Chapter 4

12 Absolute Patterns for the Analogy Section

Absolute Pattern 9. Syntax Pattern
Finding Homophony, Contraction, Grammatical Association

Q9-1. Seven is to Sandwiches as
   A) sunny is Sunday
   B) rainy is to umbrella
   C) study is to lazy
   D) dig is to tunnel
   E) supermarket is to grocery

Q9-2. There's to There is as
   A) he's is his
   B) if I were to were I
   C) she's to she will
   D) we're to we were
   E) they'd is to they have

(Q9-1) The correct answer is A

San: Q9-1 is all about sound. That's all there is to it. No meaning or logic is involved.

   Just as seven and sandwiches make the same sound, so do sunny and Sunday.

Jimin   Okay!

   if the question does not make sense at all, then I should suspect it could be Homophony Pattern.

San   Q9-2 is Contraction Pattern.

   The contraction form "There's" indicates There is/There has.

   B) is the answer.

   The contraction form "were I" indicates "If I were".

   A) The contraction form "he's" indicates he is/he has, not his.

   C) The contraction form "she's" indicates she is/she has.

   D) The contraction form "we're" indicates we are

   E) The contraction form "they'd" indicates They had/they would.

Jimin   Is that all they are asking in Syntax Pattern? What does syntax mean?

San   In fact, there are some more. This pattern basically relies on grammar, but is limited to word usage not the usage of clause or phrase.

   Syntax Pattern, meaning grammatical arrangement, will ask questions such as Contraction, Homophony, Noun/Verb or Adjective/Adverb, and Tense.

   In the next page we will practice a couple of more Syntax Patterns.

UNAUTHORIZED COPYING OR REUSE OF ANY PART OF THIS PAGE IS ILLEGAL

Chapter 4

10 Absolute Patterns for the Reading Section

Absolute Pattern 7: Understanding Attitude (Tone) Question

Jimin Is this pattern about finding what I like or dislike?

San: The most important thing about this pattern is that the answer choice must maintain the same tone and attitude with the reading passage.

Let say the tone of the main character is sad and gloomy.
In that case, you should always choose the one with the negative keyword or at least the one without positive tone. No matter how impressive the choice is to you, you don't pick the one with positive.

The author, narrator, or character in passage should give a certain impression to the reader, the other characters, or events. You should figure out the most important concern from his/her expression.
This pattern often contains subjective arguments such as positive-negative, active-passive, mental-physical tone and style.

San: It also asks you to decide the answer based on the style of the passage, paragraph, or statement. The answer can be easier if the choice includes some straightforward words such as "cynicism," "celebration," "praise," or "emphatic." But, it could be a tough question if the multiple choices contain no such a tone in the keywords such as "indirectly suggest," "imply," "mention, etc."

This Understanding Attitude pattern, however, is often subjective in the literary passage.
It's because the author, narrator, or character in a passage should give a certain impression to the reader.
Finding tone (Positive-Negative tone), thus, plays the extremely pivotal role.

Chapter 4

10 Absolute Patterns for the Reading Section

Absolute Pattern 10: Understanding the Structure of the Passage

San: This question has little to do with the content of the passage.

A Typical question is something like "What is the primary function of the first paragraph?"

If you have two competing choices: e.g.,

(A) to discuss the harmful impacts of mutation to protein,

(B) to introduce certain scientific thesis

the answer should be (B) because the major function of the first paragraph is to introduce things.

It's because it will be nonsense to asks some detail information like (A) by questioning the function of the paragraph.

The question may also ask the role of partial information.

For example, the question may ask the function of "although" clause, "however" clause, "but" clause, or the reason for saying "it seems" in the clause, etc.

You need to know the function (what it basically does), not the specific detail information in the statement.

San: Overall structural relationships question is the most complex type in this pattern.

The question normally asks relationships between paragraphs.

Therefore, the answer presents two significant distinctions between the paragraphs.

(e.g., "(A) paragraph 2 shows the critic's argument, while paragraph 3 shows the author's analyses that opposes the critic's argument")

Absolute Pattern Summary for the Reading Section

Category A: Content Question

▶ **Absolute Pattern 2: Summary Question**
Summarizing a sentence, or entire passage

▶ **Absolute Pattern 4: Example Question**
Finding the true purpose behind a specific name or idea within a sentence

▶ **Absolute Pattern 5: Word-In-Context Question**
Finding a clue word and the keyword from the sentence in question

▶ **Absolute Pattern 8: Understanding the True Purpose**
Finding the true purpose of statement

▶ **Absolute Pattern 9: Relationships Question**
Finding relations between the cause-effect, comparison-contrast, characters, and ideas

Category B: Technique Question

▶ **Absolute Pattern 1: Main Idea Question**
Finding the main idea of the entire passage, a specific paragraph, or sentences

▶ **Absolute Pattern 3: Inference Question**
Finding an indirect suggestion (or guessing)

▶ **Absolute Pattern 6: Analogy Question**
Finding a similar situation

▶ **Absolute Pattern 7: Understanding Attitude (Tone) Question**
Finding tone such as positive-negative, active-passive, mental-physical, subject-objective

▶ **Absolute Pattern 10: Understanding the Structure of the Passage**
Finding the formal intention of the entire passage or relations between the paragraphs or sentences

The Absolute Patterns for Reading summary continues in the following chapters.

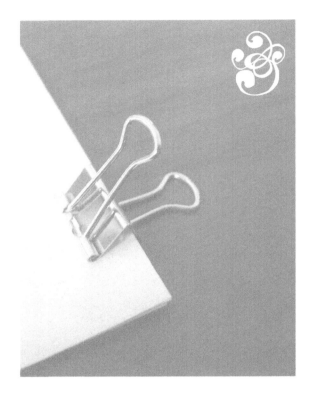

Chapter 5

1. TEST 5

2. ANSWER EXPLANATIONS for TEST 5

3. CHAPTER SUMMARY

SSAT
Reading & Verbal
Test 5

This chapter starts with the Actual Test 5.

Your goal is not getting good enough scores, but 100%.

It's your book

It's up to you to practice the Answer Explanation first.

Test 5 Reading Section
Time: 40 Minutes, 40 Questions

Directions: Each reading passage is followed by questions about it. Answer the questions that follow a passage on the basis of what is stated or implied in that passage.

Questions 1-6 are based on the following passage.

Line   New findings from NASA's Mars Reconnaissance Orbiter (MRO) provides the strongest evidence yet that liquid water flows intermittently on present-day Mars. Using an imaging spectrometer on MRO, it detected signatures of hydrated minerals on slopes where mysterious streaks are seen on the Red Planet.
   They darken and appear to flow down steep slopes during warm seasons, and then fade in cooler seasons.
5 They appear in several locations on Mars when temperatures are above minus 10 degrees Fahrenheit (minus 23 Celsius) but disappear at colder times. <u>When we search for a life,</u> our quest on Mars has been to 'follow the water,' in our search for life, and now we have convincing science that validates what we've long suspected, said John Grunsfeld, astronaut of NASA. It confirms that water is flowing today on the surface of Mars."

1

It can be inferred from the paragraph 1 that the first step the imaging spectrometer on MRO takes on is to search for

A) meaningful streaks on slopes
B) aliens
C) solid evidence of flowing water
D) any valuable minerals
E) mysterious slopes

2

It can be inferred from the paragraph 2 that the imaging spectrometer on MRO will <u>EXCLUDE</u> areas where

A) slopes with very meaningful streaks are discovered
B) slopes with potential hydrated minerals are found
C) slopes with liquid water flows are discovered
D) annual temperatures are above minus 23 Celsius
E) its permafrost naturally reserves minerals

3

Which of the following statements correctly fixes the underlined portion of the sentence "When we search for a life" (line 6)?

A) NO CHANGE
B) Because our quest on Mars was searching for water,
C) As we search for an extraterrestrial life,
D) DELETE the underlined portion, and starts the sentence with "Our quest on Mars…".
E) Because we have convincing science,

4

The passage primarily discusses

A) the process of finding aliens in the universe
B) the process of using MRO in Mars
C) a brief description about imaging spectrometer
D) the major achievement of John Grunsfeld
E) NASA's new findings about the possibility of liquid water on Mars

5

According to the passage, what has become the most significant discovery on Mars recently?

A) confirmation of water currently flowing
B) speculation of water existed in the past
C) confirmation of living things, albeit tiny molecule
D) confirmation of intelligent life on Mars
E) speculation of life other than Mars

6

It can be inferred from the passage that when NASA searches for life in other planets in our galaxy, they would most likely look for

A) humanoid
B) civilization
C) water
D) the existence of uniquely shaped slopes
E) planets with mild temperature

Questions 7-12 are based on the following passage.

Line   In the mango grove, <u>depths of shade</u> poured into his black eyes. He already knew to feel Atman in the <u>depths of his being</u>, indestructible, one with the universe.

     Joy leapt in his father's heart for his son who was quick to learn, thirsty for knowledge; he saw him growing up to become great wise man and priest, a prince among the Brahmans. Bliss leapt in his mother's breast when 5   she saw him, when she saw him walking, when she saw him sit down and get up, Siddhartha, strong, handsome, he who was walking on slender legs, greeting her with perfect respect. Love touched the hearts of the Brahmans' young daughters when Siddhartha walked through the lanes of the town with the luminous forehead, with the eye of a king, with his slim hips.

     Govinda wanted to follow Siddhartha, the beloved, the splendid. And in days to come, when Siddhartha would become a god, when he would join the glorious, then Govinda wanted to follow him as his friend, his 10   companion, his servant, his spear-carrier, his shadow. Siddhartha was thus loved by everyone. He was a source of joy for everybody, he was a delight for them all.

    <u>But he, Siddhartha, was not a source of joy for himself, he found no delight in himself</u>

7

1n Paragraph 1 (lines 1-2) Siddhartha is being described as

A) the one in the state of nirvana who realized the depth of universe

B) a great wise old man

C) a boy sees Atman inside some mango grove

D) a condescending and authoritative prodigy

E) a rascal child playing in the mango grove

8

Phrase "depths of shade" in line 1 and "depths of his being" in line 2 can be understood respectively as

A) randomness and acuteness

B) complexity and simplicity

C) darkness and innocence

D) spirituality and mentality

E) deep distance and serious quality

9

The main purpose of paragraph 2 (lines 3-8) is to demonstrate

A) Siddhartha's sexual appeal

B) Siddhartha's temperament

C) the impressive body Siddhartha possesses

D) People's applause to his fantastic body

E) People's reverence to the presence of Siddhartha

10

Govinda's attitude towards Siddhartha could be best characterized as

A) defensive

B) submissive

C) apologetic

D) condescending

E) apprehensive

11

The last sentence (line 12) reveals Siddhartha's

A) desire to look cool

B) unwillingness to meet his family and friends' wish

C) reluctance to take the current contentment

D) dissatisfaction with his family and friends

E) willingness to become a god

12

Based on the last sentence (line 12), it can be inferred that Siddhartha may

A) get married to any girl and live happily ever after

B) demand more respect and love from the people

C) live in the shade eating mango with Govinda

D) search for meaning in life

E) follow Govinda to understand life

UNAUTHORIZED COPYING OR REUSE OF ANY PART OF THIS PAGE IS ILLEGAL

Questions 13-18 are based on the following passage.

Line

An oil spill is the releases of crude oil. Cleanup and recovery from disastrous oil spill is difficult and depends upon many factors, including the type of oil spilled, the temperature of the water, and the types of shorelines and beaches involved. Oil spill accidents have initiated intense media attention and political uproar.

There is no clear relationship between the amount of oil in the aquatic environment and the likely impact on
5 biodiversity.

The bioremediation accelerator acts as a herding agent. By overspraying sheen with bioremediation accelerator, sheen is eliminated within minutes. The nutrient-rich emulsion creates a bloom of local, indigenous, pre-existing, hydrocarbon-consuming bacteria.

Those specific bacteria break down the hydrocarbons into water and carbon dioxide.
10 This innovative method, once operating cost issue is captured, will demonstrate best way to cleanup oil spill.

13

All of the oil spill issues that make clean up difficult are mentioned EXCEPT
A) the type of plumage of birds
B) the type of oil spilled
C) the temperature of the water
D) the types of shorelines
E) the types of beaches

14

The author mentions "Oil spill accidents….uproar" in line 3 mainly to
A) emphasize disastrous consequences of oil spill
B) support strong environmental activity
C) advocate current government policy
D) attack lukewarm government reaction
E) promote better cleanup technology

15

Which of the following statements correctly supports the sentence (There is no…impact on biodiversity) in lines 4-5?
A) the degree of impact is directly related to the amount of oil spill
B) a smaller spill in a sensitive environment may prove much more harmful than another environment
C) a smaller spill requires more attention to detail
D) a large spill tend to make greater impact
E) oil spill is harmful regardless of the amount

16

The author mentions "bioremediation accelerator" in line 6 as a part of
A) oil spill clean up process
B) chemicals that is contained in oil
C) agents that accelerate oil spill
D) sources that create oil spill pollution
E) recovery processes after the cleanup

17

According to the passage, bioremediation accelerator is used to
A) promote the growth of micro-organisms that degrade oil spill
B) consume bacteria
C) breakdown undetectable bacteria
D) remove oil spill from the bird plumage
E) effectively stop oil spill from spreading

18

Which of the following factors is the current limitation of using bioremediation accelerator?
A) burning the used bacteria
B) breeding bacteria
C) possible ecosystem disarrangement
D) expensive operating cost
E) harmful effect to fishery

Questions 19-24 are based on the following passage.

Line

In the early part of the year 1838, I became quite restless. I could see no reason why I should, at the end of each week, pour the reward of my toil into the purse of my master. When I carried to him my weekly wages, he would look me in the face with a robber-like fierceness, and ask, "Is this all?" He would, however, when I made him six dollars, sometimes give me six cents, to encourage me. It had the opposite effect. I regarded it as a sort
5   of admission of my right to the whole. The fact that he gave me any part of my wages was proof, to my mind, that he believed me entitled to the whole of them. I always felt worse for having received any thing; for I feared that the giving me a few cents would ease his conscience, and make him feel himself to be a pretty honorable sort of robber. My discontent grew upon me. I was ever on the look-out for means of escape; and, finding no direct means, I determined to try to hire my time, with a view of getting money with which to make my escape.
10   In the spring of 1838, when Master Thomas came to Baltimore to purchase his spring goods, I got an
        opportunity, and applied to him to allow me to hire my time. He unhesitatingly refused my request, and told me this was another stratagem by which to escape. He exhorted me to content myself, and be obedient. He told me, if I would be happy, I must lay out no plans for the future.

-From the autobiography of Frederick Douglas

19

As presented in the Passage, Frederick's desire to escape originates from

A) money

B) toiling labor

C) moral attributes to emancipate other slaves

D) desire to liberate women

E) desire to learn

20

Master Thomas refused Fredrick's request in line 11 (He unhesitatingly refused my request) mainly because

A) he knew Fredrick's idling character

B) he had a similar experience in the past

C) he felt Fredrick must be obedient in order to find contentment

D) he prepared a better plan for Fredrick

E) he felt Fredrick should lay out no plans for the future

21

The author describes Frederick's scheme to escape as

A) a way to satisfy his individual desire

B) a process that eventually changed the republic

C) a way to improve the world humanity

D) an obstacle that requires the master's agreement

E) his moral and spiritual goal

22

According to the passage, Frederick Douglas was most distressed by

A) excruciating toil

B) a robber-like fiercens of the master

C) the Master's taking his wages

D) deprive of learning

E) the Master's duplicitous behavior

23

According to line 5 (admission of my right to whole), it could have been better for Frederick if

A) he was treated as an equal human

B) he was allowed to escape

C) he didn't even receive any portion of his wages

D) he was entitled as a free man

E) he received the entire wages

24

The response from the master in the last sentence "if I would be... the future" (line 13) betrays

A) the Master's ignorance

B) the Master's hypocrisy

C) the Master's true concern for Frederick's happiness

D) the Master's irresponsible act for the future

E) the Master's feeling of obligation for others

Questions 25-30 are based on the following passage.

Line

Wherever flowering plants flourish, pollinating bees, birds, butterflies, bats, and other animals are hard at work, providing vital but often unnoticed services. But many pollinators are in serious decline. Some three-fourths of all native plants in the world require pollination most often by a native bee.

President Obama issued a memorandum establishing a Pollinator Health Task Force. The Strategy expands
5   and adds to actions already being undertaken by Federal departments to reverse pollinator losses.

Around 2006, a condition referred to as Colony Collapse Disorder (CCD) was first reported. Colonies diagnosed with CCD exhibit a rapid loss of adult worker bees, have few or no dead bees present in the colony, have excess brood and a small cluster of bees remaining with the queen bee, and have low Varroa mite and Nosema (fungal disease) levels. Colonies exhibiting CCD have insufficient numbers of bees to maintain
10 the colony and these colonies eventually die. Although USDA has currently released the report showing a positive sign in that the number of managed honey bee colonies has been relatively consistent since 2014, the level of effort by the beekeeping industry to maintain these numbers has increased.

25

The discussion of honey bees in paragraph 1 indicates

A) declining pollinators are mostly natives bees

B) other pollinators are often unnoticed

C) Colony Collapse Disorder is the major cause of the lose of honeybee

D) the public is overreacting to the loss of honeybees

E) other pollinators are in fact increasing

26

The known symptoms of Colony Collapse Disorder (CCD) include

A) loss of adult worker bees

B) sudden dead bees present in the colony

C) no signs of brood

D) overpopulation in the colony

E) sudden increase of Varroa mite

27

In lines 4-5, "The Strategy expands …pollinator losses" suggests that the current strategy

A) is not as effective as it was initially planned

B) continues to appeal to many concerned beekeepers

C) is no more valid today

D) focuses not on immediate but on long-term changes

E) focuses pollinators in general not on bees

28

Unlike paragraph 1 (lines 1-3), paragraph 3 (lines 6-12)

A) tries to focus the syndrome on CCD

B) endorses the official view of losses of Honeybees

C) criticizes the beekeeping industry because underlying syndrome is overblown

D) presents specific solution to CCD

E) believes CCD will eventually extinguish bee population

29

In line 11, the author mentions "the number of managed honey bee colonies" primarily to

A) question CCD is the major cause

B) certify that the released report is official

C) testify the beekeeping industry's effort to maintain the proper level

D) show the consistent level of honey bee colonies

E) argue the official report should not be trusted

30

It can be inferred from the passage that

A) most honey bees have completely disappeared

B) CCD was not known to outside until 2006

C) CCD symptoms did not exist before 2006

D) scientists are searching for an alternate pollinators other than honey bees

E) there is a slight correlation between CCD and the actual bee population decrease

Questions 31-35 are based on the following passage.

Line

WikiLeaks is an international non-profit journalistic organization that publishes secret information, news leaks, and classified media from anonymous sources, mainly from organizations or individuals who do not disclose their names. The group has released a number of significantly pivotal documents that have become front-page news items.

5   As of June 2009, the website had more than 1,200 registered volunteers and listed an advisory board. According to the WikiLeaks website, its goal is "to bring important news and information to the public. One of its most important activities is to publish original source material alongside news stories.

The organization's another goal is to ensure that journalists and whistleblowers are not prosecuted. The online "drop box" is described by the WikiLeaks website as "an innovative, secure and anonymous

10 way for sources to leak information to WikiLeaks journalists."

31

According to the first sentence (lines 1-3), which of the following news content would most likely be favored by WikiLeaks?

A) Former President Bush secretly donated $1 million to the charity

B) London police stops drug crime

C) U.S. gives Russia a deadline on Nuclear Treaty

D) Climate controls gets worsen

E) An unidentified high rank police officer confesses a congressman Matt is involved in a crime

32

According to the passage, all of the following people would be included as volunteers in line 5 EXCEPT

A) established journalists at New York Times

B) South African dissidents

C) anonymous newspaper reporter

D) unknown university professor

E) protesters using the group name

33

Which of the following factors does the author emphasize in line 7 (One of its important...stories)?

A) source material's evidence

B) material copyright

C) reader's point of view

D) cost-effectiveness for obtaining the news

E) economicl value of the material

34

It can be inferred that the "important news and information" (line 6) would mainly contain

A) important news unavailable through the traditional media

B) news so sensational and entertaining that requires viewer discretions

C) news no longer available in library

D) breaking news that can make a serious effect to the public

E) breaking news that are improbable to believe

35

Which of the following aspects is most important to ensure another goal in line 8?

A) working closely with the government authority

B) publishing the direct citation from the whistleblower

C) disclosing only the identified whistleblower

D) deleting all the information about the whistleblower

E) obtaining official approval concerning the leaks

Questions 36-40 are based on the following passage.

Line

There is a something in you, as in every one, that requires the tonic life of the wild. You may not know it, but there is a part of your nature that only the wild can reach. The much-housed, overheated, overdressed, and over-entertained life of most girls is artificial.

What is it about a true woodsman that instantly compels our respect, that sets him apart from the men who

5 might be of his class in village, though he may be exteriorly rough and have little or no book education? He is as conscious of his superior knowledge of the woods as an astronomer is of his knowledge of the stars. To live for a while in the wild strengthens the muscles of your mind as well as of your body. Flabby thoughts and flabby muscles depart together and are replaced by enthusiasm and vigor of purpose. To *have* seems not so desirable as to *be*.

36

The author is primarily concerned with

A) to have in the nature

B) to have in our lives

C) to live artificial life

D) to be in the wild

E) to be his class in village,

37

The author believes "book education " in lines 5 is

A) essential quality to earn respect

B) the representation of child education failure

C) the major misunderstood concept in our lives

D) inessential quality to earn respect

E) the way to achieve success in life

38

The author's tone to true woodsman is

A) undecided

B) respectful

C) despicable

D) frustrated

E) jealous

39

The passage as a whole suggests that the world of wild is

A) the holy region that should not be entered

B) a unique place to grow our deeper soul

C) a remote place that cannot be reached

D) an ideal home for most girls living artificial life

E) a rarified region where it rejects village people

40

"To_have_...to_be." in line 9 summarizes

A) the author's main point

B) the example of city life

C) most girls living in an artificial life

D) the life in hell and the life in heaven

E) all readers' conclusion

Test 5 Verbal Section   30 MINUTES, 60 QUESTIONS

Directions: the synonym questions ask you to find the most appropriate synonym to the question.

The analogy questions ask you to find the most appropriate analogy to the question.
Select the answer that best matches to the question.

Synonym Sample Question:

Q: SUPERIOR

   A higher rank

   B inferior

   C considerable

   D supermarket

   E supper

A) is the best answer because the synonym for superior is higher rank.

B) is incorrect because it applies the 'opposite concept.

C) and E) are irrelevant words.

D) is incorrect because it applies physical concept to mental concept

Test 5 Synonym questions 1 to 30

1.HACKNEYED

(A) Boring

(B) Interesting

(C) Hockey rules

(D) Surprise

(E) Requirement

2. IMPERATIVE

(A) unnecessary

(B) required

(C) king

(D) relations

(E) sadly

3. MUNDANE

(A) exciting

(B) boring

(C) Monday work

(D) weekly work

(E) tiredness

4. PLACID

(A) respect

(B) warlike

(C) peaceful

(D) placement

(E) organized

5. SPURIOUS

(A) real

(B) superior

(C) arrogant

(D) super

(E) fake

6. STEALTHY

(A) disclose

(B) gaiety

(C) excited

(D) concealment

(E) stealing

7. URBANE

(A) polite

(B) rude

(C) country like

(D) modern

(E) wasteful

8. PERFIDY

(A) friendship

(B) loyal

(C) treachery

(D) fidelity

(E) professional

9. ADVENT

(A) departure

(B) arrival

(C) venture

(D) explore

(E) advertisement

10. ITINERANT

(A) staying

(B) ticketing

(C) international

(D) understand

(E) traveling

11. CACHE

(A) open

(B) place

(C) lazy

(D) hiding place

(E) spur

12. INCITE

(A) instigate

(B) ridiculous

(C) recital

(D) citation

(E) ratio

13. APPEASE

(A) peacemaker

(B) excessive

(C) shallow

(D) anger

(E) peace

14. DUPE

(A) truth

(B) bless

(C) peace

(D) deceive

(E) cheer

15. ACME

(A) malign

(B) mail

(C) bottom

(D) pinnacle

(E) foundation

196   SSAT ABSOLUTE PATTERNS

16. DETER

(A) encourage

(B) humorous

(C) determination

(D) discourage

(E) literature

17. HOMILY

(A) deception

(B) lecture

(C) homely

(D) warm

(E) summon

18. EPICURE

(A) art of eating well

(B) manicure

(C) healing

(D) epidemic

(E) fast food

19. CAJOLE

(A) dissuade

(B) joyful

(C) excitement

(D) joint

(E) persuade

20. CHAGRIN

(A) money

(B) proud

(C) talkative

(D) Champaign

(E) humiliation

21. DOCILE

(A) tamed

(B) shock

(C) hard to control

(D) shark

(E) fish

22. VACILLATE

(A) waver

(B) dangerous

(C) difficult

(D) vaccine

(E) fixed

23. SAGE

(A) stupid

(B) wisdom

(C) aged

(D) saint

(E) ill judgment

24. BEQUEATH

(A) take back

(B) banquet

(C) generous

(D) question

(E) give

25. LAUD

(A) blame

(B) noisy

(C) long

(D) onerous

(E) praise

26. CRASS

(A) stupid

(B) smart

(C) crack

(D) buttock

(E) revamp

27. PINNACLE

(A) enormous

(B) tiny

(C) lowest point

(D) top

(E) diligent

28. RECALCITRANT

(A) obedient

(B) easy

(C) height

(D) peak

(E) stubborn

29. SQUALID

(A) tidy

(B) bad

(C) dirty

(D) new

(E) scholarly

30. NEBULOUS

(A) clear

(B) exact

(C) incredible

(D) new concept

(E) opaque

Analogy Sample Question:

Q: River is to Ocean as:

A better is to good

B rain is to cloud

C father is to mother

D city is to country

E fork is to spoon

D is the correct answer. Just as the river is smaller than the Ocean, the city is smaller than the country. The pattern applied in this question is the Degree Pattern (small to big)

A) is incorrect because the word order is flipped over.

B) is incorrect because it applies the production pattern (cloud produces rain)

C), E) are incorrect because they apply the Antonym patterns.

Test 5 Analogy questions 31 to 60

31. Arise is to arisen as

(A) awake is to awoken

(B) blow is to blew

(C) fight is to fighted

(D) lay is to layed

(E) ring is to rang

32. Inflation is to economy as music is to

(A) lyrics

(B) pitch

(C) harmony

(D) melody

(E) song

33. Market is to grocery as

(A) song is to lyrics

(B) pickle is to hamburger

(C) money is to bank

(D) actor is to movie

(E) father is to house

34. Accommodation is to motel as

(A) extrovert is character

(B) hotel is to motel

(C) guest is to lobby

(D) service is to tip

(E) personality is to introvert

35. Wedding ring is to marriage as

(A) ticket is to speeding

(B) wedding dress is to official

(C) bride is to bridegroom

(D) money is to happiness

(E) guest is to gift

36. News is to reporter as

(A) Commercial is to boring

(B) anchor is to announcer

(C) Congress is to speaker

(D) audience is to clapping

(E) T.V. is to Internet

37. Acumen is to mental as agility is to

(A) physical

(B) emotional

(C) superficial

(D) theoretical

(E) judgmental

38. Stagnant is to agility as

(A) portrait is to description

(B) often is to frequent

(C) distort is to disfigure

(D) low is to grade

(E) clear is to opaque

39. Convincing is to doubtful as

(A) confidential is to accessible

(B) persuasive is to reasonable

(C) convivial is to colorful

(D) dubious is to deceptive

(E) conviction is to belief

40. Evil is to temptation as

(A) firefighter is to flame

(B) church is to god

(C) charity is to donation

(D) credit card is to interest

(E) con man is to bait

41. Allegro is to adagio as

(A) bike is to horse carriage

(B) jet is to hang gliding

(C) motor is to pump

(D) donkey is to horse

(E) cow is to sheep

42. Proctor is to oversee as

(A) manufacturer is to produce

(B) boarder security is to screen

(C) mother is to cook

(D) brother is to annoyance

(E) baby sister is to noise

43. Experiment is to understand as beekeeping is to

(A) bee

(B) protect nature

(C) pollinate

(D) hobby

(E) preserve environment

44. Octopus is to tentacle as psychic is to

(A) lips

(B) feet

(C) prayer

(D) palm reading

(E) intuition

45. Spy is to secretive as

(A) salesman is to communicative

(B) past is to futuristic

(C) industry is to reclusive

(D) coffee is to caffeinate

(E) advancement is to definitive

46. Bewilderment is to clarity as

(A) bottom is to top

(B) brain is to muscle

(C) strong is to weak

(D) embarrassment is to proud

(E) brave is to courage

47. Violin is to cello as

(A) soprano is to alto

(B) piano is to castanets

(C) crowd is to audience

(D) saxophone is to flute

(E) semifinal is to final

48. Sympathy is to love as

(A) orange is to watermelon

(B) banana is to yellow

(C) grapefruit is to sour

(D) strawberry is to red

(E) corn is to husk

49. Reprimand is to correct as

(A) finger-wagging is to chide

(B) reconciliation is to argue

(C) work is to money

(D) tip is to service

(E) suspension is to removal

50. Baseball is to orange as

(A) sport is to vegetable

(B) vitamin C is to vitamin E

(C) tiger to giraffe

(D) pumpkin is to basketball

(E) fan is to farm

51. Complain is to resolve as

(A) tradition is to perpetuate

(B) gossip is to rumor

(C) study is to postpone

(D) friendship is to sympathy

(E) argument is to criticism

52. Prototype is to test as
(A) innovation is to revolution
(B) mass production is to sell
(C) market is to show
(D) merchant is to occupation
(E) marketplace is to noisy

53. Hobo is to humble as
(A) hustler is to secretive
(B) executive is to complicated
(C) dancer is to cognitive
(D) musician is to talented
(E) date is to embossing

54. Headache is to doctor's note as
(A) hospital is to patient
(B) product is to customer
(C) emergency is to loud
(D) speeding is to ticket
(E) crash is to accident

55. Flower is to seed as
(A) Science fiction is to alien
(B) new breed is to hybrid
(C) factory is to pollution
(D) high tech is to technology
(E) garden is to bee

56. Loyalty is to betrayal as
(A) patron is to customer
(B) supplier is to consumer
(C) patriotism is to treason
(D) supply is to demand
(E) credit card is to cash

57. Evolution is to gradual as
(A) revolution is to sudden
(B) mutation is to betterment
(C) transformation is to extinction
(D) automation is to alteration
(E) radicalization is to subtlety

58. Confiscation is to donation as
(A) annoyance is to help
(B) steal is to charity
(C) offer is to gratuitous
(D) take away is to giving
(E) blame is to praise

59. 50 dollars is to cheap as
(A) circus is to 50 dollars
(B) 50 dollars is to 5000 Korean won
(C) 50 dollars is to moderate
(D) 50 years is to five decades
(E) 50 is to age limit

60. Window frame is to aluminum as
(A) window screen is to practical
(B) window screen is to insect
(C) door hinge is to secure
(D) door hinge is to metal
(E) door hinge is to cheap metal

UNAUTHORIZED COPYING OR REUSE OF ANY PART OF THIS PAGE IS ILLEGAL

Test 5

Answer Explanations

&

The Pattern Analyses

If your Test 5 scores are unsatisfactory,

Please practice the Answer Explanations and then

solve the Actual Test 5 again.

ALL THE LOGIC AND RULES BEHIND
EVERY SINGLE SSAT QUESTION

TEST 5
READING SECTION

Please refer to the Reading Section Absolute Pattern Analyses

THE SYNONYM QUESTIONS
TEST 5 NO.1 ~ 30

1	A	16	D
2	B	17	B
3	B	18	A
4	C	19	E
5	E	20	E
6	D	21	A
7	A	22	A
8	C	23	B
9	B	24	E
10	E	25	E
11	D	26	A
12	A	27	D
13	E	28	E
14	D	29	C
15	D	30	E

THE ANALOGY QUESTIONS
TEST 5 NO. 31 ~ 60

Please refer to the Analogy Absolute Pattern Analyses

Questions 1-6 are based on the following passage.

New findings from NASA's Mars Reconnaissance Orbiter (MRO) (4 & 5) **provides the strongest evidence yet that liquid water flows intermittently** on present-day Mars. Using an imaging spectrometer on MRO, it detected signatures of hydrated minerals on slopes (1) **where mysterious streaks are seen** on the Red Planet.

They darken and appear to flow down steep slopes during warm seasons, and then fade in cooler seasons. They appear in several locations on Mars when temperatures are above minus 10 degrees Fahrenheit (minus 23 Celsius) (2) **but disappear at colder times.** When we search for a life, our quest on (6) **Mars has been to 'follow the water,'** (3) **in our search for life**, and now we have convincing science that validates what we've long suspected, said John Grunsfeld, astronaut of NASA. It confirms that water is flowing today on the surface of Mars."

Q1. Absolute Pattern 3: Inference Question Finding an indirect suggestion (or guessing)
Question Pattern: It can be inferred from the paragraph 1 that the **first step the imaging spectrometer on** MRO takes on is to search for

A) **meaningful streaks on slopes**	it detected signatures of hydrated minerals on slopes **where mysterious**
B) aliens	**streaks are seen** on the Red Planet.
C) solid evidence of flowing water	C) is incorrect because it should be the final step, not the first step.
D) any valuable minerals	D) is incorrect because water is being searched for not because it is valuable mineral.
E) mysterious slopes	

Q2. Absolute Pattern 3: Inference Question Finding an indirect suggestion (or guessing)
Question Pattern: It can be inferred from the paragraph 2 that the **imaging spectrometer on MRO will EXCLUDE** areas where

A) slopes with very meaningful streaks are discovered	They appear in several locations on Mars when
B) slopes with potential hydrated minerals are found	temperatures are above minus 10 degrees Fahrenheit
C) slopes with liquid water flows are discovered	(minus 23 Celsius) **but disappear at colder times**
D) annual temperatures are above minus 23 Celsius	
E) its permafrost naturally reserves minerals	

Q3. Absolute Pattern 10: Understanding the Structure of the Passage
Finding the structural organization of the passage or paragraph
Question Pattern: Which of the following statements correctly **fixes the underlined portion of the sentence "When we search for a life" (line 6)?**

A) NO CHANGE	When we search for a life, our quest on Mars has been
B) Because our quest on Mars was searching for water,	to 'follow the water,' **in our search for life,**
C) As we search for an extraterrestrial life,	
D) DELETE the underlined portion, and starts the	
sentence with "Our quest on Mars…".	
E) Because we have convincing science,	
D) annual temperatures are above minus 23 Celsius	
E) its permafrost naturally reserves minerals	

Q4. Absolute Pattern 1: Main Idea Question
Finding the main idea of the entire passage, a specific paragraph, or sentences
Question Pattern: The passage primarily discusses

A) the process of finding aliens in the universe B) the process of using MRO in Mars C) a brief description about imaging spectrometer D) the major achievement of John Grunsfeld **E) NASA's new findings about the possibility of liquid water on Mars**	**provides the strongest evidence yet that liquid water flows intermittently** on present-day Mars

Q5. Absolute Pattern 2: Summary Question
Summarizing a sentence or entire passage
Question Pattern: According to the passage, what has become the most **significant discovery on Mars** recently?

A) confirmation of water currently flowing B) speculation of water existed in the past C) confirmation of living things, albeit tiny molecule D) confirmation of intelligent life on Mars E) speculation of life other than Mars	**provides the strongest evidence yet that liquid water flows intermittently** on present-day Mars

Q6. Absolute Pattern 3: Inference Question Finding an indirect suggestion (or guessing)
Question Pattern: It can be inferred from the passage that when NASA searches for life in other planets in our galaxy, **they would most likely look for**

A) humanoid B) civilization **C) water** D) the existence of uniquely shaped slopes E) planets with mild temperature	Mars has been to 'follow the water, in our search for life, *Unlike the question #1, this question asks the ultimate (final) goal of Martian prove therefore, D) or E) are incorrect.

UNAUTHORIZED COPYING OR REUSE OF ANY PART OF THIS PAGE IS ILLEGAL

Questions 7-12 are based on the following passage.

In the mango grove, (8) <u>depths of shade</u> poured into his black eyes. (7) **He already knew to feel Atman in the depths of his being, indestructible, one with the universe**.

Joy leapt in his father's heart for his son who was quick to learn, thirsty for knowledge; he saw him growing up to become great wise man and priest, a prince among the Brahmans. Bliss leapt in his mother's breast when she saw him, when she saw him walking, when she saw him sit down and get up, Siddhartha, strong, handsome, he who was walking on slender legs, greeting her with perfect respect. Love touched the hearts of the Brahmans' young daughters when Siddhartha walked through the lanes of the town with (9) **the luminous forehead, with the eye of a king, with his slim hips**.

Govinda wanted to follow Siddhartha, the beloved, the splendid. And in days to come, when Siddhartha would become a god, when he would join the glorious, then Govinda wanted to follow him as his friend, his companion, (10) **his servant**, his spear-carrier, his shadow. Siddhartha was thus loved by everyone. He was a source of joy for everybody, he was a delight for them all. (11 & 12) **But he, Siddhartha, was not a source of joy for himself, he found no delight in himself**

Q7. Absolute Pattern 2: Summary Question
Question Pattern: 1n Paragraph 1(lines 1-2) **Siddhartha is** being described as

A) the one in the state of nirvana who realized the depth of universe B) a great wise old man C) a boy sees Atman inside some mango grove D) a condescending and authoritative prodigy E) a rascal child playing in the mango grove	He already knew to feel Atman in the <u>depths of his being</u>, indestructible, one with the universe

Q8. Absolute Pattern 9: Relationships Question
Question Pattern: Phrase "**depths of shade**" in line 1 and "**depths of his being**" in line 2 can be understood respectively as

A) randomness and acuteness B) complexity and simplicity C) darkness and innocence D) spirituality and mentality **E) deep distance and serious quality**	<u>depths of shade</u> poured into his black eyes. **He already knew to feel Atman in the <u>depths of his being</u>,** * The first "depth" describes physical depth of shadow, while the second "depth" describes inner quality.

Q9. Absolute Pattern 1: Main Idea Question
Question Pattern: The **main purpose of paragraph 2** (lines 3-8) is to demonstrate

A) Siddhartha's sexual appeal B) Siddhartha's temperament C) the impressive body Siddhartha possesses D) People's applause to his fantastic body **E) People's reverence to the presence of Siddhartha**	the luminous forehead, with the eye of a king, with his slim hips

Q10. Absolute Pattern 7: Understanding Attitude (Tone) Question
Question Pattern: **Govinda's attitude** towards Siddhartha could be best characterized as

A) defensive **B) submissive** C) apologetic D) condescending E) apprehensive	then Govinda wanted to follow him as his friend, his companion, **his servant**, his spear-carrier, his shadow

Q11. Absolute Pattern 7: Understanding Attitude (Tone) Question
Question Pattern: The **last sentence** (line 12) reveals Siddhartha's

A) desire to look cool B) unwillingness to meet his family and friends' wish **C) reluctance to take the current contentment** D) dissatisfaction with his family and friends E) willingness to become a god	But he, Siddhartha, was not a source of joy for himself, he found no delight in himself. B) deviates the focus of the question.

Q12. Absolute Pattern 3: Inference Question Finding an indirect suggestion (or guessing)
Question Pattern: Based on the **last sentence** (line 12), it can be inferred that **Siddhartha may**

A) get married to any girl and live happily ever after B) demand more respect and love from the people C) live in the shade eating mango with Govinda **D) search for meaning in life** E) follow Govinda to understand life	**But he, Siddhartha, was not a source of joy for himself, he found no delight in himself** * The passage doesn't describe what he will do next, but we can still infer that he would probably do (D) because he is described as a god, and all the other choices are negative.

Questions 13-18 are based on the following passage.

An oil spill is the releases of crude oil. Cleanup and recovery from (14 & 15) **disastrous oil spill is difficult and depends upon many factors**, including (13) **the type of oil spilled, the temperature of the water, and the types of shorelines and beaches** involved. Oil spill accidents have initiated intense media attention and political uproar. There is no clear relationship between the amount of oil in the aquatic environment and the likely impact on biodiversity. The bioremediation accelerator acts as (16) **a herding agent**. By overspraying sheen with bioremediation accelerator, sheen is eliminated within minutes. (17) **The nutrient-rich emulsion creates a bloom of local, indigenous, pre-existing, hydrocarbon-consuming bacteria**. Those specific bacteria break down the hydrocarbons into water and carbon dioxide.
This innovative method, (18) **once operating cost issue is captured,** will demonstrate best way to cleanup oil spill.

Q13. Absolute Pattern 2: Summary Question
Summarizing a sentence or entire passage.
Question Pattern: All of the oil **spill issues that make clean up difficult** are mentioned EXCEPT

A) the type of plumage of birds B) the type of oil spilled C) the temperature of the water D) the types of shorelines E) the types of beaches	the type of oil spilled, the temperature of the water, and the types of shorelines and beaches

Q14. Absolute Pattern 8: Understanding True Purpose
Question Pattern: The author mentions "**Oil spill accidents….uproar**" in line 3 mainly to

A) emphasize disastrous consequences of oil spill B) support strong environmental activity C) advocate current government policy D) attack lukewarm government reaction E) promote better cleanup technology	Cleanup and recovery from **disastrous an oil spill** is difficult. B), C), E) are partial information that do not directly respond to the question.

Q15. **Absolute Pattern 2: Summary Question**
Summarizing a sentence or entire passage
Question Pattern: Which of the following statements correctly supports the sentence **(there is no...impact on biodiversity)** in lines 4-5?

A) the degree of impact is directly related to the amount of oil spill **B) a smaller spill in a sensitive environment may prove much more harmful than another environment** C) a smaller spill requires more attention to detail D) a large spill tend to make greater impact E) oil spill is harmful regardless of the amount	disastrous oil spill is difficult **and depends upon many factors,** All the other choices are opposite in one way or another.

Q16. **Absolute Pattern 7: Understanding Attitude (Tone) Question**
Finding tone such as positive-negative, active-passive, mental-physical, subjective-objective.
Question Pattern: The author mentions "**bioremediation accelerator**" in line 7 as a part of

A) oil spill clean up process B) chemicals that is contained in oil C) agents that accelerate oil spill D) sources that create oil spill pollution E) recovery processes after the cleanup	The bioremediation accelerator acts as **a herding agent**

Q17. **Absolute Pattern 2: Summary Question**
Summarizing a sentence or entire passage
Question Pattern: According to the passage, **bioremediation accelerator is** used to

A) promote the growth of micro-organisms that degrade oil spill B) consume bacteria C) breakdown undetectable bacteria D) remove oil spill from the bird plumage E) effectively stop oil spill from spreading	The nutrient-rich emulsion creates a bloom of local, indigenous, pre-existing, hydrocarbon-consuming bacteria

Q18. **Absolute Pattern 4: Example Question**
Finding the true purpose behind a specific name or idea within a sentence.
Question Pattern: Which of the following factors is the current **limitation of using bioremediation accelerator**?

A) burning the used bacteria B) breeding bacteria C) possible ecosystem disarrangement **D) expensive operating cost** E) harmful effect to fishery	once operating cost issue is captured,

Questions 19-24 are based on the following passage.

In the early part of the year 1838, I became quite restless. I could see no reason why I should, at the end of each week, pour the reward of my toil into the purse of my master. (22) **When I carried to him my weekly wages, he would look me in the face with a robber-like fierceness, and ask, "Is this all?"** He would, however, when I made him six dollars, sometimes give me six cents, to encourage me. It had the opposite effect. I regarded it as a sort of admission of my right to the whole. The fact that he gave me any part of my wages was proof, to my mind, that he believed (19) **me entitled to the whole of them.** (23) **I always felt worse for having received any thing**; for I feared that the giving me a few cents would ease his conscience, and make him feel himself to be a pretty honorable sort of robber. (21 &22) My discontent grew upon me. I was ever on the look-out for means of escape; and, finding no direct means, I determined to try to hire my time, with a view of getting money with which to make my escape. In the spring of 1838, when Master Thomas came to Baltimore to purchase his spring goods, I got an opportunity, and applied to him to allow me to hire my time. He unhesitatingly refused my request, and told me (20) **this was another stratagem by which to escape.** He exhorted me to content myself, and be obedient. He told me, (24)_if I would be happy, I must lay out no plans for the future.

-From the autobiography of Frederick Douglas

Q19. Absolute Pattern 2: Summary Question
Summarizing a sentence or entire passage
Question Pattern: As presented in the Passage, Frederick's **desire to escape originates** from

A) money B) toiling labor C) moral attributes to emancipate other slaves D) desire to liberate women E) desire to learn	to my mind, that he believed **me entitled to the whole of them.**

Q20. Absolute Pattern 3: Inference Question Finding an indirect suggestion (or guessing)
Question Pattern: Master Thomas refused Fredrick's request in line 11 (He unhesitatingly refused my request) mainly because

A) he knew Fredrick's idling character **B) he had a similar experience in the past** C) he felt Fredrick must be obedient in order to find contentment D) he prepared a better plan for Fredrick E) he felt Fredrick should lay out no plans for the future	this was another stratagem by which to escape. E) is not the Master's true intention. It's only his excuse to contain him.

Q21. Absolute Pattern 7: Understanding Attitude (Tone) Question
Finding tone such as positive-negative, active-passive, mental-physical, subjective-objective
Question Pattern: The author describes **Frederick's scheme to escape** as

A) a way to satisfy his individual desire B) a process that eventually changed the republic C) a way to improve the world humanity D) an obstacle that requires the master's agreement E) his moral and spiritual goal	My discontent grew upon me. I was ever on the look-out for means of escape; Please note that this passage is about young Frederick, not the grownup heroic person.

Q22. Absolute Pattern 2: Summary Question
Summarizing a sentence or entire passage
Question Pattern: According to the passage, Frederick Douglas was **most distressed** by

A) excruciating toil B) a robber-like fiercens of the master **C) the Master's taking his wages** D) deprive of learning E) the Master's duplicitous behavior	When I carried to him my weekly wages, he would look me in the face with a robber-like fierceness, and ask, "Is this all?" My discontent grew upon me. I was ever on the look-out for means of escape;

Q23. Absolute Pattern 3: Inference Question Finding an indirect suggestion (or guessing)
Question Pattern: According to line 5 **(admission of my right to whole), it could have been better** for Frederick if

A) he was treated as an equal human B) he was allowed to escape **C) he didn't even receive any portion of his wages** D) he was entitled as a free man E) he received the entire wages	**I always felt worse for having received any thing**; for I feared that the giving me a few cents would ease his conscience

Q24. Absolute Pattern 7: Understanding Attitude (Tone) Question
Finding tone such as positive-negative, active-passive, mental-physical, subjective-objective
Question Pattern: The response from the master in the last sentence **"if I would be... the future" (line 13) betrays**

A) the Master's ignorance **B) the Master's hypocrisy** C) the Master's true concern for Frederick's happiness D) the Master's irresponsible act for the future E) the Master's feeling of obligation for others	if I would be happy, I must lay out no plans for the future. *The master wants him to keep making money for him. Therefore, B) is the answer.

Questions 25-30 are based on the following passage.

Wherever flowering plants flourish, pollinating bees, birds, butterflies, bats, and other animals are hard at work, providing vital but often unnoticed services. But many pollinators are in serious decline. Some three-fourths of all native plants in the world require pollination (25) **most often by a native bee.**

President Obama issued a memorandum establishing a Pollinator Health Task Force. The Strategy (27) expands and adds to actions already being undertaken by Federal departments to reverse pollinator losses.

Around 2006, (28 & 29) **a condition referred to as Colony Collapse Disorder (CCD) was first reported.** Colonies diagnosed with CCD exhibit a rapid (26) **loss of adult worker bees,** have few or no dead bees present in the colony, have excess brood and a small cluster of bees remaining with the queen bee, and have low Varroa mite and Nosema (fungal disease) levels. Colonies exhibiting CCD have insufficient numbers of bees to maintain the colony and these colonies eventually die. Although USDA has currently released the report showing a positive sign in that the number of managed honey bee colonies has been relatively consistent since 2014, the level of effort by the beekeeping industry to (29) **maintain these numbers has increased.**

Q25. Absolute Pattern 2: Summary Question
Question Pattern: The discussion of **honey bees in paragraph 1** indicates

A) declining pollinators are mostly natives bees B) other pollinators are often unnoticed C) Colony Collapse Disorder is the major cause of the lose of honeybee D) the public is overreacting to the loss of honeybees E) other pollinators are in fact increasing	Some three-fourths of all native plants in the world require pollination **most often by a native bee.** C) is incorrect because the question asks the paragraph 1, not 3.

Q26. Absolute Pattern 2: Summary Question
Question Pattern: The **known symptoms** of Colony Collapse Disorder (CCD) include

A) loss of adult worker bees B) sudden dead bees present in the colony C) no signs of brood D) overpopulation in the colony E) sudden increase of Varroa mite	loss of adult worker bees. have **few or no dead bees** present in the colony, **have excess brood** and a **small cluster of bees remaining** with the queen bee, and have **low Varroa** mite and Nosema (fungal disease) levels

---

Q27. Absolute Pattern 3: Inference Question Finding an indirect suggestion (or guessing)
Question Pattern: In lines 4-5, "**The Strategy expands …pollinator losses**" suggests that the current strategy

A) is not as effective as it was initially planned B) continues to appeal to many concerned beekeepers C) is no more valid today D) focuses not on immediate but on long-term changes E) focuses pollinators in general not on bees	The Strategy **expands and adds to actions already being undertaken…** *"**Expands and adds**" implies the current strategy is not as effective as it was planned.

Q28. Absolute Pattern 10: Understanding the Structure of the Passage
Question Pattern: Unlike paragraph 1 (lines 1-3), **paragraph 3 (lines 3-12)**

A) tries to focus the syndrome on CCD B) endorses the official view of losses of Honeybees C) criticizes the beekeeping industry because underlying syndrome is overblown D) presents specific solution to CCD E) believes CCD will eventually extinguish bee population	a condition referred to as Colony Collapse Disorder (CCD) was first reported. *The 3rd paragraph mainly discusses CCD.

Q29. **Absolute Pattern 8: Understanding True Purpose**
Question Pattern: In line 11, the author mentions **"the number of managed honey bee colonies"** primarily to

A) question CCD is the major cause B) certify that the released report is official C) **testify the beekeeping industry's effort to maintain the proper level** D) show the consistent level of honey bee colonies E) argue the official report should not be trusted	the level of effort by the beekeeping industry to **maintain these numbers has increased**.

Q30. **Absolute Pattern 3: Inference Question** Finding an indirect suggestion (or guessing)
Question Pattern: It can be **inferred** from the passage that

A) most honey bees have completely disappeared B) **CCD was not known to outside until 2006** C) CCD symptoms did not exist before 2006 D) scientists are searching for an alternate pollinators other than honey bees E) there is a slight correlation between CCD and the actual bee population decrease	a condition referred to as Colony Collapse Disorder (CCD) was **first reported**. * In other words, CCD was not known until 2006, it doesn't mean it didn't exist then. C) is incorrect because it could have existed without knowing it.

Questions 31-35 are based on the following passage.

WikiLeaks is an international non-profit journalistic organization that (31 & 34) **publishes secret information, news leaks, and classified media from anonymous sources,** mainly from organizations or individuals (32) **who do not disclose their names.** The group has released a number of significantly pivotal documents that have become front-page news items. As of June 2009, the website had more than 1,200 registered volunteers and listed an advisory board. According to the WikiLeaks website, its goal is "to bring important news and information to the public. One of its most important activities is to publish (33) **original source material** alongside news stories. The organization's another goal is to ensure that journalists and whistleblowers are not prosecuted. The online "drop box" is described by the WikiLeaks website as "an innovative, (35) **secure and anonymous way** for sources to leak information to WikiLeaks journalists."

Q31. **Absolute Pattern 3: Inference Question** Finding an indirect suggestion (or guessing)
Question Pattern: According to the first sentence (lines 1-3), which of the following **news content would most likely be favored by WikiLeaks**?

A) Former President Bush secretly donated $1 million to the charity B) London police stops drug crime C) U.S. gives Russia a deadline on Nuclear Treaty D) Climate controls gets worsen E) **An unidentified high rank police officer confesses a congressman Matt is involved in a crime**	publishes secret information, news leaks, and classified media from anonymous sources,

Q32 Absolute Pattern 3: Inference Question   Finding an indirect suggestion (or guessing)
Question Pattern: According to the passage, all of the following **people would be included as volunteers** in line 5 **EXCEPT**

A) **established journalists at New York Times** B) South African dissidents C) anonymous newspaper reporter D) unknown university professor E) protesters using the group name	**publishes secret information, news leaks, and classified media from anonymous sources,** mainly from organizations or individuals **who do not disclose their names.** A) is opposite. B) is vague.

Q33. Absolute Pattern 2: Summary Question
Summarizing a sentence or entire passage
Question Pattern: Which of the following factors does the author emphasize in line 7 **(One of its important… stories)?**

A) **source material's evidence** B) material copyright C) reader's point of view D) cost-effectiveness for obtaining the news E) economic value of the material	One of its most important activities is to publish **original source material** alongside news stories.

Q34. Absolute Pattern 3: Inference Question   Finding an indirect suggestion (or guessing)
Question Pattern: It can be inferred that the **"important news and information" (line 6)?**ould mainly contain

A) **important news unavailable through the traditional media** B) news so sensational and entertaining that requires viewer discretions C) news no longer available in library D) breaking news that can make a serious effect to the public E) breaking news that are improbable to believe	publishes secret information, news leaks, and classified media from **anonymous sources,**

Q35. Absolute Pattern 3: Inference Question   Finding an indirect suggestion (or guessing)
Question Pattern: Which of the following aspects is most important to ensure **another goal in line 8**?

A) working closely with the government authority B) publishing the direct citation from the whistleblower C) disclosing only the identified whistleblower D) **deleting all the information about the whistleblower** E) obtaining official approval concerning the leaks	The online "drop box" is described by the WikiLeaks website as "an innovative, **secure and anonymous way** for sources to leak information to WikiLeaks journalists."

Questions 36-40 are based on the following passage.

There is a something in you, as in every one, that requires the tonic life of the wild. You may not know it, but there is a part of your nature that only the wild can reach. The much-housed, overheated, overdressed, and over-entertained life of most girls is artificial. What is it about a true woodsman that instantly compels (Q38) **our respect**, that sets him apart from the men who might be of his class in village, (Q37) **though he may be** exteriorly rough and have little or no **book education**? He is as conscious of his superior knowledge of the woods as an astronomer is of his knowledge of the stars, To live for a while (Q39) **in the wild strengthens the muscles of your mind** as well as of your body. Flabby thoughts and flabby muscles depart together and are replaced by enthusiasm and vigor of purpose. (Q36 & Q40) **To *have* seems not so desirable as to *be*.**

Q36. Absolute Pattern 1: Main Idea Question
Question Pattern: The author is **primarily concerned** with

A) to have in the nature B) to have in our lives C) to live artificial life **D) to be in the wild** E) to be his class in village,	(TOPIC) There is a something in you, as in every one, that requires the tonic life of the wild. (CONLCUSION) To *have* seems not so desirable as to *be*. By combining the topic and the conclusion sentences, we can see that the author favors (D)

Q37. Absolute Pattern 7: Understanding Attitude (Tone) Question
Question Pattern: The author believes "**book education** " in lines 6 is

A) essential quality to earn respect B) the representation of child education failure C) the major misunderstood concept in our lives **D) inessential quality to earn respect** E) the way to achieve success in life	*The concessional part (though he may be…)of the sentence implies something is an inessential part, not the main part. The author argues the woodsman earns our respect although he has no book education. That is, book is inessential

Q38. Absolute Pattern 7: Understanding Attitude (Tone) Question
Question Pattern: The **author's tone** to true woodsman is

A) undecided **B) respectful** C) despicable D) frustrated E) jealous	What is it about a true woodsman that instantly compels **our respect**

Q39. Absolute Pattern 2: Summary Question
Question Pattern: The passage as a whole suggests that the **world of wild** is

A) the holy region that should not be entered **B) a unique place to grow our deeper soul** C) a remote place that cannot be reached D) an ideal home for most girls living artificial life E) a rarified region where it rejects village people	To live for a while in the wild strengthens the **muscles of your mind** as well as of your body. A), E) are opposite.

Q40. Absolute Pattern 8: Understanding True Purpose
Question Pattern: "To_have_...to_be." in line 9 summarizes

A) the author's main point B) the example of city life C) most girls living in an artificial life D) the life in hell and the life in heaven E) all readers' conclusion	replaced by enthusiasm and vigor of purpose. **To *have* seems not so desirable as to *be*.** The last sentence represents the author's main point.

Test 5 Absolute Patterns for the Analogy Section

Absolute Pattern 9. Syntax Pattern
Finding Homophony, Contraction, Grammatical Association

Q31. A is the Best Answer. The past participle of arise is arisen as that of awake is awoken.

Absolute Pattern 4. Characteristic Pattern
Finding Characteristic of Person, Place, Object, or Idea and its Associated Action

Q32. B is the Best Answer. Inflation is increase of price in economy. Similar term in music is pitch.

Absolute Pattern 1. Category Pattern
Finding Part/Whole, Same Type/Kind, Association   Absolute Pattern

Q33. A is the Best Answer. Market contains grocery as (A) song contains lyrics

Absolute Pattern 1. Category Pattern
Finding Part/Whole, Same Type/Kind, Association   Absolute Pattern

Q34. E is the Best Answer. Motel is a type of accommodation as introvert is a type of personality. (A) is flipped.

Absolute Pattern 4. Characteristic Pattern
Finding Characteristic of Person, Place, Object, or Idea and its Associated Action

Q35. A is the Best Answer. Wedding ring is the proof of marriage as is (A) ticket to speeding.

Absolute Pattern 3. Purpose (Tool) Pattern
Finding Relationships between the Purpose of Individual to Object, to its Function, its User, its Use, and its Association

Q36. C is the Best Answer. This question asks aboutthe purpose of someone and also is seeking the similar job:
Reporter announces news as (C) speaker announces congressional issue. (B) is synonym.

6. Definition Pattern
Finding Definition/Concept of person, place, thing, and emotion

Q37. A is the Best Answer. Acumen is mental sharpness. Agility, like acumen, describes swift movement.

Absolute Pattern 2. Synonym/Antonym
Finding a similar or an opposite meaning between words

Q38. E is the Best Answer. Stagnant is an antonym to agility as is (E) clear to opaque

Absolute Pattern 2. Synonym/Antonym
Finding a similar or an opposite meaning between words

Q39. A is the Best Answer. Convincing is an antonym to doubtful as (A) confidential is to accessible

Absolute Pattern 4. Characteristic Pattern
Finding Characteristic of Person, Place, Object, or Idea and its Associated Action

Q40. E is the Best Answer. Temptation and bait are synonym. Evil and con man are a similar concept.

Absolute Pattern 5. Degree Pattern
Finding a Degree and a Shape in person, place, thing, and emotion

Q41. B is the Best Answer. This question asks about Degree Pattern moving fast to slow.
Allegro is faster than adagio as (B) jet is to hang gliding. (D) is opposite.

Absolute Pattern 3. Purpose (Tool) Pattern
Finding Relationships between the Purpose of Individual to Object, to its Function, its User, its Use, and its Association

Q42. B is the Best Answer. Both proctor and (B) boarder security perform the similar functions: oversee or screen.

Absolute Pattern 3. Purpose (Tool) Pattern
Finding Relationships between the Purpose of Individual to Object, to its Function, its User, its Use, and its Association

Q43. C is the Best Answer. The purpose of Experiment is to understand as that of beekeeping is to (C) pollinate.

Absolute Pattern 4. Characteristic Pattern
Finding Characteristic of Person, Place, Object, or Idea and its Associated Action

Q44. E is the Best Answer. Octopus uses tentacle as psychic uses (E) intuition

Absolute Pattern 6. Definition Pattern
Finding Definition/Concept of person, place, thing, and emotion

Q45. A is the Best Answer. The questions is based on how we define things or activity.
Spy is secretive as (A) salesman is communicative.

Absolute Pattern 7. Mental (Emotion) Pattern
Finding Feeling/Mental Concept and its Emotion

Q46. D is the Best Answer. Bewilderment and clarity refer to our mental activity and also they are opposite concept. Embarrassment and proud apply a similar concept.
(A), (B), and (C) are physical. (E) is synonym, not like the question with antonym concept.

Absolute Pattern 4. Characteristic Pattern
Finding Characteristic of Person, Place, Object, or Idea and its Associated Action

Q47. D is the Best Answer. Violin and cello are string musical instrument (D) saxophone is to flute are wind instruments.

Absolute Pattern 5. Degree Pattern
Finding a Degree and a Shape in person, place, thing, and emotion

Q48. A is the Best Answer. Sympathy is smaller than love as (A) orange is smaller than watermelon.

Absolute Pattern 3. Purpose (Tool) Pattern
Finding Relationships between the Purpose of Individual to Object, to its Function, its User, its Use, and its Association

Q49. A is the Best Answer. Reprimand is the gesture to correct. (A) finger-wagging is to chide. (B) is opposite. The other choices do not contain gesture.

Absolute Pattern 5. Degree Pattern
Finding a Degree and a Shape in person, place, thing, and emotion

Q50. D is the Best Answer. Baseball is about the size of orange as (D) pumpkin is to basketball

Absolute Pattern 3. Purpose (Tool) Pattern
Finding Relationships between the Purpose of Individual to Object, to its Function, its User, its Use, and its Association

Q51. A is the Best Answer. This question asks about what (Noun) needs to be done to do what (Verb). Complain (Noun) needs to be resolved (Verb) as tradition (Noun) needs to be perpetuated (Verb).

Absolute Pattern 3. Purpose (Tool) Pattern
Finding Relationships between the Purpose of Individual to Object, to its Function, its User, its Use, and its Association

Q52. B is the Best Answer. The purpose of prototype is to test product as (B) mass production is to sell.

Absolute Pattern 4. Characteristic Pattern
Finding Characteristic of Person, Place, Object, or Idea and its Associated Action

Q53. A is the Best Answer.
Hobo is characteristically humble as (A) hustler is to secretive. The other choices are not necessarily the primary characteristics of each individual.

Absolute Pattern 8. Production Pattern
Finding Cause-and-Effect in Person, Concept, and Object

Q54. D is the Best Answer. Headache requires doctor's note as (D) speeding causes ticket

Absolute Pattern 8. Production Pattern
Finding Cause-and-Effect in Person, Concept, and Object

Q55. B is the Best Answer. Flower is produced by Seed as (B) new breed is by hybrid

Absolute Pattern 2. Synonym/Antonym
Finding a similar or an opposite meaning between words

Q56. C is the Best Answer. Loyalty is an antonym to betrayal. Patriotism is an antonym to treason. They are a similar concept. (B) and (D) are antonym but not in the question category.

Absolute Pattern 6. Definition Pattern
Finding Definition/Concept of person, place, thing, and emotion

Q57. A is the Best Answer. Evolution is gradual advancement. Revolution is sudden movement. (B) mutation doesn't necessarily generate better generation. (E) is opposite.

Absolute Pattern 6. Definition Pattern
Finding Definition/Concept of person, place, thing, and emotion

Q58. D is the Best Answer. Confiscation means take away. Donation means giving.

Absolute Pattern 11. Subjective-Objective Pattern
Finding Quality-Quantity, Tangible-Intangible Association

Q59. C is the Best Answer. Both cheap and moderate are subjective value.

All the other choices have quantifiers or objective value (age limit).

Absolute Pattern 4. Characteristic Pattern
Finding Characteristic of Person, Place, Object, or Idea and its Associated Action

Q60. D is the Best Answer. Both aluminum and metal are substances of materials. (E) cheap metal is subjective value.

Chapter 5 Summary

The Chapter Summary contains equal portions of

12 Absolute Patterns for Analogy Section and

10 Absolute Patterns for Reading Section.

You may study all at once to significantly

improve your understanding and your scores.

Chapter 5

12 Absolute Patterns for the Analogy Section

Absolute Pattern 9. Syntax Pattern
Finding Homophony, Contraction, Grammatical Association

Q9-3. Departure is to go as computer is to

A) calculate

B) calculator

C) electronics

D) expensive

E) computation

Q9-4. Blow is to blew as choose is

A) chosen

B) chose

C) choice

D) choosy

E) choosed

(Q9-3) The correct answer is A

San: Q9-3: Departure (noun); go (verb). Computer (noun); calculate (verb)—they are synonyms.

It may appear to be Synonym Pattern, but you will never be able to solve it from that Pattern because it asks Noun/Verb Pattern within synonyms.

Do you know the answer for Q9-2?

Jimin   You go ahead!

San   Q9-2 is (B)

The question asks present tense vs. past tense.

The past tense of blow is blew. The past tense of choose is chose.

Jimin   Is there any other type in this Syntax Pattern, San?

San   Yes! It may ask you to distinguish adjective and adverb or the usage of adjective.

Adjective will appear a lot because it represents the concept and idea.

Jimin   How about spelling? Do they ask spelling too?

San   Not really!

But they will ask you some confusing words like the difference between "there" and "their."

SSAT ABSOLUTE PATTERNS

Chapter 5

12 Absolute Patterns for the Analogy Section

Absolute Pattern 10. Positive-Negative Pattern
Finding Positive-Negative Value from Antonym Category

Q10. Evil is to God

    A) north is to south

    B) lion is to zebra

    C) dark is to light

    D) medicine is to poison

    E) man is to woman

The correct answer is C

San: Evil is negative value and God is positive value so as dark is to light.

    This pattern appears to be Antonym Pattern, but in fact it is one level higher than that.

Jimin   Do you mean that A), B), and E) are definitely opposite pair of words but have no clear Positive-Negative Value? Is that what you're saying?

San   Exactly! Take a look at A) for instance.

    North and South are definitely Opposite words, but there's no Negative-Positive Value in there.

    The big difference between Evil and God, on the other hand, although Opposite, comes from their clear Negative-Positive Concept.

    That's what we are looking for!

    Don't forget D) is using the Positive-Negative Pattern but also uses a flipping trick.

UNAUTHORIZED COPYING OR REUSE OF ANY PART OF THIS PAGE IS ILLEGAL

Chapter 5

12 Absolute Patterns for the Analogy Section

Absolute Pattern 11. Subjective-Objective Pattern
Finding Quality-Quantity, Tangible-Intangible Association

Q11-1. Temperature is to 10°F degree as
  A) Jane is to tall
  B) the movie is to good
  C) student is to school uniform code
  D) last year is to 2018
  E) happiness is to money

Q11-2. Book is to knowledge
  A) age is to wisdom
  B) dime is to ten cents
  C) friend is to friendship
  D) centennial is to 100 years
  E) boiling point is to 100 degree

(Q11-1) The correct answer is D

San: 10°F degree contains a number that can be quantified or counted.
        Only Choice D) has the same value.

Jimin   How about E)? Money can be counted too! Can you be more specific?

San   Money is concept.
        To make it a correct answer you should show a definite amount of money.
        That is, data, numbers, money, or years… all of these values can be quantified by numbers.
        In broader sense, it can include Objective value too.

Jimin   Objective value? What do you mean?

San   Take a look at choice C).
        School uniform code is objective value without showing the exact numbers.
        For instance, school uniform can be blue color, or a nylon type of fabric, or 30 inches of waistline, etc.
        When you compare choice C), choice A) tall and B) good are Subjective value that has no standard.
        Therefore, (C) is closer to the answer than (A) or (B). Were there no D), what should you choose?

Jimin   C)?

San   That's right! (To be continued in the next page)

Chapter 5

12 Absolute Patterns for the Analogy Section

Absolute Pattern 11. Subjective-Objective Pattern
Finding Quality-Quantity, Tangible-Intangible Association

San: The actual question may not be that difficult. Just keep in mind though that almost all adjectives are Subjective concept such as tall, fast, cheap, quick, expensive, beautiful.

Just one more thing!

Subjective Value and Mental Value can be further divided into the Passive-Active Value.

We will discuss this in the following pattern.

Do you know the answer for Q11-2?

Jimin   Is it A)?

San   The answer is C).

A book (Tangible object), knowledge (Intangible, Objective)

Friend (Tangible), friendship (Intangible)

For A) age is Intangible concept. It is not an object like book or friend.

Jimin   I thought this question was the production pattern.

San   If it were that easy, virtually every choice should be the answer.

Choice B), D) and E) are incorrect because they have quantity value (numbers) too.

The Absolute Patterns for Analogy summary continues in the following chapters.

Chapter 5

20 Common Patterns for *In*correct Choices
For the Reading Section

San: Now armed with more strategic understanding in the reading questions, we will learn how to isolate the dusty four incorrect choices with less wrinkles on your face using the following 20 incorrect common patterns.

20 Common Patterns for *Incorrect* Choices

1 Positive-Negative Tone (value)

This rule is simple but very powerful tool.

All you need is to identify the keywords in each multiple choice.

Think if the keyword in the multiple choices is positive or negative, then match with the reading passage's keywords based on positive-negative value. This will lead you the answer concretely.

Practically majority of the questions are solved by using this single pattern.

2 Antonym or Opposite Perception

This pattern, next to the above positive-negative tone, appears most frequently.

The vast majority of incorrect choices, especially "EXCEPT", "NOT" questions apply antonym or opposite concept.

So readily applicable is the usage of antonym as incorrect choices that almost all questions apply this.

3 Active-Passive Value

Let's suppose we have two competing choices A) sympathy B) sadness

Can you tell the difference?

Not immediately, right?

Let's suppose you are watching a strange movie. In the movie, a woman character is dying in a bed. Do you feel sad? No, you will be sympathetic at most.

Let's suppose your close friend died suddenly. Do you feel sympathetic to her? No, you will be sad at the least.

Identifying the tone—whether it is active or passive—is very important.

*Please note that this active-Passive value is not the same thing as the active-passive voice in Grammar.

UNAUTHORIZED COPYING OR REUSE OF ANY PART OF THIS PAGE IS ILLEGAL

20 Common Patterns for *In*correct Options

 Not stated in the passage (incl. Future Prediction)

Some incorrect choices use not stated words in the passage. It rather uses our familiar common senses.

One representative example is exploiting a well-known fact or criticizing a heroic figure.

Students may be extremely confused if the passage described the benefits of war or accused

Martin Luther King Jr.

New information, however tempting, should not be an answer.

 Minor or Unrelated Example

This type appears frequently with the question Pattern 1: Main idea Question.

For example, the answer for the main idea question contains a relatively general and therefore neutral keyword so that it could be fit into the general message in the passage, while maintaining the objective tone.

On the contrary, were the keyword too specific, it becomes a minor idea or unrelated choice to the question.

 Insufficient Information

Some multiple choices could be both correct and incorrect at the same time.

"What does that mean?"

For instance, if choice (A) contains one correct keyword while (B), two keywords, then choice (A) is incorrect because information is insufficient or only partially correct compared to (B).

This type is the main culprit that put you in a quandary situation between two options.

The Absolute Patterns for Reading summary continues in the following chapters.

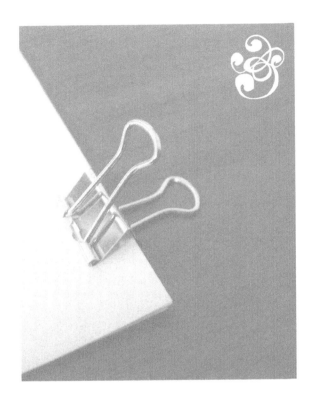

Chapter 6

1. TEST 6

2. ANSWER EXPLANATIONS for TEST 6

3. CHAPTER SUMMARY

SSAT
Reading & Verbal
Test 6

This chapter starts with the Actual Test 6.

Your goal is not getting good enough scores, but 100%.

It's your book

It's up to you to practice the Answer Explanation first.

Test 6 Reading Section
Time: 40 Minutes, 40 Questions

Directions: Each reading passage is followed by questions about it. Answer the questions that follow a passage on the basis of what is stated or implied in that passage.

Questions 1-6 are based on the following passage.

Line

Cat cafés are quite popular in Japan, with Tokyo being home to 58 cat cafés as of 2015. There are various types of cat café in Japan, some feature specific categories of cat such as black cats, fat cats, rare breed cats or house keeping cats. Japanese cat cafés feature strict rules to ensure cleanliness and <u>animal welfare</u>, in particular seeking to ensure that the cats are not disturbed by excessive and unwanted attention by young

5 Children.

Cat cafés have been spreading across North America. Cat cafés in North America differ from Japan. If the goal in Japanese cat café is to find relaxing companionship with cat from stressful and lonely urban life, Cat cafes in North America help get cats adopted by partnering with local cat rescuers. For example, Le Café des Chats/Cat Café Montreal in Montreal, Canada opened its doors to the public <u>in August 2014,</u> [QUESTION 4]

10 Hundreds of animals have been adopted through their efforts.

1

The author finds the popularity of Cat Cafés in Japan from

A) companionship with animal

B) forbidding tradition

C) stress from rats

D) adoption

E) affordability than dogs

2

Which of the following analogies resembles the animal welfare issue mentioned in the first paragraph?

A) a dog beaten by its owner

B) a parrot abandoned by its owner

C) a tortoise stopped feeding by its owner

D) a hamster being played like a toy by a child

E) a cat that has no medical insurance

3

The main difference between Cat Cafes in Japan and that in North America is that North America focuses more on

A) stray cats

B) pet owner's welfare

C) strict rules

D) child education

E) companionship

4

Which of the following statements would be most appropriate to complete the sentence after "in August 2014," in line 9?

A) with 8 cats adopted from local shelters.

B) with 10 lovely Persian cats.

C) with 12 black cats similar to the Egyptian status.

D) for those who feel lonely and need companionship

E) for those people getting stress from rats in house

5

The main difference between Japanese Cat café and North America's can be summarized respectively as

A) companionship vs. familiarity

B) tradition vs. companionship

C) companionship vs. practicality

D) official vs. unofficial

E) humanity vs. inhumanity

6

It can be inferred that Cat Cafes in North America have

A) no cute cats at all

B) mostly companionable cats

C) mainly rare-breed cats

D) mostly dogs

E) mostly abandoned cats

Questions 7-12 are based on the following passage.

Line

You will rejoice to hear that no disaster has accompanied the commencement of an enterprise which you have regarded with such evil forebodings. I arrived here yesterday, and my first task is to assure my dear sister of my welfare and increasing confidence in the success of my undertaking. I am already far north of London, and as I walk in the streets of Petersburgh, I feel a cold northern breeze play upon my cheeks, which braces my

5 nerves and fills me with delight. Do you understand this feeling? Inspirited by this <u>wind of promise</u>, my daydreams become more fervent and vivid. <u>I try in vain to be persuaded that the pole is the seat of frost and desolation; it ever presents itself to my imagination as the region of beauty and delight.</u> There, Margaret, the sun is forever visible, its broad disk just skirting the horizon and diffusing a perpetual splendour. There–for with your leave, my sister, I will put some trust in preceding navigators–there snow and frost are banished.

7

The passage is narrated from the point of view of

A) an observer who did not know the narrator initially

B) a sister who is traveling

C) an observer who has partial knowledge of the narrator

D) a narrator under the name Margaret

E) one of the sailors

8

The passage alludes the narrator is heading to

A) the narrator's hometown

B) the South Pole

C) the North Pole

D) an unknown place

E) wherever wind leads

9

The passage indicates that the narrator is traveling to a place

A) visited by many people

B) less inhabitable

C) ideal for sailing

D) attempted by many sailors previously

E) promised to sister

10

The literary device used in line 5 (wind of promise) is

A) oxymoron

B) simile

C) metaphor

D) extended metaphor

E) irony

11

The contrasting view in line 6-7 (I try in vain...and delight) can be signified as one of

A) juxtaposition

B) allusion

C) flashback

D) hyperbole

E) irony

12

Which of the following analogies resembles the narrator's emotion in 6-7?

A) a foreigner discovers a fancy restaurant in unknown village

B) a disagreeable weather challenges the tourist

C) an artist finds beauty from the aftermath of war

D) twins start to understand more about each other

E) a mother knows how to control her spoiled child

Questions 13-18 are based on the following passage.

Line   Mutation is the permanent alteration of the nucleotide sequence of the genome of an organism. Mutations result from errors during DNA replication. Mutations may produce discernible changes in the observable characteristics of an organism. Mutations play a part in both normal and abnormal biological processes. <u>Mutations in genes can either have no effect, alter the product of a gene, or prevent the gene from functioning</u>
5   <u>properly or completely, may cause damaging effects on genes.</u>
    One study on genetic variations between different species of *Drosophila* suggests that, if a mutation changes a protein produced by a gene, the result is likely to be harmful, with an estimated two-thirds of amino acid polymorphisms that have damaging effects, and the remainder being either neutral or marginally beneficial.
    Natural selection such as height can be categorized into three different types. The first is directional
10 selection, which is a shift in the average value of a trait over time—for example, organisms slowly getting taller. Secondly, disruptive selection is selection for extreme trait values and often results in two different values becoming most common, with selection against the average value. This would be when either short or tall organisms had an advantage, but not those of medium height. Finally, in stabilizing selection there is selection against extreme trait values on both ends.
15   Most loss of function mutations are selected against. But when selection is weak, mutation bias towards loss of function can affect evolution. For example, pigments are no longer useful when <u>animals</u> live in the darkness caves, and tend to be lost. This kind of loss of function can occur because of mutation bias.

13

Paragraph 1 defines mutation process as EXCEPT
A) lasting alternation of the nucleotide sequence
B) mostly beneficial to organism
C) errors of DNA replication process
D) normal and abnormal biological processes
E) observable changes in organism's characteristics

14

Based on explanation in lines 4-5, Mutations in genes
A) stabilize the product of a gene
B) may prevent the gene from malfunctioning
C) largely benefit the organism
D) may have damaging effects on genes
E) should always influence on organism through lifetime

15

According to paragraph 2 (lines 6-8), which pairing best represents the different ratios of harmful amino acid polymorphisms and the remainder respectively?
A) 70 percent and 30 percent
B) 50 percent and 50 percent
C) 10 percent and 30 percent
D) 90 percent and 10 percent
E) 10 percent and 90 percent

16

According to paragraph 2 (lines 6-8), mutation that alters a protein would very likely
A) have almost no effect on the organism
B) produce damaging effects
C) benefit the organism
D) remain neutral permanently
E) undergo weak mutation selection process

17

It can be inferred from paragraph 3 (lines 9-14) that if Leaf-eating deer migrates to Giraffe habitat, deer must undergo
  I. Directional selection
  II. Disruptive selection
  III. Stabilizing section
A) I
B) II
C) III
D) I and III
E) II and III

18

The author mentions "animals" in line 16 primarily to exemplify
A) mutation bias through evolution
B) the benefit of bats living in caves
C) the loss of function through evolution
D) the evolution of species
E) animals that cause our fear

Questions 19-23 are based on the following passage.

Line
    The Islamic State of Iraq (ISIL) is a Salafi jihadist militant group.
The group has been designated a terrorist organization by the United Nations. ISIL is widely known for its videos of beheadings and other types of executions of both soldiers and civilians.
    The group proclaimed itself a worldwide caliphate and began referring to itself as the Islamic State in 2014.
5   As a caliphate, it claims religious, political and military authority over all Muslims worldwide.
It held a large area in western Iraq and eastern Syria, containing an estimated 2.8 to 8 million people, where it enforced its interpretation of sharia law. ISIL is believed to be operational in 18 countries across the world.
In 2015, ISIL was estimated to have a force of more than 30,000 fighters.
    In July 2017, the group lost control of its largest city, Mosul. On 10 December 2017, Iraq's Prime Minister
10 Haider al-Abadi said that Iraqi forces had driven the last remnants of Islamic State from the country, three years after the militant group captured about a third of Iraq's territory.

19

The first sentence (lines 1) mainly describes the Islamic State of Iraq's

A) heinous terrorist acts

B) brutality

C) motivation

D) background identity

E) history

20

The author's main point when he says "ISIL is widely known for its videos of beheadings" (line 2) is that ISIL is

A) gaining popularity from Youtube

B) difficult to contain

C) actually beheading civilians

D) spectacular in using Youtube video

E) strategically promoting their heinous activities

21

The group's proclamation itself a worldwide caliphate (line 4) betrays ISIL's need for

A) reclusive isolation

B) official approval from worldwide

C) unhindered interaction with other countries

D) the worldwide recognition of their morality

E) respect from all other Muslims

22

In paragraph 2 (lines 4-8), the author mainly focuses on ISIL's

A) difficulty to control its worldwide organization

B) degree to which it has grown worldwide

C) strong 30,000 fighters

D) size of population

E) way of believing Muslim

23

The overall tone of the last paragraph (lines 9-11), is one of

A) awe

B) terror

C) irate

D) relief

E) concern

Questions 24-31 are based on the following passage.

Line
   The San Francisco Bay Area has seen tremendous growth and is expected to grow by an additional 25% in population and employment. The region's employment and output outpaced the nation's. Here, employment is growing faster than population and the population faster than housing units. Growth has posed enormous transportation challenges as it relates to the safety, mobility, environment and economic productivity.

5   Some of the key trends include current population growth, increase in number of older citizens and shift of people to mega-regions. These challenges are now impacting the citizens of San Francisco. Travel in the City is very time-consuming and expensive. Problems will get worse. Freight demand is also on the rise. Increased deliveries in San Francisco have created safety conflicts, double parking, and blocked access with large trucks that are incompatible on the roads of a city like San Francisco.

10   To solve this issue, Incorporate Connected and Automated vehicle technology will be proven to be safe to further reduce travel costs, eliminate collisions and fatalities, and reduce parking demand sufficiently.

24

Currently, the biggest concern in San Francisco is probably

A) growing number of citizens

B) the number of housing units

C) employment output

D) the employment rate

E) transportation system

25

The author describes one of the advantages of San Francisco as?

A) growing number of older citizens

B) housing affordability

C) housing unit availability

D) the employment rate

E) transportation system

26

Which of the following benefits can be expected from " Incorporate Connected and Automated vehicle technology in line 10?

I.   traveling cost efficiency

II. solution to parking demand

III. pollution elimination

A) I only

B) II, only

C) III only

D) I, II only

E) I, II, III

27

The freight demand issues include all of the following EXCEPT

A) mega-regions

B) delivery

C) safety

D) parking

E) road access

28

The author mentions "Some of the key trends" (line 5) in order to indicate

A) significant challenges in the city

B) limited impact to the city

C) short-term manageable problems

D) main factors that benefit the city

E) reasons for the tremendous growth of the city

29

The main purpose of the first paragraph (lines 1-4) is to

A) celebrate the current and the future growth of the city of San Francisco

B) present the city's irresolvable issues

C) indicate growing transportation challenge

D) emphasize the city's fascinating features

E) warn the debacle in economy due to the transportation issues

30

In line 2-3 (Here, employment....units). the author conveys the tone of

A) celebration

B) concern

C) jubilation

D) irritation

E) appreciation

31

This passage would probably be taken from

A) the City of San Francisco Education Ministry

B) White House annual report

C) San Francisco traveling guide

D) San Francisco metro transportation committee

E) The History of modern San Francisco

Questions 32-37 are based on the following passage.

Line   It was on the way to Sandown Park that I met him first, on that horribly wet July afternoon.
He sat opposite to me in the train going down, and my attention was first attracted to him by the marked contrast between his appearance and his attire: he had not thought fit to adopt the regulation costume for such occasions, and I think I never saw a man who had made himself more horsey; he wore extremely tight
5   trousers. Somehow, he aroused compassion rather than any sense of the ludicrous. He puzzled me so much that I did my best to enter into conversation with him, only to be baffled by the jerky embarrassment.

32

The intended effect of the portrayal of a man's attire (lines 4-5) is to show

A) an inescapable fate with the narrator

B) the person's weird looking

C) the origin of the companionship

D) there's a beast inside the man

E) the person's brutality

33

The author's initial feeling toward the man was one of

A) annoyance

B) curiosity

C) indifference

D) intellectual assessment

E) hatred

34

The passage as a whole is written by the narrator who?

A) speculates about the stranger

B) is the member of the same family

C) reflects his younger days

D) is the stranger himself

E) knows everything about the man

35

In lines 5-6 "He puzzled me… ", the narrator's feeling shifts from puzzlement to

A) courage

B) curiosity

C) determination

D) uncertainty

E) humiliation

36

The author writes the story based on

A) personal speculation

B) well-known fact

C) long familiarity

D) scholarly analysis

E) social phenomenon

37

It can be inferred from the passage that the man might have reacted to the narrator's advancement as

A) a tactical invasion

B) a romantic courtship

C) a humorous attempt

D) a friendly invitation

E) an annoying intrusion

Questions 38-40 are based on the following passage.

Line
What is the peculiar charm of that mighty, snow-capped sea of mountains, whose stupendous waves tossed far into the heavens seem ever about to overwhelm the level wheat-fields of Western Canada? The lure of the mountains defies analysis. The rolling foothills in the foreground seem tangible and comprehensible, but above the towering outer wave of the
5 mountains, float silvery outlines that seem to be the fabric of some outer purer world.

One who has seen this vision may not resist the insistent call to explore the mountain world. The call has been working in the hearts of men for generations. They came alone in the early days, each man fighting his way up through some doorway that led into the heart of the Glittering Mountains.

38

"The lure of the mountains defies analysis" (line 3)

can also be interpreted as

A) mountains need further analysis

B) there's something beyond our analysis

C) anything attractive needs not be analyzed

D) all the mountains are subject to analysis

E) mountain climbing requires analytical skills

39

The author mentions "The rolling foothills" in

line 3 in order to

A) warn those kids wishing to roll in the mountains

B) visualize foothills that is actually moving

C) show mountains within our reach to comprehend

D) tell the reader that the mountains are a purer world

E) warn people to avoid mountain climbing

40

"the hearts" in line 7 refers to

A) a desire to climb the mountains

B) a wish to camp in the foothills

C) a dream of becoming a heart surgeon

D) a hesitation to analyze the mountains

E) a heart to brave difficult weather

Test 6 Verbal Section   30 MINUTES, 60 QUESTIONS

Directions: the synonym questions ask you to find the most appropriate synonym to the question.

The analogy questions ask you to find the most appropriate analogy to the question.
Select the answer that best matches to the question.

Synonym Sample Question:

Q: SUPERIOR

 A higher rank

 B inferior

 C considerable

 D supermarket

 E supper

A) is the best answer because the synonym for superior is higher rank.

B) is incorrect because it applies the 'opposite concept.

C) and E) are irrelevant words.

D) is incorrect because it applies physical concept to mental concept

---

Test 6 Synonym questions 1 to 30

1. EERIE
(A) ear
(B) check
(C) correction
(D) error
(E) frightening

2. ELUDE
(A) lure
(B) luminary
(C) evade
(D) exit
(E) meeting

3. EFFICIENT
(A) efficacious
(B) evolve
(C) expansive
(D) fuse
(E) unusual

4. ESTEEM
(A) heat
(B) respect
(C) standing out
(D) clear
(E) stymie

5. EXPLOIT
(A) use
(B) moving
(C) explosion
(D) reach out
(E) late

6. EXTRACT

(A) removal

(B) traction

(C) factor

(D) extrapolation

(E) exterminate

7. INGENIOUS

(A) engender

(B) genuine

(C) innocent

(D) generations

(E) gentle

8. INNOVATION

(A) novel

(B) noble

(C) cultivation

(D) trust

(E) notorious

9. LIBERATE

(A) leverage

(B) life

(C) free

(D) vibrate

(E) shackle

10. INTIMIDATION

(A) hostility

(B) intimacy

(C) precision

(D) combination

(E) round

11. JOVIAL

(A) promise

(B) cheerful

(C) capitalization

(D) mood

(E) relation

12. INCIDENTAL

(A) dependent

(B) minor

(C) untrue

(D) stylish

(E) loaded

13. REPLICA

(A) item

(B) motion

(C) worry

(D) function

(E) copy

14. INTERSECT

(A) recognize

(B) obtain

(C) predict

(D) converge

(E) dilute

15. FRETFUL

(A) provoked

(B) occupied

(C) worried

(D) masked

(E) ruined

16. MAYHEM

(A) reform

 (B) hustle

(C) disorder

(D) notion

(E) preference

17. MAR

(A) attach

(B) decide

(C) hustle

(D) broaden

(E) spoil

18. DISCREET

(A) pleasing

(B) tactful

(C) uneasy

(D) guarded

(E) vigilant

19. TEMPERANCE

(A) logic

(B) irritation

(C) hospitality

(D) restraint

(E) protection

20. LIBERATE

(A) release

(B) bond

(C) transfer

(D) conceive

(E) answer

21. EXQUISITE

(A) generous

(B) precise

(C) elegant

(D) noteworthy

(E) justifying

22. PIGMENT

(A) farm feed

(B) color source

(C) blunt object

(D) animal skin

(E) busy schedule

23. PROLOGUE

(A) extension

(B) nonessential part

(C) humorous play

(D) introduction

(E) sequel

24. PLAUSIBLE

(A) reasonable

(B) inventive

(C) momentary

(D) discourteous

(E) overconfident

25. SUBSEQUENT

(A) understanding

(B) following

(C) danger

(D) discrepancy

(E) overwhelming

26. SUPPLEMENT

(A) extra

(B) join

(C) teacher

(D) complement

(E) end

27. SWARM

(A) flock

(B) swimming

(C) warm

(D) individual

(E) boss

28. TANGIBLE

(A) touchable

(B) intangible

(C) attainable

(D) audible

(E) admissible

29. TERMINATE

(A) discontinue

(B) criticize

(C) gather

(D) build

(E) replace

30. TERRAIN

(A) body

(B) track

(C) land

(D) rainforest

(E) piece

Analogy Sample Question:

Q: River is to Ocean as:

A better is to good

B rain is to cloud

C father is to mother

D city is to country

E fork is to spoon

D is the correct answer. Just as the river is smaller than the Ocean, the city is smaller than the country. The pattern applied in this question is the Degree Pattern (small to big)

A) is incorrect because the word order is flipped over.

B) is incorrect because it applies the production pattern (cloud produces rain)

C), E) are incorrect because they apply the Antonym patterns.

Test 6 Analogy questions 31 to 60

31. Ice is to snow as

(A) coffee is to melt

(B) cold is to warm

(C) freeze is to melt

(D) cream is to white

(E) land is to tire

32. Government is to policy as military is to

(A) general

(B) army

(C) command

(D) solder

(E) war

33. Boat is to horse as dock is to

(A) bird

(B) water

(C) stable

(D) staple

(E) duck

34. Taste is bitter as

(A) caustic is to personality

(B) touch is to intangible

(C) sight is to nostalgic

(D) smell is to belligerent

(E) hearing is to myopia

35. North is to South as

(A) iron is to lead

(B) polar bear is to cola

(C) printer is to melody

(D) sink is to vehicle

(E) old is to elder

36. Employee is to resume as

(A) factory work is to work order

(B) job is to profession

(C) professional is to skilled worker

(D) reputation is to reference

(E) occupation is to livelihood

37. Flattery is to adulation as pardon is to

(A) excuse

(B) please

(C) subservient

(D) reason

(E) behavior

38. Absolute is to conditional as

(A) purification is to relief

(B) provisional is to categorical

(C) solution is to understand

(D) gas is to vaporization

(E) limit is to standard

39. Employee is to company as

(A) pressure is to steam engine

(B) employer is to owner

(C) firm is to organization

(D) staff is to bonus

(E) clock is to timing

40. Key is to lock as

(A) door is to protection

(B) reporter is to newspaper

(C) internet is to domain

(D) ticket is to concert entrance

(E) insurance is to automobile

41. Assistant is to boss as

(A) soprano is to alto

(B) voice is to instrument

(C) speed is to tempo

(D) humming is to opera

(E) king is to prime minister

42. Market is to exchange as Internet is to

(A) fast

(B) free

(C) connect

(D) online

(E) transfer

43. Border is to boundary as national park is to

(A) preservation

(B) amusement

(C) family trip

(D) inconvenience

(E) diversification

44. Tourist is to attraction as archeologist is to

(A) papers

(B) remnants

(C) honor

(D) academy

(E) pride

45. Paris is to romantic as Egypt is to

(A) archaic

(B) sphinx

(C) mummy

(D) desert

(E) treasure

46. Grandma is to boy as

(A) kindergarten is to university

(B) elementary is to middle school

(C) grade 1 is to grade 11

(D) teacher is to professor

(E) principal is to student

47. Supporting actress is to actor

(A) director is to movie

(B) waiter is to waitress

(C) table clothe is to silverware

(D) tip is to tax

(E) customer is to manager

48. California is to largest state

(A) Puerto Rico is to oldest state

(B) New York is to very expensive state

(C) Hawaii is to pleasant state

(D) Utah is to desert state

(E) Alaska is to coldest state

49. Advice is to hint

(A) expel is to warning

(B) chalk is to marker

(C) program is to curriculum

(D) science is to math

(E) announcement is to memo

50. Movie is to symphony as

(A) spare tire is to car

(B) theater is to seat

(C) director is to movie

(D) scene is to movement

(E) melody is to music

51. Farm work is to difficult as

(A) Google is to fast

(B) last year was 2018

(C) Christmas is to December

(D) Renaissance is to Italy

(E) apple is to fruit

52. Vigilant is to night watchman as

(A) capital punishment is to shoplifting

(B) tense is to military checkpoint

(C) dictator is to tyrant

(D) grant is to membership

(E) school discipline is to child

53. Counselor is to advice as

(A) newspaper is to issue

(B) greed is to money

(C) friend is to tip

(D) rhythm is to dance

(E) flame is to fire

54. Magic is to applause as

(A) audience is to crowd

(B) magician is to hustler

(C) victim is to condolence

(D) wand is to hocus-pocus

(E) skill is to practice

55. Import is to payment

(A) salesman is to promotion

(B) boss is to plan

(C) assistant is to help

(D) driver is to driving

(E) sales is to income

56. Melancholy is to tear as

(A) iron is to rust

(B) bread is to mold

(C) cheese is to smell

(D) orange is to rotten

(E) hot-temper is to anger

57. Craftsmanship is to genuine article as

(A) autobiography is to vicarious experience

(B) factory is to mass products

(C) mass media is to information

(D) writer is to story

(E) singer is to melody

58. Gale is to snail as

(A) life is to death

(B) wind is to gust

(C) insect is to nature

(D) animal is to speed

(E) weather is to animal

59. Penthouse is to luxury as

(A) uptown is to expensive

(B) high rise building is to over 25 story.

(C) chandelier is to above 10feet

(D) building code is to 1200 sections

(E) penthouse is to 2500 square feet requirement

60. Infatuated is to veneration as

(A) annoyed is to vexation

(B) caring is to loving

(C) rejected is to alarmed

(D) aggravated is to painful

(E) grumpy is to old

Test 6

Answer Explanations

&

The Pattern Analyses

If your Test 6 scores are unsatisfactory,

Practice the Answer Explanations and then solve

the Actual Test 6 again.

ALL THE LOGIC AND RULES BEHIND
EVERY SINGLE SSAT QUESTION

UNAUTHORIZED COPYING OR REUSE OF ANY PART OF THIS PAGE IS ILLEGAL

TEST 6
READING SECTION

Please refer to the Reading Section Absolute Pattern Analyses

THE SYNONYM QUESTIONS THE ANALOGY QUESTIONS

TEST 6 NO.1 ~ 30.   TEST 6 NO. 31 ~ 60

				Please refer to the Analogy Section Absolute Pattern Analyses
1	E	16	C	
2	C	17	E	
3	A	18	D	
4	B	19	D	
5	A	20	A	
6	A	21	C	
7	C	22	B	
8	A	23	D	
9	C	24	A	
10	A	25	B	
11	B	26	A	
12	B	27	A	
13	E	28	A	
14	D	29	A	
15	C	30	C	

Questions 1-6 are based on the following passage.

Cat cafés are quite popular in Japan, with Tokyo being home to 58 cat cafés as of 2015. There are various types of cat café in Japan, some feature specific categories of cat such as black cats, fat cats, rare breed cats or house keeping cats. Japanese cat cafés feature strict rules to ensure cleanliness and animal welfare, in particular seeking to ensure that the cats are not disturbed by (2) **excessive and unwanted attention by young Children.**

Cat cafés have been spreading across North America. Cat cafés in North America differ from Japan. (5) If the goal in Japanese cat café is to find relaxing (1) **companionship with cat** from stressful and lonely urban life, Cat cafes in North America help get (3 & 6) **cats adopted by partnering with local cat rescuers**. For example, Le Café des Chats/Cat Café Montreal in Montreal, Canada opened its doors to the public in August 2014, [QUESTION 4] (4) **Hundreds of animals have been adopted through their efforts.**

Q1 . Absolute Pattern 2: Summary Question
Question Pattern: The author finds the **popularity of Cat Cafés** in Japan from

A) companionship with animal B) forbidding tradition C) stress from rats D) adoption E) affordability than dogs	If the goal in Japanese cat café is to find relaxing **companionship with cat** from stressful and lonely urban life,

---

Q2. Absolute Pattern 6: Analogy Question Finding a similar situation
Question Pattern: Which of the following **analogies resembles the animal welfare** mentioned in the first paragraph?

A) a dog beaten by its owner B) a parrot abandoned by its owner C) a tortoise stopped feeding by its owner **D) a hamster being played like a toy by a child** E) a cat that has no medical insurance	excessive and unwanted attention by young Children.

Q3. Absolute Pattern 9: Relationships Question
Question Pattern: The main difference between Cat Cafes in Japan and that in North America is that **North America** focuses more on

A) stray cats B) pet owner's welfare C) strict rules D) child education E) companionship	cats adopted by partnering with local cat rescuers

---

Q4. Absolute Pattern 2: Summary Question
Question Pattern: Which of the following statements would be most appropriate to **complete the sentence after "in August 2014,"** in line 9?

A) with 8 cats adopted from local shelters. B) with 10 lovely Persian cats. C) with 12 black cats similar to the Egyptian status. D) for those who feel lonely and need companionship E) for those people getting stress from rats in house	Cat Café Montreal in Montreal, Canada opened its doors to the public in August 2014, **A) with 8 cats adopted from local shelters. Hundreds of animals have been adopted through their efforts.**

Q5. Absolute Pattern 9: Relationships Question
Question Pattern: The main difference between **Japanese Cat café and North America's** can be summarized respectively as

A) companionship vs. familiarity B) tradition vs. companionship **C) companionship vs. practicality** D) official vs. unofficial E) humanity vs. inhumanity	If the goal in Japanese cat café is to find relaxing **companionship with cat** from stressful and lonely urban life, Cat cafes in North America help get **cats adopted by partnering with local cat rescuers**.

Q6. Absolute Pattern 3: Inference Question Finding an indirect suggestion (or guessing)
Question Pattern: It can be inferred that **Cat Cafes in North America have**

A) no cute cats at all B) mostly companionable cats C) mainly rare-breed cats D) mostly dogs **E) mostly abandoned cats**	Cat cafes in North America help get **cats adopted by partnering with local cat rescuers**.

Questions 7-12 are based on the following passage.

You will rejoice to hear that no disaster has accompanied the commencement of an enterprise which you have regarded with such evil forebodings. I arrived here yesterday, and my first task is to assure (7) **my dear sister** of my welfare and increasing confidence in the success of my undertaking. I am already far north of London, and as I walk in the streets of Petersburgh, I feel a cold northern breeze play upon my cheeks, which braces my nerves and fills me with delight.

Do you understand this feeling? Inspirited by this (10) **wind of promise,** my daydreams become more fervent and vivid. (11 & 12) **I try in vain to be persuaded that** (8) **the pole is** (9) **the seat of frost and desolation; it ever presents itself to my imagination as the region of beauty and delight**. There, Margaret, the sun is forever visible, its broad disk just skirting the horizon and diffusing a perpetual splendor. There—for with your leave, my sister, I will put some trust in preceding navigators—there snow and frost are banished.

Q7 . Absolute Pattern 10: Understanding the Structure of the Passage
Question Pattern: The passage is **narrated** from the point of view of

A) an observer who did not know the narrator initially **B) a sister who is traveling** C) an observer who has partial knowledge of the narrator D) a narrator under the name Margaret E) one of the sailors	my first task is to assure **my dear sister** of my welfare and increasing confidence in the success of my undertaking

Q8. Absolute Pattern 3: Inference Question Finding an indirect suggestion (or guessing)
Question Pattern: The passage alludes the **narrator is heading to**

A) the narrator's hometown B) the South Pole **C) the North Pole** D) an unknown place E) wherever wind leads	I am already far **north of London**, ... I try in vain to be persuaded that **the pole** is the seat of frost and desolation;

Q9 . **Absolute Pattern 2: Summary Question**
Summarizing a sentence or entire passage
Question Pattern: The passage indicates that the **narrator is traveling to a place**

A) visited by many people **B) less inhabitable** C) ideal for sailing D) attempted by many sailors previously E) promised to sister	I try in vain to be persuaded that **the pole** is **the seat of frost and desolation**; it ever presents itself to my imagination as the region of beauty and delight

Q10. **Absolute Pattern 5: Word-In-Context Question**
Finding a clue word and the keyword from the sentence in question
Question Pattern: The literary device used in line 5 (**wind of promise**) is

A) oxymoron B) simile **C) metaphor** D) extended metaphor E) irony	wind of promise,… is metaphor. *Metaphor is a figure of speech in which a word or phrase is applied to an object or action to which it is not literally applicable.

Q11 . **Absolute Pattern 5: Word-In-Context Question**
Finding a clue word and the keyword from the sentence in question
Question Pattern: The contrasting view in line 6-7 (I try in vain...and delight) can be signified as one of

A) juxtaposition B) allusion C) flashback D) hyperbole E) irony	I try in vain to be persuaded that the pole is **the seat of frost and desolation**; it ever presents itself to my imagination as the region of **beauty and delight** * The phrase shows the juxtaposition of these two images. Juxtaposition is the fact of two things being seen or placed close together with contrasting effect.

Q12. **Absolute Pattern 6: Analogy Question** Finding a similar situation
Question Pattern: Which of the following **analogies resembles the narrator's emotion** in 6-7?

A) a foreigner discovers a fancy restaurant in unknown village B) a disagreeable weather challenges the tourist **C) an artist finds beauty from the aftermath of war** D) twins start to understand more about each other E) a mother knows how to control her spoiled child	I try in vain to be persuaded that the pole is **the seat of frost and desolation**; it ever presents itself to my imagination as the region of **beauty and delight.**

Questions 13-18 are based on the following passage.

Mutation is the permanent alteration of the nucleotide sequence of the genome of an organism. Mutations result from errors during DNA replication. Mutations may produce discernible changes in the observable characteristics of an organism. Mutations play a part in both normal and abnormal biological processes. Mutations in genes can either have no effect, alter the product of a gene, or prevent the gene from functioning properly or completely, (13 &14) **may cause damaging effects on genes.**

One study on genetic variations between different species of *Drosophila* suggests that, if a mutation changes a (16) **protein produced by a gene, the result is likely to be harmful,** with an estimated (15) **two-thirds of amino acid polymorphisms that have damaging effects, and the remainder being either neutral or marginally** beneficial.   Natural selection such as height can be categorized into three different types. The first is (17) **directional selection, which is a shift in the average value of a trait over time—for example, organisms slowly getting taller.** Secondly, disruptive selection is selection for extreme trait values and often results in two different values becoming most common, with selection against the average value. This would be when either short or tall organisms had an advantage, but not those of medium height. Finally, in stabilizing selection there is selection against extreme trait values on both ends.

Most loss of function mutations are selected against. (18) **But when selection is weak, mutation bias towards loss of function can affect evolution**. For example, pigments are no longer useful when animals live in the darkness of caves, and tend to be lost. This kind of loss of function can occur because of mutation bias.

Q13. **Absolute Pattern 2: Summary Question**
Summarizing a sentence or entire passage
Question Pattern: Paragraph 1 defines **mutation process as EXCEPT**

A) lasting alternation of the nucleotide sequence **B) mostly beneficial to organism** C) errors of DNA replication process D) normal and abnormal biological processes E) observable changes in organism's characteristics	may cause damaging effects on genes.

Q14. **Absolute Pattern 2: Summary Question**
Summarizing a sentence or entire passage
Question Pattern: Based on explanation in lines 4-5, **Mutations in genes**

A) stabilize the product of a gene B) may prevent the gene from malfunctioning C) largely benefit the organism **D) may have damaging effects on genes** E) should always influence on organism through lifetime	may cause damaging effects on genes. All the remaining choices are opposite.

Q15. **Absolute Pattern 9: Relationships Question**
Finding relations between the cause-effect, comparison-contrast, characters, and ideas
Question Pattern: According to paragraph 2 (lines 6-8), which pairing best represents the different **ratios of harmful amino acid polymorphisms and the remainder** respectively?

A) 70 percent and 30 percent B) 50 percent and 50 percent C) 10 percent and 30 percent D) 90 percent and 10 percent E) 10 percent and 90 percent	two-thirds of amino acid polymorphisms that have damaging effects, and the remainder being either neutral or marginally

Q16.**Absolute Pattern 2: Summary Question**
Summarizing a sentence or entire passage
Question Pattern: According to paragraph 2 (lines 6-8), mutation that **alters a protein** would very likely

A) have almost no effect on the organism **B) produce damaging effects** C) benefit the organism D) remain neutral permanently E) undergo weak mutation selection process	protein produced by a gene, the result is likely to be harmful,

Q17. **Absolute Pattern 3: Inference Question** Finding an indirect suggestion (or guessing)
Question Pattern: It can be inferred from paragraph 3 (lines 9-14) that **if Leaf-eating deer migrates to Giraffe habitat, deer must undergo**

I. Directional selection II. Disruptive selection III. Stabilizing section **A) I** B) II C) III D) I and III E) II and III	directional selection, which is a shift in the average value of a trait over time—for example, organisms **slowly getting taller.**

Q18. **Absolute Pattern 8: Understanding True Purpose**
Finding the true purpose of statement, sentences, or the entire paragraph
Question Pattern: The author mentions **"animals"** in line 16 primarily to exemplify

A) mutation bias through evolution B) the benefit of bats living in caves C) the loss of function through evolution D) the evolution of species E) animals that cause our fear	Most loss of function mutations are selected against. **But when selection is weak, mutation bias towards loss of function can affect evolution**.

Questions 19-23 are based on the following passage.

The Islamic State of Iraq (ISIL) is (19) **a Salafi jihadist militant group.**
The group has been designated a terrorist organization by the United Nations. ISIL is (20) **widely known for its videos of beheadings and other types of executions** of both soldiers and civilians.

The group proclaimed itself a worldwide caliphate and began referring to itself as the Islamic State in 2014. As a caliphate, (21) **it claims religious, political and military authority** over all Muslims worldwide.

It held a large area in western Iraq and eastern Syria, containing an estimated (22) **2.8 to 8 million people, where it enforced its interpretation of sharia law. ISIL is believed to be operational in 18 countries across the world. In 2015, ISIL was estimated to have a force of more than 30,000 fighters.**

In July 2017, the group lost control of its largest city, Mosul. On 10 December 2017, Iraq's Prime Minister Haider al-Abadi said that Iraqi forces had driven the (23) **last remnants of Islamic State from the country**, three years after the militant group captured about a third of Iraq's territory.

Q19. Absolute Pattern 2: Summary Question
Question Pattern: The **first sentence** (lines 1) mainly describes the Islamic State of Iraq's

A) heinous terrorist acts B) brutality C) motivation **D) background identity** E) history	The Islamic State of Iraq (ISIL) is (19) **a Salafi jihadist militant group.**

Q20. Absolute Pattern 7: Understanding Attitude (Tone) Question
Question Pattern: The author's main point when he says "ISIL is widely known for its **videos of beheadings**" (line 2) is that ISIL is

A) gaining popularity from Youtube B) difficult to contain C) actually beheading civilians D) spectacular in using Youtube video **E) strategically promoting their heinous activities**	widely <u>known for its videos of beheadings</u> and other types of executions of both soldiers and civilians. "widely known for" implies that the main purpose is to promote their activities, not killing itself.

Q21. Absolute Pattern 8: Understanding True Purpose
Question Pattern: The group's proclamation itself a worldwide caliphate (line 4) betrays ISIL's need for

A) reclusive isolation **B) official approval from worldwide** C) unhindered interaction with other countries D) the worldwide recognition of their morality E) respect from all other Muslims	it claims religious, political and military authority over all Muslims worldwide.

Q22. Absolute Pattern 2: Summary Question
Summarizing a sentence or entire passage
Question Pattern: In **paragraph 2** (lines 4-8), the author mainly focuses on ISIL's

A) difficulty to control its worldwide organization **B) degree to which it has grown worldwide** C) strong 30,000 fighters D) size of population E) way of believing Muslim	**2.8 to 8 million** people, where it enforced its interpretation of sharia law. ISIL is believed to be operational in **18 countries** across the world. In 2015, ISIL was estimated to have a force of more than **30,000 fighters**. C) is a part of the answer B).

Q23. Absolute Pattern 7: Understanding Attitude (Tone) Question
Finding tone such as positive-negative, active-passive, mental-physical, subjective-objective
Question Pattern: The overall **tone of the last paragraph** (lines 9-11), is one of

A) awe B) terror C) irate **D) relief** E) concern	that Iraqi forces had driven the **last remnants of Islamic State from the country**, three years after the militant group captured about a third of Iraq's territory.

Questions 24-31 are based on the following passage.

The San Francisco Bay Area has seen tremendous growth and is expected to grow by an additional 25% in population and (25) **employment.** The region's employment and output outpaced the nation's. (30) Here, employment is growing faster than population and the **population faster than housing units.** Growth has posed (24 &29) **enormous transportation challenges** as it relates to the safety, mobility, environment and economic productivity.

Some of the key trends include current population growth, increase in number of older citizens and shift of people to mega-regions. (28) **These challenges are now impacting the citizens of San Francisco**. Travel in the City is very time-consuming and expensive. Problems will get worse. Freight demand is also on the rise. (27) Increased **deliveries** in San Francisco have created **safety conflicts, double parking, and blocked access** with large trucks that are incompatible on the roads of a city like San Francisco.

(31) **To solve this issue,** Incorporate Connected and Automated vehicle technology will be proven to be safe to further reduce (26) **travel costs**, eliminate collisions and fatalities, and reduce **parking demand** sufficiently.

Q24. Absolute Pattern 2: Summary Question
Summarizing a sentence or entire passage
Question Pattern: "Currently, **the biggest concern** in San Francisco is probably

A) growing number of citizens B) the number of housing units C) employment output D) the employment rate **E) transportation system**	Growth has posed **enormous transportation challenges** as it relates to the safety, mobility, environment and economic productivity.

Q25. Absolute Pattern 2: Summary Question
Summarizing a sentence or entire passage
Question Pattern: The author describes one of the **advantages of San Francisco** as?

A) growing number of older citizens B) housing affordability C) housing unit availability **D) the employment rate** E) transportation system	The San Francisco Bay Area has seen tremendous growth and is expected to grow by an additional 25% in population and **employment.** All the other choices are problems.

UNAUTHORIZED COPYING OR REUSE OF ANY PART OF THIS PAGE IS ILLEGAL

Q26. Absolute Pattern 2: Summary Question
Summarizing a sentence or entire passage
Question Pattern: Which of the following **benefits** can be expected from " Incorporate **Connected and Automated vehicle technology** in line 10?

I. traveling cost efficiency
  II. solution to parking demand
  III. pollution elimination
A) I only
B) II, only
C) III only
D) I, II only
E) I, II, III
	Incorporate Connected and Automated vehicle technology will be proven to be safe to further reduce **travel costs**, eliminate collisions and fatalities, and reduce **parking demand** sufficiently.

Q27. Absolute Pattern 2: Summary Question
Summarizing a sentence or entire passage
Question Pattern: The **freight demand issues include** all of the following **EXCEPT**

A) mega-regions B) delivery C) safety D) parking E) road access	Freight demand is also on the rise. Increased **deliveries** in San Francisco have created **safety conflicts, double parking, and blocked access** with large trucks

Q28. Absolute Pattern 4: Example Question
Finding the true purpose behind a specific name or idea within a sentence
Question Pattern: The author mentions "**Some of the key trends**" (line 5) in order to indicate

A) significant challenges in the city B) limited impact to the city C) short-term manageable problems D) main factors that benefit the city E) reasons for the tremendous growth of the city	Some of the key trends include current population growth, increase in number of older citizens and shift of people to mega-regions. **These challenges a**re now impacting the citizens of San Francisco *"These challenges" is functioning as the amplifier.

Q29. Absolute Pattern 1: Main Idea Question
Finding the main idea of the entire passage, a specific paragraph, or sentences
Question Pattern: The main purpose of the **first paragraph** (lines 1-4) is to

A) celebrate the current and the future growth of the city of San Francisco B) present the city's irresolvable issues **C) indicate growing transportation challenge** D) emphasize the city's fascinating features E) warn the debacle in economy due to the transportation issues	**enormous transportation challenges** as it relates to the safety, mobility, environment and economic productivity.

Q30. Absolute Pattern 7: Understanding Attitude (Tone) Question
Finding tone such as positive-negative, active-passive, mental-physical, subjective-objective.
Question Pattern: In line 2-3 (**Here, employment….units**). the author conveys the **tone** of

A) celebration **B) concern** C) jubilation D) irritation E) appreciation	Here, employment is growing faster than population and the **population faster than housing units.** Employment growing faster than population causes the shortage of workers.

Q31. Absolute Pattern 3: Inference Question Finding an indirect suggestion (or guessing)
Question Pattern: This **passage would probably be taken** from

A) the City of San Francisco Education Ministry B) White House annual report C) San Francisco traveling guide **D) San Francisco metro transportation committee** E) The History of modern San Francisco	**To solve this issue,** Incorporate Connected and Automated vehicle technology will be proven to be safe to further reduce **travel costs**, eliminate collisions and fatalities, and reduce **parking demand** sufficiently.

Questions 32-37 are based on the following passage.

It was on the way to Sandown Park that I met him first, on that horribly wet July afternoon. He sat opposite to me in the train going down, and my attention was first (Q33)**attracted to him** by the marked contrast between his appearance and his attire: he had not thought fit to adopt the regulation costume for such occasions, and I think (Q32)**I never saw a man who had made himself** more horsey; he wore extremely tight trousers. Somehow, he aroused compassion rather than any sense of the ludicrous. (Q34 & Q36) **He puzzled me so much** that I did my best to enter into conversation with him, only to be baffled by the (Q35 & Q37)**jerky embarrassment.**

Q32. Absolute Pattern 8: Understanding True Purpose
Finding the true purpose of statement, sentences, or the entire paragraph
Question Pattern: The intended effect of the portrayal of a **man's attire** (lines 3-5) is to show

A) an inescapable fate with the narrator **B) the person's weird looking** C) the origin of the companionship D) there's a beast inside the man E) the person's brutality	...and I think I never saw a man who had made himself more aggressively horsey. the portrayal of a man focuses on his outfit in weird way.

Q33. Absolute Pattern 7: Understanding Attitude (Tone) Question
Finding tone such as positive-negative, active-passive, mental-physical, subjective-objective.
Question Pattern: The **author's initial feeling** toward the man was one of

A) annoyance **B) curiosity** C) indifference D) intellectual assessment E) hatred	He puzzled and interested me (CURIOSITY) so much that I did my best to enter into conversation with him, ...

Q34. Absolute Pattern 10: Understanding the Structure of the Passage
Finding the structural organization of the passage or paragraph
Question Pattern: The passage as a whole **is written by the narrator who**?

A) **speculates about the stranger** B) is the member of the same family C) reflects his younger days D) is the stranger himself E) knows everything about the man	**I never saw a man who had made himself** more horsey; he wore extremely… The story begins by describing a stranger's weird outfits. Therefore, the narrator speculates about the stranger.

Q35. Absolute Pattern 7: Understanding Attitude (Tone) Question
Finding tone such as positive-negative, active-passive, mental-physical, subjective-objective.
Question Pattern: In lines 6-7 "He puzzled me… ", the narrator's **feeling shifts from puzzlement to**

A) courage B) curiosity C) determination D) uncertainty **E) humiliation**	He puzzled and interested me so much that I did my best to enter into conversation with him, only to be baffled <u>by the jerky embarrassment (HUMILIATION)</u>

Q36. Absolute Pattern 10: Understanding the Structure of the Passage
Finding the structural organization of the passage or paragraph
Question Pattern: The **author writes the story** based on

A) **personal speculation** B) well-known fact C) long familiarity D) scholarly analysis E) social phenomenon	The story begins by describing a stranger's weird outfits. Therefore, the narrator speculates about the stranger.

Q37. Absolute Pattern 3: Inference Question Finding an indirect suggestion (or guessing)
Question Pattern: It can be inferred from the passage that **the man might have reacted** to the narrator's advancement as

A) a tactical invasion B) a romantic courtship C) a humorous attempt D) a friendly invitation **E) an annoying intrusion**	He puzzled and interested me so much that I did my best to enter into conversation with him, only to be baffled <u>by the jerky embarrassment (HUMILIATION)</u> The reason for the narrator's embarrassment must have been the harsh reaction of the stranger. A) is too extreme.

Questions 38-40 are based on the following passage.

What is the peculiar charm of that mighty, snow-capped sea of mountains, whose stupendous waves tossed far into the heavens seem ever about to overwhelm the level wheat-fields of Western Canada? The lure of the **mountains (Q38) defies analysis**. **The rolling foothills** in the Foreground (Q39) **seem tangible and comprehensible,** but above the towering outer wave of the mountains, float **silvery outlines** that seem to be the fabric of some outer purer world. One who has seen this vision may not resist the insistent (Q40) **call to explore the mountain** world. The call has been working in the hearts of men for generations. They came alone in the early days, each man fighting his way up through some **doorway that led into the heart of the Glittering Mountains**.

Q38. Absolute Pattern 3: Inference Question Finding an indirect suggestion (or guessing)

Question Pattern: "The lure of the mountains **defies analysis**" (line 3) can also be interpreted as

A) mountains need further analysis **B) there's something beyond our analysis** C) anything attractive needs not be analyzed D) all the mountains are subject to analysis E) mountain climbing requires analytical skills	"Defies" explains something of mountains beyond human understanding or analysis.

Q39. Absolute Pattern 8: Understanding True Purpose
Finding the true purpose of statement, sentences, or the entire paragraph

Question Pattern: The author mentions "The **rolling foothills"** in line 3 in order to

A) warn those kids wishing to roll in the mountains B) visualize foothills that is actually moving **C) show mountains within our reach to comprehend** D) tell the reader that the mountains are a purer world E) warn people to avoid mountain climbing	**The rolling foothills** in the Foreground **seem tangible and comprehensible.** Seems tangible means within our reach.

Q40. Absolute Pattern 3: Inference Question Finding an indirect suggestion (or guessing)

Question Pattern: "**the hearts**" in line 7 refers to

A) a desire to climb the mountains B) a wish to camp in the foothills C) a dream of becoming a heart surgeon D) a hesitation to analyze the mountains E) a heart to brave difficult weather	One who has seen this vision may not resist the insistent **call to explore the mountain** world. The call has been working in the hearts of men for generations.

Test 6 Absolute Patterns for the Analogy Section

Absolute Pattern 4. Characteristic Pattern
Finding Characteristic of Person, Place, Object, or Idea and its Associated Action

Q31. C is the Best Answer. Ice characteristically freezes and snow characteristically melts.

Absolute Pattern 3. Purpose (Tool) Pattern
Finding Relationships between the Purpose of Individual to Object, to its Function, its User, its Use, and its Association

Q32 C is the Best Answer. Government uses policy as military uses (C) command.
Policy and command have the similar functionality.

Absolute Pattern 3. Purpose (Tool) Pattern
Finding Relationships between the Purpose of Individual to Object, to its Function, its User, its Use, and its Association

Q33. C is the Best Answer. Boat is kept in dock as horse is in (C) stable.

Absolute Pattern 1. Category Pattern
Finding Part/Whole, Same Type/Kind, Association   Absolute Pattern

Q34. A is the Best Answer. Taste is bitter can be transferred to caustic personality, a similar concept.
Albeit sensory concept, all the other choices applied improper descriptions.

Absolute Pattern 1. Category Pattern
Finding Part/Whole, Same Type/Kind, Association   Absolute Pattern

Q35. A is the Best Answer. North and South belong to direction as (A) iron and lead belong to metal

Absolute Pattern 3. Purpose (Tool) Pattern
Finding Relationships between the Purpose of Individual to Object, to its Function, its User, its Use, and its Association

Q36. A is the Best Answer. Resume describes work experience of individual employee.
(A) work order describes work process of goods.

Absolute Pattern 2. Synonym/Antonym
Finding a similar or an opposite meaning between words

Q37. A is the Best Answer. Flattery is a synonym to adulation as pardon is a synonym to (A) excuse

Absolute Pattern 2. Synonym/Antonym
Finding a similar or an opposite meaning between words

Q38. B is the Best Answer. Absolute is an antonym to conditional as (B) provisional is to categorical. They are all synonym to each other.

Absolute Pattern 3. Purpose (Tool) Pattern
Finding Relationships between the Purpose of Individual to Object, to its Function, its User, its Use, and its Association

Q39. A is the Best Answer. Company uses employee as (A) steam engine uses pressure. (E) is flipped over.

Absolute Pattern 3. Purpose (Tool) Pattern
Finding Relationships between the Purpose of Individual to Object, to its Function, its User, its Use, and its Association

Q40. D is the Best Answer. Key releases lock as (D) ticket allows to enter a concert

Absolute Pattern 5. Degree Pattern
Finding a Degree and a Shape in person, place, thing, and emotion

Q41. D is the Best Answer. Assistant is a lower rank than boss as (D) humming is quieter than opera.

Absolute Pattern 3. Purpose (Tool) Pattern
Finding Relationships between the Purpose of Individual to Object, to its Function, its User, its Use, and its Association

Q42. C is the Best Answer. Market exchanges goods as Internet (C) connects information.

Absolute Pattern 3. Purpose (Tool) Pattern
Finding Relationships between the Purpose of Individual to Object, to its Function, its User, its Use, and its Association

Q43. A is the Best Answer. Border is to set boundary as national park is for (A) preservation.

Absolute Pattern 3. Purpose (Tool) Pattern
Finding Relationships between the Purpose of Individual to Object, to its Function, its User, its Use, and its Association

Q44. B is the Best Answer. Tourist is looking for attraction as archeologist is looking for (B) remnants.

Absolute Pattern 4. Characteristic Pattern
Finding Characteristic of Person, Place, Object, or Idea and its Associated Action

Q45. A is the Best Answer. Paris is characteristically known for (romantic) place as Egypt is for (A) archaic place.

Absolute Pattern 5. Degree Pattern
Finding a Degree and a Shape in person, place, thing, and emotion

Q46. E is the Best Answer. Grandma is older than boy as (E) principal is older than to student. The other choices are flipped over.

Absolute Pattern 1. Category Pattern
Finding Part/Whole, Same Type/Kind, Association   Absolute Pattern

Q47. A is the Best Answer. Supporting actress, actor, director are all movie category.

UNAUTHORIZED COPYING OR REUSE OF ANY PART OF THIS PAGE IS ILLEGAL

Absolute Pattern 11. Subjective-Objective Pattern
Finding Quality-Quantity, Tangible-Intangible Association

Q48. E is the Best Answer. California is the largest state (E) Alaska is to coldest state. (A) is territory, not a state and not the oldest.

6. Definition Pattern
Finding Definition/Concept of person, place, thing, and emotion

Q49. E is the Best Answer. The question asks about what is official and what is casual.

Advice (official) is to hint (casual) as (E) announcement is to memo. They are the same speech category.

Absolute Pattern 1. Category Pattern
Finding Part/Whole, Same Type/Kind, Association   Absolute Pattern

Q50. D is the Best Answer. Movie has individual scene (part) and symphony has individual movement (part)

Absolute Pattern 11. Subjective-Objective Pattern
Finding Quality-Quantity, Tangible-Intangible Association

Q51. A is the Best Answer. Difficult and fast are subjective value. All the other choices are objective.

6. Definition Pattern
Finding Definition/Concept of person, place, thing, and emotion

Q52 B is the Best Answer. The question asks about what we feel about someone or something. Nightwatchman is vigilant (that's how we feel) as (B) military checkpoint is tense.

Absolute Pattern 6. Definition Pattern
Finding Definition/Concept of person, place, thing, and emotion

Q53. C is the Best Answer. The question asks about what is official and what is casual.

Counselor is to advice is official as (C) friend is to tip is casual. They are all synonym or similar situation.

Absolute Pattern 7. Mental (Emotion) Pattern
Finding Feeling/Mental Concept and its Emotion

Q54. C is the Best Answer. Applause is our emotion to magic as (C) condolence is our emotion to victim.

Absolute Pattern 8. Production Pattern
Finding Cause-and-Effect in Person, Concept, and Object

Q55. E is the Best Answer. Import produces payment as (E) sales (export) produces income.

Both Import and sales proceed money category.

Absolute Pattern 7. Mental (Emotion) Pattern
Finding Feeling/Mental Concept and its Emotion

Q56. E is the Best Answer. Melancholy produces tear as (E) hot-temper produces anger.
The other choices are not emotion category.

Absolute Pattern 1. Category Pattern
Finding Part/Whole, Same Type/Kind, Association   Absolute Pattern

Q57. B is the Best Answer. Craftsmanship produces genuine article as (B) factory produces mass products.
The other choices are intangible value.

Absolute Pattern 1. Category Pattern
Finding Part/Whole, Same Type/Kind, Association   Absolute Pattern

Q58 E is the Best Answer. Gale is (E) weather as snail is animal.

Absolute Pattern 11. Subjective-Objective Pattern
Finding Quality-Quantity, Tangible-Intangible Association

Q59. A is the Best Answer. luxury is subjective view, so as expensive.
All the other choices contain numeric quantifiers.

Absolute Pattern 5. Degree Pattern
Finding a Degree and a Shape in person, place, thing, and emotion

Q60. B is the Best Answer. Infatuated is less degree of liking than veneration as (B) caring is to loving

Chapter 6 Summary

The Chapter Summary contains equal portions of

12 Absolute Patterns for Analogy Section and

10 Absolute Patterns for Reading Section.

You may study all at once to significantly

improve your understanding and your scores.

Chapter 6

12 Absolute Patterns for the Analogy Section

Absolute Pattern 12. Human-Nonhuman Pattern
Finding Active-Passive/Human-Nonhuman Association

Q12-1. Goalie is to Champion as

    A) zebra is to stripe

    B) beaver is to dam

    C) thief is to police

    D) host is to guest

    E) bee is to sting

Q12-2 Baby is cute as battery is

    A) dead

    B) discharged

    C) gone

    D) deceased

    E) lifeless

(Q12-1) The correct answer is C

San: Goalie and thief are Passive Concept as champion and police are Active Concept.

    First of all, these are all human category.

    For choice A), B), and E) they are all animal category.

    Therefore, we should eliminate A), B), and E) from the choices.

    Choice D) is flipped over. Host, compared to guest, is Active.

    You may also think that A) zebra and B) beaver are Passive Concept compared to E) Bee.

    As you can see from above, it is critical to subdivide the concept into the minimal level.

    This pattern is applied in the entire patterns we have discussed so far.

San   For Q12-2, B) is the answer.

    Baby is cute; battery is discharged

    We often use the word "dead" when the battery is discharged.

    We also often say like "Hey, San! You need to recharge your battery.

    We, however, should distinguish the proper word usage between human and nonhuman concept.

Jimin   We have euphemism or metaphor though.

San   No! We don't. The entire Analogy-stems that you see from the test use the first definition unless

    the Analogy-stem itself contains such a nuance.

    As an example, If you see the question "Fire is to flame," it means literal fire ignited by the chemical

---

Chapter 6

12 Absolute Patterns for the Analogy Section

San: reaction that produces flame.

You should never euphemistically interpret the fire like "I'm in love."

When the euphemism or metaphor is the main theme of the question, you will notice it immediately.

We've already discussed this in Definition Pattern that contains adjective concept.

The Reading Section

20 Common Patterns for *Incorrect* Options

7 Unrelated Word or Issue

The most evident examples can be seen in the Pattern 5: Word-in-Context Question.

Common incorrect choices in this pattern usually employ the followings:

(a) Switch figurative meaning word with the literal meaning (i.e., I'm on fire)

(b) Place an impressive flamboyant adverb or adjective right next the plain keyword such as 'it' so that you can focus on the unrelated pretty baits instead of the keyword.

(c) Put a difficult vocabulary that requires your vocabulary knowledge.

8 Inconsistency with Question

This pattern employs the inconsistency trick.

It often distracts the student by putting a true, but totally unrelated statement in the passage.

It is your job to limit the reading scope.

For instance, you should not find the answer from paragraph 2 when the question asks paragraph 1.

9 Unknown Prediction

Some incorrect choices include a verb in future tense or adverb such as 'likely to be' or regular verb or noun that contains the future meaning such as 'seem', 'will', 'anticipation'.

It is not your job to predict the future without having a logically written cause-effect situation in the passage.

Even inference question is anchored in the cause-effect logic.

Those unknown choices already have congenital defects when they were born.

20 Common Patterns for *In*correct Options

10 Too Specific Example

Pattern 1: Main Idea Question, for instance, does not seek out the answer from too specific example.

If you must choose the answer between too general and too specific, choose the former.

As an example, a specific name, place, thing, time, history, etc. does not necessarily add more value to the answer for the main idea question. It often works as a reverse agent.

11 Too Objective Word Usage

This is the opposite situation from the above statement.

Some choices stop short at explaining the fact, making the phrase too objective and vague.

Pattern 7: Understanding Attitude (Tone) Question requires a keyword that illustrates a decisive tone (subjective, positive-negative), not too broad and objective word.

12 Extreme Word Usage

Incorrect choices using extreme words are relatively easy when it involves adverbs such as "always", "only", "never", etc.

Can you instantly compare the nature of the words like "dwindling", "compromised", "extinct", or "failed"?

If not, you still need to practice with this book.

13 Shifting the Argument

Argument can change between paragraphs or within the passage.

For example, in paragraph 1, critics will argue with one thing, for which the author will later oppose in paragraph 2 or 3. In more complex question, the author himself suddenly changes his opinion.

The Absolute Patterns for Reading summary continues in the following chapters.

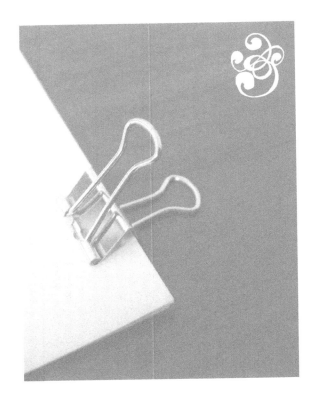

Chapter 7

1. TEST 7

2. ANSWER EXPLANATIONS for TEST 7

3. CHAPTER SUMMARY

SSAT

Reading & Verbal

Test 7

This chapter starts with the Actual Test 7.

Your goal is not getting good enough scores, but 100%.

It's your book

It's up to you to practice the Answer Explanation first.

Test 7 Reading Section
Time: 40 Minutes, 40 Questions

Directions: Each reading passage is followed by questions about it. Answer the questions that follow a passage on the basis of what is stated or implied in that passage.

Questions 1-6 are based on the following passage.

Line

An unmanned aerial vehicle (UAV), commonly known as a drone, is an aircraft without a human pilot aboard. A UAV is defined as a powered, aerial vehicle that does not carry a human operator, uses aerodynamic forces to provide vehicle lift, can fly autonomously or be piloted remotely, and carry a lethal or nonlethal payload. UAVs originated mostly in <u>military combat applications</u>, although their use is expanding in
5   commercial, scientific, recreational, agricultural and surveillance. The term more widely used by the public, "drone was given in reference to the resemblance of male bee that makes loud and regular sounds.

The US held a 60% military-market share in 2006. It operated over 9,000 UAVs in 2014. From 1985 to 2014, exported drones came predominantly from Israel (60.7%) and the United States (23.9%).

1

Based on the passage, which of the following examples is NOT considered as an UAV?

A) an aircraft without a pilot
B) an autonomous aircraft controlled remotely
C) an onboard computer controlled drone
D) a drone lifts with rubber band propeller
E) an unmanned military aircraft

2

The author mentions UAV's origin from military application (line 4). Which statement best exemplifies the UAV's original purpose in military?

A) military mission that is too dangerous to humans
B) army camp life that can generate entertainment
C) military service that generates commercial interest
D) army base with the lack of agricultural sustenance
E) army base with the lack of drone support

3

All of the following are referred to as UAV's expansion areas EXCEPT

A) commercial
B) scientific
C) recreational
D) military
E) agricultural

4

Which sensory device was used when UAV's commonly known name 'drone' was adopted?

A) hearing
B) sight
C) touch
D) smell
E) taste

5

The author's tone about drone in the last sentence is

A) entertaining
B) cheerful
C) openly hostile
D) statistical
E) scientific

6

Which of the following sentences is LEAST applicable as the topic sentence for the last paragraph (lines 7-8)?

A) The UAV's global market is dominated by the U.S.
B) As technology improves, there has been expansion in the UAV's global market in less than a decade
C) UAV's global market, however, faces some serious privacy issues as it expands exponentially.
D) The statistics shows the U.S. as the largest market controller
E) U.S. exports drone and UAVs around the world

Questions 7-12 are based on the following passage.

Line

After I had been living for the past two years in the French capital, whilst in the company of several army officers, to meet an <u>Austrian gentleman</u> who entertained us with the recital of his experiences during the Tonquin campaign of 1883-85. Owing to an affaire de coeur, he had enlisted in the Foreign Legion, had risen to the rank of sergeant-major, was twice wounded, and had been decorated with the médaille militaire for
5 bravery in action. This narrative so excited my imagination and desire for adventure that I fell into slumber that night only after having decided on taking a similar course.

The next morning I put my project into execution, and, as aforesaid, went to the fountain-head for information. Perhaps <u>the officials may have had serious doubts</u> as to whether I was in my right mind, for it is not every day that an individual comes to the Ministère, and in a matter-of-fact manner asks to enlist to a
10 foreign army, in just such a way as one might ask for a room at an hotel. Whatever their thoughts may have been, they were exceedingly obliging, and informed me that I must go to the Rue St Dominique, the central recruiting office. Knowing that I should be likely to meet and mix with all conditions of men in the road I had chosen, on taking <u>my decision</u> I had determined to accept things as they were without complaint, so long as the <u>life would bring me new experiences.</u> Yet never once during the five years of my service did I regret the step taken and wish it retraced.

7

The narrator felt that the life of Austrian gentleman in line 2 was

A) adventurous

B) humble

C) lack of entertainment

D) puzzling

E) reclusive

8

In developing the paragraph 1 (lines 1-6), the narrator states all of the following EXCEPT

A) description of his current living

B) recollection of conversation

C) reference to another person's background

D) enthusiasm to chart his life course

E) nostalgia to his hometown

9

The officials in line 8 reacted to the narrator as if he were

A) heroic

B) crazy

C) serious

D) humorous

E) intellectual

10

In line 8 "the officials have had serious doubts" because they

A) were concerned about the narrator's future

B) thought the narrator concealed something

C) did not understand the narrator's language well

D) found the narrator was a foreigner

E) did not trust the narrator

11

When mentioning "my decision" in line 13, the narrator's tone is

A) argumentative

B) somber

C) decisive

D) laudatory

E) conciliatory

12

Which best describes the interaction between the narrator and the officials in lines 8-10 (Perhaps the officials...may have been)?

A) Both are attentive to say what they truly think

B) Both realize the Great War is coming

C) The narrator respects the officials' advice

D) Both officials and the narrator are reluctant to say any further

E) The narrator doubts whether officials are in right minds.

Questions 13-18 are based on the following passage.

Line   Sunspots are dark spots on the sun's photosphere. This phenomena has approximately 11-year cycle. The first scientific periodicity of this phenomena is ascribed to an European observer, Galileo Galilee in 1610.
        Although the records made by then <u>Chinese naked-eye observers</u> contradict it, Sun went through a period of inactivity in the late 17th century. This period is known as the Maunder Minimum. Without having a concrete
5   evidence, the Maunder Minimum, from 1645 to 1715, is defined as the prolonged sunspot inactivity period.
        The reason that the Maunder Minimum invites a special attention to scientists is because this period also corresponds to a climatic period called the "Little Ice Age." Throughout the Maunder Minimum, terrestrial temperature was abnormally cold at lower altitudes. Although sunspots themselves produce only minor effects on solar emissions, the magnetic activity that accompanies the sunspots can produce dramatic changes in <u>the</u>
10 <u>ultraviolet and soft x-ray emission levels</u>. These changes over the solar cycle have important consequences for the Earth's upper atmosphere. As revealed on the discrepancy between Chinese naked-eye observers and the later European scientists concerning the Maunder Minimum, whether sunspot activity is a transient phenomenon or long-lived feature due to unsustainable decomposition of the Sun's magnetic field remains elusive.

13

The passage defines solar activity cycle as
A) an enduring but not yet fully confirmed theory
B) significant to the modern global warming
C) transient phenomena and therefore insignificant
D) a basic theory
E) a mysterious supernatural phenomena

14

According to the last paragraph, which of the possible research projects would further ascertain the Sunspot activity is unsustainable feature of the Sun?
A) Finding how fast the sun's magnetic field decomposes
B) Identifying whether the sun's magnetic field is sustainable or unsustainable
C) Confirming that the sunspot activity is a transient
D) Finding that the sunspot activity is related to the Maunder Minimum
E) Confirming that the sunspot activity doesn't exist

15

The reference to the "Chinese naked-eye observers" (line 3) primarily serves to
A) solidify Maunder Minimum theory
B) respect the 16th century Chinese scientists
C) disqualify Maunder Minimum
D) provide a certain kind of zealotry
E) confirm Maunder Minimum is long-lived feature

16

Why do scientists pay special attention to the Maunder Minimum?
A) because they know the Ice Age is coming
B) because the period is related with the Little Ice Age
C) because the sun's inactivity is related with it
D) because the single sunspot is as wide as the earth diameter that can threaten the earth
E) because the sun's inactivity has never been reported

17

According to line 3, it can be inferred that the Chinese naked-eye observers
A) felt noticeably cold temperature during the period
B) were mocked by later European scientists
C) experienced little temperature drop
D) observed a period of inactivity of the sun but not the temperature drop
E) agreed mostly with the European observers

18

Understanding the ultraviolet and soft x-ray emission levels in line 10 is important because
A) they have significant consequences for the earth's upper atmosphere.
B) they have significant consequences to the air pollution
D) they decompose the sun's magnetic field fast
E) they affect the greenhouse and air quality

Questions 19-24 are based on the following passage.

Line   Louis Armstrong was an American trumpeter, composer, singer, and actor. He is considered as the most influential figures in jazz. His career spanned five decades, from the 1920s to the 1960s ,different eras in jazz.
        Coming to prominence in the 1920s as an "inventive" trumpet player, Armstrong was not officially trained in jazz, shifting the focus of the music from collective improvisation to solo performance. He was one of the first
5   truly popular African-American entertainers to "cross over," whose skin color was secondary to his music in likeminded fans' passion. His artistry and personality *allowed* him socially *acceptable* to *access* the upper echelons of American society which were highly *open* for black men of his *era.*
        He hardly looked back at his youth as the worst of times but drew inspiration from it instead: "Every time I close my eyes blowing trumpet of mine—I look right in the heart of good old New Orleans. [QUESTION 24]

19

The first paragraph (lines 1-2) mainly focuses on
A) a musician's longevity
B) a musician's divided interest
C) a musician's insight into many other nonmusical areas
D) a musician's impressively long career in various jazz
E) a musician who lived for five different decades.

20

Which of the following statement most correctly describes the second paragraph (lines 3-7)?
A) Armstrong was genuinely talented improviser
B) Armstrong was only one of few officially trained jazz musicians among black people
C) Armstrong adhered to the valuable musical heritage
D) Armstrong focused on solo performance
E) Armstrong was the inventor of trumpet

21

Which of the following statements explicitly conveys the author's respect to the later life of the musician?
A) Armstrong was not officially trained in jazz
B) Armstrong was born when United State of America was racially the Divided States of America.
C) Armstrong's beginning position was unenviable
D) Armstrong earned racially divided respect
E) Armstrong was among the great jazz players

22

The word "cross over" (line 5) mainly refers to
A) race convergence in music
B) music for winter sports
C) a prototype sports utility vehicle in 1920s
D) a musician's legal violation
E) race segregation in music

23

Which italicized word in the sentence in lines 6-7 is incorrectly used?
A) allowed
B) acceptable
C) access
D) open
E) era

24

Consider the last underlined sentence (line 9) is not truly the last sentence. Which choice would most effectively conclude the final paragraph?
A) It had given me something to live for."
B) Well...New Orleans gave me a lot of trouble."
C) I regret I should have been a well-behaved kid."
D) Who knew I would make so much money and live like a king?"
E) I wish I could turn back time and start all over."

Questions 25-30 are based on the following passage.

Line

From the early 20th century, developing mass media technologies, such as radio and film, were credited with an almost irresistible power to mold an audience's beliefs according to the communicators' will. The basic assumption of strong media effects theory was that audiences were passive and homogeneous. This assumption was not based on empirical evidence but on assumptions of human nature. There were two
5   main explanations for this perception of mass media effects. First, mass broadcasting technologies were acquiring a widespread audience, even among average households. People were astonished by the speed of information dissemination. Secondly, short-term propaganda techniques were implemented during the war time by several governments as a powerful tool for uniting their people. "This propaganda exemplified strong, but ill-effect of communication" said the political scientist Harold Lasswell, who focused on the early media effects.
10   With the new variables added to research, it was difficult to isolate media influence that resulted in any media effects to an audience's cognition, attitude and behavior. As Berelson summed up: "Some kinds of communication on some kinds of issues have brought to the attention of some kinds of people under some kinds of conditions have some kinds of effect." The media play an indispensable role in the proper functioning of a modern democracy. Without mass media, openness and accountability are very tough to reach in contemporary democracies.

25

The author views media effects theory in line 3 as

A) an evidence with plenty of data and statistics

B) a fundamental concept that needs further research

C) a perception that cannot be proven

D) a familiar concept shared by several other theories

E) problematic to call it a theory

26

Which of the following assertions corresponds LEAST with the author's argument concerning the effects of mass media in lines 1-9?

A) It helped mold an audience's view

B) Communicators made the audience to be passive

C) Communicators made the audience to be homogeneous

D) Average households were excluded from obtaining mass media information

E) Government implemented short-term propaganda

27

Based on line 14, the role of media in modern democratic society serves chiefly to

A) mold public opinion

B) disclose reliable information

C) represent government propaganda

D) offer information to selective pubic

E) make public passive and homogeneous

28

The author mentions Harold lasswell in line 9 mainly to

A) give an authority to his opinion

B) exemplify how mass media well performed back then

C) raise concern about political involvement in mass media

D) interpret the media effects in the 21th century

E) show how important mass media is to the public

29

Harold Lasswell in line 9 may view "the communicators" in line 2 with?

A) respect

B) concern

C) analytical

D) greedy

E) naïve

30

The quotation from Berellson (line11-13) indicates that media effects

A) cannot be defined in a single term or value

B) can be determined transparently

C) should be isolated from the government propaganda theory

D) remain as the most powerful influence on the public

E) use different method depending on the audience

Questions 31-35 are based on the following passage.

Line   First let us say something belongs to what we call the mind and others to what we call matter. Let us suppose the matter to be entirely and absolutely homogeneous. Things may be classified according to their color, their shape, their weight, the pleasure they give us, their quality of being alive or dead, and so on; one much given to classification would only be troubled by the number of possible distinctions.

5   Since so many divisions are possible, at which shall we stop and say: this is the one which corresponds exactly to the opposition of mind and matter. It must be supposed that we shall do so by means of a criterion. Otherwise, we should only be acting fantastically.

31

According to the author, matter can basically be understood as

A) homogeneous

B) heterogeneous

C) a problem

D) an issue

E) a science

32

All of the following elements can be classified as a matter EXCEPT

A) color

B) shape

C) weight

D) pleasure

E) weight

33

In line 7, when the author says "acting fantastically", it can be understood as acting

A) theoretically

B) beautifully

C) magically

D) critically

E) randomly

34

The author suggests that the mind and matter are

A) entirely mysterious

B) somewhat different

C) two oppositions

D) one single criterion

E) fantastically homogeneous

35

According to the author, which of the following statement is true?

A) matter need not be classified

B) all matters are heterogeneous

C) matter in the passage is synonym to problem

D) the mind cannot be classified

E) mind is matter as well

Questions 36-40 are based on the following passage.

Line

Several years ago, at the one of the major engineering societies, the president of the society gave expression to a thought so startling that the few laymen who were seated in the auditorium fairly gasped. "since engineers had got the world into war, it was the duty of engineers to get the world out of war."

I mention this merely to bring to the reader's attention the tremendous power which engineers wield in world

5 affairs. The profession of engineering adapts discoveries in science to the uses of mankind, but is a peculiarly isolated one. Very little is known about it among those outside of the profession. Laymen know something about law, a little about medicine. But laymen know nothing about engineering. Average layman cannot differentiate between the man who runs a locomotive and the man who designs a locomotive. In ordinary parlance both are called engineers.

10 Yet there is a difference between them--a difference as between day and night.

36

Why does the President believe as he said in lines 2-3, ("since engineers ...world out of war")

A) Engineers were all German

B) War utilized engineers' knowledge

C) Engineers served as freedom fighters at war

D) Engineers supported the war for money

E) Engineers are destructive in nature

37

"the tremendous power" (line 4), focuses primarily on which aspect of engineers?

A) Their ability to adapt discoveries in science

B) Their desire to use it for the mankind

C) Their peculiarly isolated personality

D) The fact they don't know they are being used

E) Their ability to adapt discoveries in arts

38

In line 8-9 ("Average layman …locomotive"), the author compares which of the following aspects?

A) war and peace

B) engineer and non-engineer

C) benefit and harm

D) practicality and impracticality

E) job and hobby

39

Why did the few laymen in line 2 gasp?

A) They were not prepared to hear such a remark

B) They were not engineers

C) They were in fact engineers

D) They thought nobody knew about it

E) They felt threatened by the president's speech

40

The author refers "law and medicine" in line 7 because they

A) equally contributed to mankind

B) are relatively easy to understand

C) do not use science

D) also have duty to get the world out of war

E) are harder than engineering

Test 7 Verbal Section   30 MINUTES, 60 QUESTIONS

Directions: the synonym questions ask you to find the most appropriate synonym to the question.

The analogy questions ask you to find the most appropriate analogy to the question.
Select the answer that best matches to the question.

Synonym Sample Question:

Q: SUPERIOR

A higher rank

B inferior

C considerable

D supermarket

E supper

A) is the best answer because the synonym for superior is higher rank.

B) is incorrect because it applies the 'opposite concept.

C) and E) are irrelevant words.

D) is incorrect because it applies physical concept to mental concept

Test 7 Synonym questions 1 to 30

1. MANUFACTURE

(A) make

(B) copy

(C) print

(D) fabricate

(E) elect

2. WHOLEHEARTEDLY

(A) entirely

(B) duplicity

(C) sincerely

(D) deadly

(E) gladly

3. REVEAL

(A) abate

(B) giving

(C) clandestine

(D) divulge

(E) generate

4. RECKLESSLY

(A) rashly

(B) subside

(C) reduce

(D) lackey

(E) embarrassingly

5. PUSH

(A) impoverish

(B) step

(C) throb

(D) abdicate

(E) propel

UNAUTHORIZED COPYING OR REUSE OF ANY PART OF THIS PAGE IS ILLEGAL

6. ABERRATION

(A) attentive

(B) abhorrence

(C) typical

(D) deviation

(E) power

7. ERRATIC

(A) error

(B) standard

(C) inconsistent

(D) rhythmic

(E) habitual

8. SPECIFY

(A) end

(B) rescue

(C) special

(D) state

(E) pacify

9. ABJECT

(A) hopeless

(B) poverty

(C) reject

(D) unimportant

(E) disbelief

10. AGILE

(A) transparent

(B) quick

(C) slow

(D) agree

(E) again

11. NAIVE

(A) complex

(B) kind

(C) kid

(D) generous

(E) unsophisticated

12. ABNEGATE

(A) begin

(B) reject

(C) remove

(D) negate

(E) abnormal

13. TRIVIAL

(A) valuable

(B) fast

(C) trifle

(D) serious

(E) triumvirate

14. ABORTIVE

(A) deliver baby

(B) unsuccessful

(C) aboard

(D) boating

(E) abridge

15. MOTIVE

(A) force

(B) happy

(C) moving

(D) reason

(E) motor

16. BEWILDERED

(A) wild

(B) confused

(C) forested

(D) vegetated

(E) natural

17. SPECULATION

(A) speed

(B) stall

(C) think

(D) see

(E) spectacle

18. ABSOLVE

(A) forgive

(B) solve

(C) regret

(D) add

(E) know

19. OBSESSED

(A) seeded

(B) grown

(C) natural

(D) oversized

(E) overly concerned

20. ABSTINENT

(A) standing low

(B) abysmal

(C) approving

(D) useful

(E) avoiding

21. VARY

(A) slow

(B) change

(C) full

(D) extremely

(E) very

22. DIGNITY

(A) honor

(B) degree

(C) design

(D) notice

(E) advice

23. PASSIVE

(A) slow

(B) submissive

(C) hiding

(D) passionate

(E) artificial

24. ABSTRACT

(A) theoretical

(B) track

(C) straight

(D) abysmal

(E) abound

25. OPPORTUNITY

(A) luck

(B) fortune

(C) basic

(D) turn

(E) a good chance

26. ABSTRUSE

(A) difficult to understand

(B) bottom

(C) structure

(D) baseless

(E) transitional

27. PERPLEXITY

(A) laxity

(B) clear

(C) elegance

(D) confusion

(E) purple

28. DRAB

(A) easy

(B) dull

(C) clear

(D) puzzle

(E) drain

29. VERSATILE

(A) argumentative

(B) changing

(C) colorful

(D) verisimilitude

(E) satellite

30. HARDY

(A) tough

(B) unchanging

(C) complex

(D) ossified

(E) dangerous

Analogy Sample Question:

Q: River is to Ocean as:

A better is to good

B rain is to cloud

C father is to mother

D city is to country

E fork is to spoon

D is the correct answer. Just as the river is smaller than the Ocean, the city is smaller than the country. The pattern applied in this question is the Degree Pattern (small to big)

A) is incorrect because the word order is flipped over.

B) is incorrect because it applies the production pattern (cloud produces rain)

C), E) are incorrect because they apply the Antonym patterns.

Test 7 Analogy questions 31 to 60

31. Knife is to scissors as butcher is to

(A) tailor

(B) architect

(C) teacher

(D) scientist

(E) banker

SSAT UPPER LEVEL 7 PRACTICE TESTS WITH THE ABSOLUTE PATTERNS

32. Technology is to innovation as tradition is to

(A) discovery
(B) record
(C) chronicle
(D) preservation
(E) ancient

33. Game is to rule as

(A) automobile is to monthly payment
(B) signal is to traffic
(C) concrete is to building
(D) cooking is to recipe
(E) report card is to student

34. Spinach is to orange as

(A) vitamin is to vitality
(B) salad is to dressing
(C) vegetable is to tomato
(D) vegetarian is to healthy
(E) grapes is to cucumber

35. Hinge is to door

(A) spoke is to wheel
(B) rubber is to tire
(C) lock is to key
(D) clip is to paper
(E) nail is to hammer

36. Milky way is to solar system

(A) school is to student
(B) sun is to lunar
(C) moon is to solar
(D) chocolate is to snack
(E) universe is to astronomy

37. Adverse is to weather as malignant is to

(A) disease
(B) day
(C) rain
(D) message
(E) cure

38. Outdated is to Brand new as

(A) fight is to brawl
(B) winter is to spring
(C) wind is to rain
(D) obsolete is to innovative
(E) human is to mammal

39. Supervisor is to oversee as

(A) bottle is to preserve
(B) employer is to boss
(C) worker is to direct
(D) oversea is to international
(E) company is to conglomerate

40. Painter is to inspiration as

(A) artist is to brush
(B) writer is to chalk
(C) physician is to drug
(D) mathematician is to logic
(E) solder is to warfare

41. Desperation is to wish as

(A) worship is to follow
(B) gift is to present
(C) poetry is to short
(D) winter is to autumn
(E) ocean is to river

UNAUTHORIZED COPYING OR REUSE OF ANY PART OF THIS PAGE IS ILLEGAL

281

42. Alarm clock is to alert as lullaby

(A) timer

(B) cry

(C) rest

(D) wake

(E) calm

43. Bluetooth is to integration as marketplace is

(A) interaction

(B) integrity

(C) introvert

(D) tradition

(E) introspection

44. Underwear is to comfort as uniform is to

(A) colorful

(B) diversity

(C) identity

(D) sales

(E) coverage

45. Leader is to charisma as servant is to

(A) flattery

(B) poverty

(C) Christmas break

(D) obedience

(E) unintelligence

46. Monastery is to confinement as

(A) museum is to innovation

(B) bank is to generosity

(C) school is to contest

(D) amusement park is to exhilaration

(E) church is to sleep conducive

47. Suspension is to expel

(A) quiz is to final exam

(B) summer break is to spring break

(C) principal is to teacher

(D) school year is to term

(E) diploma is to certificate

48. Try-out is to tenacity as

(A) liter is to gallon

(B) quart is to pint

(C) kilometer is to meter

(D) pound is to ounce

(E) mile is to inch

49. Quench is to seep as

(A) tumult is to confusion

(B) eat is to devour

(C) opaque is to lucid

(D) surprise is to consternation

(E) engagement is to marriage

50. Pastoral is to peaceful as

(A) church is to busy

(B) industrial zone is to polluted

(C) commercial area is to beneficiary

(D) rural is to country-like

(E) folk is to advanced

51. Sensitive is to careful as

(A) ordinary is to ignore

(B) difficult is to enjoy

(C) easy is to avoid

(D) tricky is to accept

(E) extra is to cautious

52. Awakening is to March as

(A) new year celebration is to January

(B) family is to May

(C) camping is to July

(D) beer fast is to October

(E) hibernation is to November

53. Rain is to cloud as

(A) chef is to meal

(B) baby is to mother

(C) summer sports is swimming

(D) boy is to youth

(E) Hawaii is to subzero temperature

54. Volcano is to lava as

(A) wood is to woods

(B) arid is to climate

(C) fire is to flame

(D) moon is to sun

(E) hard work is to diligence

55. Paramedic is to emergency treatment as

(A) nurse is to vitality check

(B) hospital is to sanitation

(C) medicine is to cure

(D) infection is to virus

(E) injury is to trauma

56. Rehabilitator is to regimen as

(A) predator is to prey

(B) surgeon is to green

(C) doctor is to prescription

(D) nurse is to white

(E) food is to energy

57 Dance is to step as

(A) pebble is to sand

(B) song is to rhythm

(C) construction is to building

(D) book is to knowledge

(E) personality is to character

58. Fire is to pungent as

(A) soup is to bland

(B) candy is to friend

(C) chocolate is to romance

(D) vinegar is to acrid

(E) orange is to juicy

59. Autumn is to quiet as

(A) elephant is to mammal

(B) skin is to dermatologist

(C) chair is to leather

(D) Halloween movie is to scary

(E) Christmas is to December

60. Elephant is to smart as

(A) elephant tusk is to illegal

(B) elephant is to human-like

(C) adult elephant is to over 600pounds

(D) young elephant is to below age five

(E) zoo animal is to domesticated animal

Test 7

Answer Explanations

&

The Pattern Analyses

If your Test 7 scores are unsatisfactory,

Practice the Answer Explanations and then solve

the Actual Test 7 again.

ALL THE LOGIC AND RULES BEHIND

EVERY SINGLE SSAT QUESTION

TEST 7
READING SECTION

Please refer to the Reading Section Absolute Pattern Analyses

THE SYNONYM QUESTIONS NO.1 ~ 30				THE ANALOGY QUESTIONS NO.31 ~ 60.

Please refer to the Analogy Section Absolute Pattern Analyses

1	A	16	B
2	C	17	C
3	D	18	A
4	A	19	E
5	E	20	E
6	D	21	B
7	C	22	A
8	D	23	B
9	A	24	A
10	B	25	E
11	E	26	A
12	B	27	D
13	C	28	B
14	B	29	B
15	A	30	A

Questions 1-6 are based on the following passage.

An unmanned aerial vehicle (UAV), commonly known as a drone, is an aircraft **without a human pilot aboard.** A UAV is defined as (1) a **powered,** aerial vehicle that **does not carry a human operator,** uses **aerodynamic forces to provide vehicle lift, can fly autonomously or be piloted remotely,** and carry a lethal or nonlethal payload. UAVs originated mostly in (2) **military combat applications,** although their use is (3) expanding in commercial, scientific, recreational, agricultural and surveillance. The term more widely used by the public, "drone was given in reference to the resemblance of male bee that makes (4) **loud and regular sounds.**

(5 & 6) **The US held a 60% military-market share in 2006.** It operated over 9,000 UAVs in 2014. From 1985 to 2014, exported drones came predominantly from Israel (60.7%) and the United States (23.9%).

Q1. Absolute Pattern 2: Summary Question
Summarizing a sentence or entire passage
Question Pattern: Based on the passage, which of the following examples is **NOT considered as an UAV**?

A) an aircraft without a pilot B) an autonomous aircraft controlled remotely C) an onboard computer controlled drone **D) a drone lifts with rubber band propeller** E) an unmanned military aircraft	without a human pilot aboard. A UAV is defined as **a powered,** aerial vehicle that does not carry a human operator, uses **aerodynamic forces to provide vehicle lift**, can fly autonomously or be piloted remotely,

---

Q2. Absolute Pattern 3: Inference Question Finding an indirect suggestion (or guessing)
Question Pattern: Which statement best exemplifies the UAV's original **purpose in military**?

A) military mission that is too dangerous to humans B) army camp life that can generate entertainment C) military service that generates commercial interest D) army base with the lack of agricultural sustenance E) army base with the lack of drone support	UAVs originated mostly in **military combat applications**

Q3. Absolute Pattern 2: Summary Question
Question Pattern: All of the following are referred to as **UAV's expansion areas EXCEPT**

A) commercial B) scientific C) recreational **D) military** E) agricultural	**originated mostly in <u>military applications</u>,** although their use is expanding in commercial, scientific, recreational, agricultural and surveillance. *The passage didn't say drone's expansion in military.

Q4. Absolute Pattern 2: Summary Question
Question Pattern: Which **sensory device** was used when UAV's commonly known name 'drone' was adopted?

A) hearing B) sight C) touch D) smell E) taste	male bee that makes **loud and regular sounds.**

Q5. Absolute Pattern 7: Understanding Attitude (Tone) Question
Finding tone such as positive-negative, active-passive, mental-physical, subjective-objective
Question Pattern: The author's **tone about drone** in the last sentence is

A) entertaining B) cheerful C) openly hostile **D) statistical** E) scientific	The US held a 60% military-market share in 2006. It operated over 9,000 UAVs in 2014

Q6. Absolute Pattern 1: Main Idea Question
Finding the main idea of the entire passage, a specific paragraph, or sentences
Question Pattern: Which of the following sentences is **LEAST applicable as the topic sentence for the last paragraph (lines 7-8)?**

A) The UAV's global market is dominated by the U.S. B) As technology improves, there has been expansion in the UAV's global market in less than a decade **C) UAV's global market, however, faces some serious privacy issues as it expands exponentially.** D) The statistics shows the U.S. as the largest market controller E) U.S. exports drone and UAVs around the world	The US held a 60% military-market share in 2006. It operated over 9,000 UAVs in 2014. From 1985 to 2014, exported drones came predominantly from Israel (60.7%) and the United States (23.9%). *C) "privacy issues" is not only unrelated but also negative tone.

Questions 7-12 are based on the following passage.

(8) **After I had been living for the past two years in the French** capital, whilst in the company of several army officers, to meet an <u>Austrian gentleman</u> who entertained us with the recital of his experiences during the Tonquin campaign of 1883-85. Owing to an affaire de coeur, he had (7) **enlisted in the Foreign Legion, had risen to the rank of sergeant-major, was twice wounded, and had been decorated with the médaille militaire for bravery in action**. This narrative so excited my imagination and desire for adventure that I fell into slumber that night only after having decided on taking a similar course.

The next morning I put my project into execution, and, as aforesaid, went to the fountain-head for information. Perhaps <u>the officials may have had serious doubts</u> as to whether (9) **I was in my right mind**, for it is not every day that an individual comes to the Ministère, and in a matter-of-fact manner asks (10) **to enlist to a foreign army, in just such a way as one might ask for a room at an hotel.** (12) **Whatever their thoughts may have been,** they were exceedingly obliging, and informed me that I must go to the Rue St Dominique, the central recruiting office. Knowing that I should be likely to meet and mix with all conditions of men in the road I had chosen, on taking <u>my decision</u> I had (11) **determined to accept things as they were without complaint**, so long as the <u>life would bring me new experiences.</u> Yet never once during the five years of my service did I regret the step taken and wish it retraced.

Q7. Absolute Pattern 7: Understanding Attitude (Tone) Question
Finding tone such as positive-negative, active-passive, mental-physical, subjective-objective
Question Pattern: The narrator felt that the **life of Austrian gentleman** in line 2 was

A) adventurous B) humble C) lack of entertainment D) puzzling E) reclusive	enlisted in the Foreign Legion, had risen to the rank of sergeant-major, was twice wounded, and had been decorated with the médaille militaire for bravery in action

Q8. Absolute Pattern 2: Summary Question
Summarizing a sentence or entire passage
Question Pattern: In developing **the paragraph 1** (lines 1-6), the narrator states all of the following **EXCEPT**

A) description of his current living B) recollection of conversation C) reference to another person's background D) enthusiasm to chart his life course **E) nostalgia to his hometown**	After I had been living for the past two years…... meet an Austrian gentleman …during the Tonquin campaign of 1883-85. …I fell into slumber that night only after having decided on taking a similar course

Q9. Absolute Pattern 7: Understanding Attitude (Tone) Question
Finding tone such as positive-negative, active-passive, mental-physical, subjective-objective.
Question Pattern: The **officials in line 8 reacted to the narrator** as if he were

A) heroic **B) crazy** C) serious D) humorous E) intellectual	Perhaps <u>the officials may have had serious doubts</u> as to whether **I was in my right mind**

Q10. Absolute Pattern 2: Summary Question Summarizing a sentence or entire passage.
Question Pattern: In line 8 **"the officials have had serious doubts"** because they

A) were concerned about the narrator's future B) thought the narrator concealed something C) did not understand the narrator's language well **D) found the narrator was a foreigner** E) did not trust the narrator	**to enlist to a foreign army,** in just such a way as one might ask for a room at an hotel

Q11. Absolute Pattern 7: Understanding Attitude (Tone) Question
Finding tone such as positive-negative, active-passive, mental-physical, subjective-objective
Question Pattern: When mentioning **"my decision"** in line 13, the **narrator's tone is**

A) argumentative B) somber **C) decisive** D) laudatory E) conciliatory	determined to accept things as they were without complaint

Q12. Absolute Pattern 9: Relationships Question
Finding relations between the cause-effect, comparison-contrast, characters, and ideas
Question Pattern: Which best describes **the interaction between the narrator and the officials** in lines 8-10 (Perhaps the officials...the central recruiting office)?

A) Both are attentive to say what they truly think B) Both realize the Great War is coming C) The narrator respects the officials' advice **D) Both officials and the narrator are reluctant to say any further** E) The narrator doubts whether officials are in right minds.	<u>Perhaps the officials may have had serious doubts as</u> ... Whatever their thoughts were...

Questions 13-18 are based on the following passage.

Sunspots are dark spots on the sun's photosphere. This phenomena has approximately 11-year cycle. The first scientific periodicity of this phenomena is ascribed to an European observer, Galileo Galilee in 1610.

Although the records made by then <u>Chinese naked-eye observers (15 & 17)</u> **contradict it, Sun went through a period of inactivity in the late 17th century.** This period is known as the Maunder Minimum. Without having a concrete evidence, the Maunder Minimum, from 1645 to 1715, is defined as the prolonged sunspot inactivity period.

The reason that the Maunder Minimum invites a (16) **special attention to scientists is because this period also corresponds to a climatic period called the "Little Ice Age."** Throughout the Maunder Minimum, terrestrial temperature was abnormally cold at lower altitudes. Although sunspots themselves produce only minor effects on solar emissions, the magnetic activity that accompanies the sunspots can produce dramatic changes in <u>the ultraviolet and soft x-ray emission levels</u>. These changes over the solar cycle have (18) **important consequences for the Earth's upper atmosphere**. As revealed on the discrepancy between Chinese naked-eye observers and the later European scientists concerning the Maunder Minimum, whether sunspot activity is a transient phenomenon or long-lived feature (14) **due to unsustainable decomposition of the Sun's magnetic field** (13) **remains elusive.**

Q13. Absolute Pattern 2: Summary Question
Summarizing a sentence or entire passage
Question Pattern: The passage defines **solar activity cycle** as

A) an enduring but not yet fully confirmed theory B) significant to the modern global warming C) transient phenomena and therefore insignificant D) a basic theory E) a mysterious supernatural phenomena	whether sunspot activity is a transient phenomenon or long-lived feature due to unsustainable decomposition of the Sun's magnetic field **remains elusive**

Q14. Absolute Pattern 2: Summary Question Summarizing a sentence or entire passage.
Question Pattern: According to the last paragraph, which of the possible research projects would further **ascertain the Sunspot activity is unsustainable feature** of the Sun?

A) Finding how fast the sun's magnetic field decomposes B) Identifying whether the sun's magnetic field is sustainable or unsustainable C) Confirming that the sunspot activity is a transient D) Finding that the sunspot activity is related to the Maunder Minimum E) Confirming that the sunspot activity doesn't exist	or long-lived feature **due to unsustainable decomposition of the Sun's magnetic field remains elusive**

Q15. Absolute Pattern 9: Relationships Question
Finding relations between the cause-effect, comparison-contrast, characters, and ideas
Question Pattern: The reference to the **"Chinese naked-eye observers"** (line 3) primarily serves to

A) solidify Maunder Minimum theory B) respect the 16th century Chinese scientists **C) disqualify Maunder Minimum** D) provide a certain kind of zealotry E) confirm Maunder Minimum is long-lived feature	Although the records made by then <u>Chinese naked-eye observers</u> **contradict it, Sun went through a period of inactivity in the late 17th century.** In the phrase "Although contradict it", "it" refers to the following period of inactivity. Therefore, Chinese observers disqualified Maunder Minimum or sunspot inactivity.

Q16. **Absolute Pattern 8: Understanding True Purpose**
Finding the true purpose of statement, sentences, or the entire paragraph
Question Pattern: Why do scientists pay special attention to the Maunder Minimum?

A) because they know the Ice Age is coming **B) because the period is related with the Little Ice Age** C) because the sun's inactivity is related with it D) because the single sunspot is as wide as the earth diameter that can threaten the earth E) because the sun's inactivity has never been reported	...special attention to scientists is because this period also corresponds to a climatic period called the "Little Ice Age C) is incorrect because Maunder Minimum is the sun's inactivity itself. Therefore, repeating the question.

Q17. **Absolute Pattern 3: Inference Question** Finding an indirect suggestion (or guessing)
Question Pattern: According to line 3, it can be inferred that the **Chinese naked-eye observers**

A) felt noticeably cold temperature during the period B) were mocked by later European scientists **C) experienced little temperature drop** D) observed a period of inactivity of the sun but not the temperature drop E) agreed mostly with the European observers	Although the records made by then <u>Chinese naked-eye observers</u> **contradict it, Sun went through a period of inactivity in the late 17th century.** In "Although contradict it", "it" refers to the following period of inactivity. Therefore, Chinese observers disqualified Maunder Minimum or sunspot inactivity.

Q18. **Absolute Pattern 8: Understanding True Purpose**
Finding the true purpose of statement, sentences, or the entire paragraph
Question Pattern: Understanding the **ultraviolet and soft x-ray** emission levels in line 10 is important **because**

A) they have significant consequences for the earth's upper atmosphere. B) they have significant consequences to the air pollution D) they decompose the sun's magnetic field fast E) they affect the greenhouse and air quality	important consequences for the Earth's upper atmosphere

Questions 19-24 are based on the following passage.

Louis Armstrong was an American trumpeter, composer, singer, and actor. He is considered as the most influential figures in jazz. **(19) His career spanned five decades, from the 1920s to the 1960s ,different eras in jazz.**

Coming to prominence in the 1920s as an "inventive" trumpet player, Armstrong was not officially trained in jazz, shifting the focus of the music from collective improvisation to **(20) solo performance. (21) He was one of the first truly popular African-American entertainers to "crossover," (22) whose skin color was secondary to his music in likeminded fans' passion.** His artistry and personality *allowed* him socially *acceptable* to *access* the upper echelons of American society which were **(23) highly *open* for black men** of his *era*.

He hardly looked back at his youth as the worst of times but drew inspiration from it instead: "Every time I close my eyes blowing that trumpet of mine—(24) **I look right in the heart of good old New Orleans...**

Q19. Absolute Pattern 1: Main Idea Question
Finding the main idea of the entire passage, a specific paragraph, or sentences
Question Pattern: The first paragraph (lines 1-2) mainly focuses on

A) a musician's longevity B) a musician's divided interest C) a musician's insight into many other nonmusical areas **D) a musician's impressively long career in various jazz** E) a musician who lived for five different decades	His career spanned five decades, from the 1920s to the 1960s ,different eras in jazz. E) is incorrect because it belongs to D)

Q20. Absolute Pattern 2: Summary Question
Summarizing a sentence or entire passage
Question Pattern: Which of the following statement most correctly describes the second paragraph (lines 3-7)?

A) Armstrong was genuinely talented improviser B) Armstrong was only one of few officially trained jazz musicians among black people C) Armstrong adhered to the valuable musical heritage **D) Armstrong focused on solo performance** E) Armstrong was the inventor of trumpet	shifting the focus of the music from collective improvisation to **solo performance**

Q21. Absolute Pattern 7: Understanding Attitude (Tone) Question
Finding tone such as positive-negative, active-passive, mental-physical, subjective-objective.
Question Pattern: Which of the following statements explicitly conveys the author's respect to the <u>later life</u> of the musician?

A) Armstrong was not officially trained in jazz B) Armstrong was born when United State of America was racially the Divided States of America. C) Armstrong's beginning position was unenviable D) Armstrong earned racially divided respect **E) Armstrong was among the great jazz players**	**He was one of the first truly popular African-American entertainers** to "crossover

Q22. Absolute Pattern 5: Word-In-Context Question
Finding a clue word and the keyword from the sentence in question
Question Pattern: The word "crossover" (line 5) mainly refers to

A) race convergence in music B) music for winter sports C) a prototype sports utility vehicle in 1920s D) a musician's legal violation E) race segregation in music	**whose skin color was secondary** to his music in likeminded fans' passion

Q23. Absolute Pattern 5: Word-In-Context Question
Finding a clue word and the keyword from the sentence in question
Question Pattern: Which italicized word in the sentence in lines 6-7 is incorrectly used?

A) allowed B) acceptable C) access **D) open** E) era	His artistry and personality *allowed* him socially *acceptable* to *access* the upper echelons of American society which were **highly unacceptable for black men** of his *era*.

Q24. Absolute Pattern 2: Summary Question
Summarizing a sentence or entire passage.
Question Pattern: Consider the last underlined sentence (line 9) is not truly the last sentence. Which choice would most effectively **conclude the final paragraph**?

A) It had given me something to live for." B) Well...New Orleans gave me a lot of trouble." C) I regret I should have been a well-behaved kid." D) Who knew I would make so much money and live like a king?" E) I wish I could turn back time and start all over."	I look right in the heart of good old New Orleans. **A) It had given me something to live for."**

Questions 25-30 are based on the following passage.

From the early 20th century, developing mass media technologies, such as radio and film, were credited with an almost irresistible power to mold an audience's beliefs according to the communicators' will. The basic assumption of strong media effects theory was that audiences were passive and homogeneous. This assumption was (25) **not based on empirical evidence but on assumptions of human nature**. There were two main explanations for this perception of mass media effects. First, mass broadcasting technologies were acquiring a widespread audience, (26) **even among average households.** People were astonished by the speed of information dissemination. Secondly, short-term propaganda techniques were implemented during the war time by several governments as a powerful tool for uniting their people. (28) **"This propaganda exemplified strong, but ill-effect of communication"** said the political scientist Harold Lasswell, who focused on the early media effects.

With the new variables added to research, (30) **it was difficult to isolate media influence** that resulted in any media effects to an audience's cognition, attitude and behavior. As Berelson summed up: "Some kinds of communication on some kinds of issues have brought to the attention of some kinds of people under some kinds of conditions have some kinds of effect." The media play an indispensable role in the proper functioning of a modern democracy. Without mass media, (27) **openness and accountability are very tough to reach** in contemporary democracies.

Q25. **Absolute Pattern 7: Understanding Attitude (Tone) Question**
Finding tone such as positive-negative, active-passive, mental-physical, subjective-objective
Question Pattern: The author views **media effects theory** in line 3 as

A) an evidence with plenty of data and statistics B) a fundamental concept that needs further research **C) a perception that cannot be proven** D) a familiar concept shared by several other theories E) problematic to call it a theory	not based on empirical evidence but on assumptions of human nature

Q26. **Absolute Pattern 2: Summary Question** Summarizing a sentence or entire passage.
Question Pattern: Which of the following assertions corresponds **LEAST with the author's argument concerning the effects of mass media** in lines 1-9?

A) It helped mold an audience's view B) Communicators made the audience to be passive C) Communicators made the audience to be homogeneous **D) Average households were excluded from obtaining mass media information** E) Government implemented short-term propaganda	There were two main explanations for this perception of mass media effects. First, mass broadcasting technologies were acquiring a widespread audience, **even among average households**

Q27. **Absolute Pattern 2: Summary Question**
Summarizing a sentence or entire passage.
Question Pattern: Based on line 14, **the role of media in modern democratic society** serves chiefly to

A) mold public opinion **B) disclose reliable information** C) represent government propaganda D) offer information to selective pubic E) make public passive and homogeneous	Without mass media, **openness and accountability are very tough to reach** in contemporary democracies

UNAUTHORIZED COPYING OR REUSE OF ANY PART OF THIS PAGE IS ILLEGAL

Q28. **Absolute Pattern 4: Example Question**
Finding the true purpose behind a specific name or idea within a sentence
Question Pattern: The author mentions **Harold lasswell** in line 9 mainly to

A) give an authority to his opinion B) exemplify how mass media well performed back then **C) raise concern about political involvement in mass media** D) interpret the media effects in the 21th century E) show how important mass media is to the public	**"This propaganda exemplified strong, but ill-effect of communication"** said the political scientist Harold Lasswell

Q29. **Absolute Pattern 7: Understanding Attitude (Tone) Question**
Finding tone such as positive-negative, active-passive, mental-physical, subjective-objective
Question Pattern: Harold Lasswell in line 9 may view **"the communicators"** in line 2 with?

A) respect **B) concern** C) analytical D) greedy E) naïve	**"This propaganda exemplified strong, but ill-effect of communication"** said the political scientist Harold Lasswell

Q30. **Absolute Pattern 2: Summary Question**
Summarizing a sentence or entire passage.
Question Pattern: The quotation from **Berellson** (line11-13) indicates that media effects

A) cannot be defined in a single term or value B) can be determined transparently C) should be isolated from the government propaganda theory D) remain as the most powerful influence on the public E) use different method depending on the audience	**it was difficult to isolate media influence** that resulted in any media effects to an audience's cognition, attitude and behavior. As Berelson summed up: "Some kinds of communication on some kinds of issues have brought to the attention of some kinds of people under some kinds of conditions have some kinds of effect."

Questions 32-35 are based on the following passage.

First let us say something belongs to what we call the mind and others to what we call matter. Let us suppose the matter to be entirely and absolutely (Q31) **homogeneous**. Things may be classified according to their color, their shape, their weight, (Q32) **the pleasure they give us**, their quality of being alive or dead, and so on; one much given to classification would only be troubled by the number of possible distinctions. Since so many divisions are possible, at which shall we stop and say: this is the one which corresponds (Q34 & Q35) **exactly to the opposition of mind and matter.** It must be supposed that we shall do so by means of a criterion. (Q33)**Otherwise, we should only be acting fantastically.**

Q31. Absolute Pattern 2: Summary Question Summarizing a sentence or entire passage.
Question Pattern: According to the author, **matter can basically be understood** as

A) homogeneous B) heterogeneous C) a problem D) an issue E) a science	Let us suppose the matter to be entirely and absolutely **homogeneous**.

Q32. Absolute Pattern 2: Summary Question
Summarizing a sentence or entire passage.
Question Pattern: All of the following elements can be **classified as a matter** EXCEPT

A) color B) shape C) weight **D) pleasure** E) weight	**the pleasure they give us. The matter has no pleasure.** * It is we who feel pleasure.

Q33. Absolute Pattern 5: Word-In-Context Question
Finding a clue word and the keyword from the sentence in question
Question Pattern: In line 8, when the author says "**acting fantastically,**" it can be understood as acting

A) theoretically B) beautifully C) magically D) critically **E) randomly**	It must be supposed that we shall do so by means of a criterion. **Otherwise,** we should only be acting fantastically. **"Otherwise" is the keyword here.** The opposite meaning for criterion should be random. The author uses the word, 'fantastically' to compare the difference between criterion (the group) and the other (non-group). Therefore, fantastically must be a negative word.

Q34. Absolute Pattern 9: Relationships Question
Finding relations between the cause-effect, comparison-contrast, characters, and ideas
Question Pattern: The author suggests that **the mind and matter** are

A) entirely mysterious B) somewhat different **C) two oppositions** D) one single criterion E) fantastically homogeneous	Since so many divisions are possible, at which shall we stop and say: this is the one which corresponds **exactly to the opposition of mind and matter.**

UNAUTHORIZED COPYING OR REUSE OF ANY PART OF THIS PAGE IS ILLEGAL

Q35. **Absolute Pattern 2: Summary Question** Summarizing a sentence or entire passage.
Question Pattern: According to the author, which of the following **statement is true**?

A) matter need not be classified B) all matters are heterogeneous C) matter in the passage is a synonym to problem **D) the mind cannot be classified** E) mind is matter as well	Since so many divisions are possible, at which shall we stop and say: this is the one which corresponds **exactly to the opposition of mind and matter.** The author believes matter can be divided so many times, while exactly opposite is true to the mind. That is, mind cannot be classified. A), B), C), E) are all opposite statement

Questions 36-40 are based on the following passage.

Several years ago, at the one of the major engineering societies, the president of the society gave expression to a thought so startling that the **few laymen** who were seated in the auditorium fairly (Q39) **gasped. "since engineers had got the world into war, it was the duty of engineers to get the world out of war."**

I mention this merely to bring to the reader's attention the tremendous power which engineers wield in world affairs. (Q36 & Q37) **The profession of engineering adapts discoveries in science** to the uses of mankind, but is a peculiarly isolated one. Very little is known about it among those outside of the profession. (Q40) **Laymen know** something about **law, a little about medicine**. But laymen know nothing about engineering. (Q38) **Average layman cannot differentiate between the man who runs a locomotive and the man who designs a locomotive**. In ordinary parlance both are called engineers. Yet there is a difference between them--a difference as between day and night.

Q36. **Absolute Pattern 8: Understanding True Purpose**
Finding the true purpose of statement, sentences, or the entire paragraph
Question Pattern: Why does the President believe as he said in lines 2-3, ("since engineers ...world out of war")

A) Engineers were all German **B) War utilized engineers' knowledge** C) Engineers served as freedom fighters at war D) Engineers supported the war for money E) Engineers are destructive in nature	**The profession of engineering adapts discoveries in science** to the uses of mankind… *The passage doesn't directly state how engineers are responsible for the war. Compared to the lack of information, the rest are too specific and therefore incorrect.

Q37. **Absolute Pattern 8: Understanding True Purpose**
Finding the true purpose of statement, sentences, or the entire paragraph
Question Pattern: "the **tremendous power**" (line 4), focuses primarily on which aspect of engineers?

A) Their ability to adapt discoveries in science B) Their desire to use it for the mankind C) Their peculiarly isolated personality D) The fact they don't know they are being used E) Their ability to adapt discoveries in arts	I mention this merely to bring to the reader's attention the **tremendous power** which engineers wield in world affairs. **The profession of engineering adapts discoveries in science** to the uses of mankind… B) is not stated. C) does not respond to the question.

SSAT UPPER LEVEL 7 PRACTICE TESTS WITH THE ABSOLUTE PATTERNS

Q38. Absolute Pattern 9: Relationships Question
Finding relations between the cause-effect, comparison-contrast, characters, and ideas
Question Pattern: In line 7-8 ("Average layman …locomotive"), **the author compares**?

A) war and peace **B) engineer and non-engineer** C) benefit and harm D) practicality and impracticality E) job and hobby	Average layman cannot differentiate between the man **who runs a locomotive and the man who designs a locomotive.** This example sentence describes driver and engineer.

Q39. Absolute Pattern 3: Inference Question Finding an indirect suggestion (or guessing)
Question Pattern: Why did the **few laymen in line 2 gasp**?

A) They were not prepared to hear such a remark B) They were not engineers C) They were in fact engineers D) They thought nobody knew about it E) They felt threatened by the president's speech	Several years ago, at the one of the major engineering societies, the president of the society gave expression to a thought so **startling** that the **few laymen** who were seated in the auditorium fairly **gasped.** *They startled and gasped. This emotional state explains that they were not prepared to hear such a remark. B) is distraction. The fact that laymen gasp is not related with whether they are engineers or non-engineers.

Q40. Absolute Pattern 9: Relationships Question
Finding relations between the cause-effect, comparison-contrast, characters, and ideas
Question Pattern: The author refers to "**law and medicine**" in line 7 because they

A) equally contributed to mankind **B) are relatively easy to understand** C) do not use science D) also have duty to get the world out of war E) are harder than engineering	**Laymen know** something about **law, a little about medicine**. But laymen know nothing about engineering

Test 7 Absolute Patterns for the Analogy Section

Absolute Pattern 3. Purpose (Tool) Pattern
Finding Relationships between the Purpose of Individual to Object, to its Function, its User, its Use, and its Association

Q31. A is the Best Answer. Butcher uses knife as (A) tailor uses scissors.

Absolute Pattern 6. Definition Pattern
Finding Definition/Concept of person, place, thing, and emotion

Q32. D is the Best Answer. Technology focuses on innovation as does tradition on (D) preservation

Absolute Pattern 3. Purpose (Tool) Pattern
Finding Relationships between the Purpose of Individual to Object, to its Function, its User, its Use, and its Association

Q33. D is the Best Answer. Game uses rule as (D) does cooking to recipe, similar procedures and concept.

Absolute Pattern 1. Category Pattern
Finding Part/Whole, Same Type/Kind, Association   Absolute Pattern

Q34 E is the Best Answer. Spinach and cucumber are vegetable category and grapes and orange are fruits.

Absolute Pattern 3. Purpose (Tool) Pattern
Finding Relationships between the Purpose of Individual to Object, to its Function, its User, its Use, and its Association

Q35. D is the Best Answer. Hinge holds door as (D) clip does on paper.

Absolute Pattern 1. Category Pattern
Finding Part/Whole, Same Type/Kind, Association   Absolute Pattern

Q36 A is the Best Answer. Milky way (whole) is to solar system (part) as (A) school is to student.

Absolute Pattern 9. Syntax Pattern
Finding Homophony, Contraction, Grammatical Association

Q37. A is the Best Answer. Adverse normally refers to unfavorable weather as does malignant to disease.

Absolute Pattern 6. Definition Pattern
Finding Definition/Concept of person, place, thing, and emotion

Q38. D is the Best Answer. Obsolete, no longer practical and outdated. Innovation is brand new.

Absolute Pattern 3. Purpose (Tool) Pattern
Finding Relationships between the Purpose of Individual to Object, to its Function, its User, its Use, and its Association

Q39. A is the Best Answer. The purpose of Supervisor is to oversee as (A) that of bottle is to hold.

Absolute Pattern 3. Purpose (Tool) Pattern
Finding Relationships between the Purpose of Individual to Object, to its Function, its User, its Use, and its Association

Q40. D is the Best Answer. Painter uses inspiration as (D) mathematician uses logic.

Make sure "inspiration" is conceptual, not materials like the other choices.

Absolute Pattern 7. Mental (Emotion) Pattern
Finding Feeling/Mental Concept and its Emotion

Q41 A is the Best Answer. Desperation is greater degree than wish as (A) worship is to follow.

They are both mental concept and (E) is ruled out for that reason.

Absolute Pattern 3. Purpose (Tool) Pattern
Finding Relationships between the Purpose of Individual to Object, to its Function, its User, its Use, and its Association

Q42 E is the Best Answer. The purpose of Alarm clock is to alert as lullaby (E) is to calm.

Absolute Pattern 6. Definition Pattern
Finding Definition/Concept of person, place, thing, and emotion

Q43 A is the Best Answer. The purpose of Bluetooth is for integration as that of marketplace is (A)
Interaction (exchange goods), a a similar concept.

Absolute Pattern 4. Characteristic Pattern
Finding Characteristic of Person, Place, Object, or Idea and its Associated Action

Q44 C is the Best Answer. Underwear gives comfort as uniform gives (C) identity

Absolute Pattern 4. Characteristic Pattern
Finding Characteristic of Person, Place, Object, or Idea and its Associated Action

Q45 D is the Best Answer. Leader possesses charisma as servant is (D) obedient

Absolute Pattern 4. Characteristic Pattern
Finding Characteristic of Person, Place, Object, or Idea and its Associated Action

Q46 D is the Best Answer. Monastery is filled with confinement as (D) amusement park, with exhilaration.

Absolute Pattern 5. Degree Pattern
Finding a Degree and a Shape in person, place, thing, and emotion

Q47. A is the Best Answer. Suspension is less punishment than expel. Quiz is smaller exam than final.

Absolute Pattern 5. Degree Pattern
Finding a Degree and a Shape in person, place, thing, and emotion

Q48. A is the Best Answer. Try-out is only once. Tenacity is continuation. (A) liter is only 1/4 of gallon

Absolute Pattern 5. Degree Pattern
Finding a Degree and a Shape in person, place, thing, and emotion

Q49. A is the Best Answer. Quench is greater amount of drinking than seep as in (A) tumult is to confusion

Absolute Pattern 4. Characteristic Pattern
Finding Characteristic of Person, Place, Object, or Idea and its Associated Action

Q50 B is the Best Answer. Pastoral is characteristically peaceful as (B) industrial zone is polluted.

Absolute Pattern 4. Characteristic Pattern
Finding Characteristic of Person, Place, Object, or Idea and its Associated Action

Q51 A is the Best Answer. We are careful to Sensitive matter as we (A) ignore to ordinary matter.

Absolute Pattern 4. Characteristic Pattern
Finding Characteristic of Person, Place, Object, or Idea and its Associated Action

Q52 E is the Best Answer. Awakening (of animal) in March and hibernation in November describe seasonal norm in nature.

Absolute Pattern 8. Production Pattern
Finding Cause-and-Effect in Person, Concept, and Object

Q53 B is the Best Answer. Cloud produces rain as (B) mother produces baby.

Absolute Pattern 8. Production Pattern
Finding Cause-and-Effect in Person, Concept, and Object

Q54 C is the Best Answer. Volcano makes lava as fire produces flame

Absolute Pattern 8. Production Pattern
Finding Cause-and-Effect in Person, Concept, and Object

Q55 A is the Best Answer. Paramedic performs emergency treatment as nurse does vitality check. Both are professional medical staff.

Absolute Pattern 8. Production Pattern
Finding Cause-and-Effect in Person, Concept, and Object

Q56 C is the Best Answer. Rehabilitator provides regimen as doctor gives prescription. Both are medical professional staff.

Absolute Pattern 4. Characteristic Pattern
Finding Characteristic of Person, Place, Object, or Idea and its Associated Action

Q57 B is the Best Answer. Dance uses step. Song uses rhythm, the same musical genre and concept.

Absolute Pattern 1. Category Pattern
Finding Part/Whole, Same Type/Kind, Association   Absolute Pattern

Q58 D is the Best Answer. Fire makes pungent smell and vinegar makes acrid smell. Both pungent and acrid are synonym. (A) is taste.

Absolute Pattern 7. Mental (Emotion) Pattern
Finding Feeling/Mental Concept and its Emotion

Q59 D is the Best Answer. Autumn is quiet, emotionally. Halloween movie is scary, emotionally.

Absolute Pattern 11. Subjective-Objective Pattern
Finding Quality-Quantity, Tangible-Intangible Association

Q60 B is the Best Answer. Elephant is to smart (Subjective view) and (B) elephant is to human-like are subjective value. (A) and (E) are objective; (C) and (D) contain quantifiers.

UNAUTHORIZED COPYING OR REUSE OF ANY PART OF THIS PAGE IS ILLEGAL

Chapter 7 Summary

The Chapter Summary contains equal portions of

12 Absolute Patterns for Analogy Section and

10 Absolute Patterns for Reading Section.

You may study all at once to significantly

improve your understanding and your scores.

Chapter 7

SSAT Analogy Absolute Pattern Summary

Absolute Pattern 1. Category Pattern
Finding Part/Whole, Same Type/Kind, Association

Absolute Pattern 2. Synonym/Antonym
Finding similar or opposite meaning between words

Absolute Pattern 3. Purpose (Tool) Pattern
Finding Relationships between the Purpose of Individual to Object, to its Function, its User, its Use, and its Association

Absolute Pattern 4. Characteristic Pattern
Finding Characteristic of Person, Place, Object, or Idea and its Associated Action

Absolute Pattern 5. Degree Pattern
Finding Degree and Shape in person, place, thing, and emotion

Absolute Pattern 6. Definition Pattern
Finding Definition/Concept of person, place, thing, and emotion

Absolute Pattern 7. Mental (Emotion) Pattern
Finding Feeling/Mental Concept and its Emotion

Absolute Pattern 8. Production Pattern
Finding Cause-and-Effect in Person, Concept, and Object

Absolute Pattern 9. Syntax Pattern
Finding Homophony, Contraction, Grammatical Association

Absolute Pattern 10. Positive-Negative Pattern
Finding Positive-Negative Value from Antonym Category

Absolute Pattern 11. Subjective-Objective Pattern
Finding Quality-Quantity, Tangible-Intangible Association

Absolute Pattern 12. Human-Nonhuman Pattern
Finding Active-Passive/Human-Nonhuman Association

20 Common Patterns for *In*correct Options
The Reading Section

14 | Repeating the Question

Fooling students can never be easier when choices paraphrase the question instead of answering it.

Some questions may look extremely easy at first sight because the choice paraphrases the question.

15 | Synonym or Similar Perception

Virtually, the majority of the correct answers rely on the synonym pattern.

However, some choices simply place opposite adjective or adverb right next to the keyword (the synonym) that eventually changes the meaning of the choice.

For example, can you distinguish between "acceptance" and "mild acceptance" and "guarded acceptance"

All three are so different that only one—depending on situation—can be the answer.

16 | Concept Comparison

Concept comparison pattern normally presents two opposing concepts.

This pattern can be subcategorized such as the "Physical-Mental", "Negative-Positive", "Passive-Active", "Part-Whole", "A single individual involvement-Two individuals involvement", etc.

Without properly understanding the concept comparison, every choice may look the same.

20 Common Patterns for *Incorrect* Options
The Reading Section

17 Quantity-Quality Concept

Some keywords contain quantity concept, while others are quality.

As an example, the word "comics" inspires us a low quality, while "one-fourth" tells us the quantity.

18 Personal-Group Perspective

Personal perspective is usually represented by the first person 'I'.

A social or group perspective uses more objective tone and general writing style.

The incorrect choices may confuse you between these two perspectives.

Therefore, check if the passage is written by the first person perspective "I" or the third person in general.

19 Part-Whole Relations

Imagine one paragraph (total of 15 lines) is made of single long sentence.

You should know that this single sentence can be broken down into all five choices.

Please remember you are assigned to read only the line that is given to you such as out of total 15 lines,

(A) lines 1-2, (B) lines 3-5, (C) lines 6-10, (D) lines 11-12, (E) lines 13-15, not the whole chunk of it.

Please do not read and judge beyond the exact line provided for you.

20 Characteristics

You should be ready to translate abstract concept.

Some keywords characterize the idea or object using our five senses (smell, hearing, touch, see, taste).

For instance, instead of saying "onion", the option will write "an edible bulb plant with a pungent taste and smell."

UNAUTHORIZED COPYING OR REUSE OF ANY PART OF THIS PAGE IS ILLEGAL

ABSOLUTE PATTERN SERIES

SAT Absolute Patterns 7 Practice Tests

SAT 11 Absolute Patterns in Reading Section
The entire 47 questions in the reading section, both literary and informational passages, can be categorized into three parts: Category A: Content Question; Category B:Technique Question; Category C: Integrated Question. These three categories can be subcategorized into eleven patterns.
Applying these 11 patterns—mostly one pattern per question —plus 20 incorrect choice patterns will be absolutely the most effective and systemic way to improve your scores.

SAT Absolute Patterns 12 Practice Tests Writing & Language

24 Patterns in Writing & Language Section
The entire Writing and Language Section uses these patterns.
CollegeBoard SAT creates questions based on these patterns.
Instead of solving each individual question endlessly without knowing the patterns and logic, assume that each question is made of a unique formula. For the perfect score, memorize 24 patterns in this book. Practice until every pattern becomes natural to you.

PSAT & SAT STARTER'S Absolute Patterns 3Practice

When you are entering SAT for the first time, you would probably rely heavily on your own strategy. Inside the mechanism of SAT, however, is just a little bit more complex so that it requires not only how much time you deal with the problems but also how systematically you can handle them.
To thoroughly understand the patterns, please solve one question at a time and check the answer using the step-by-step pattern explanations without a time limit.

SSAT Absolute Patterns Middle Level 8 Practice Tests

SSAT 15 Hidden Patterns in the Analogy Section
The entire Analogy Section uses these 15 Absolute Patterns.
The official SSAT creates the questions based on these patterns.
Instead of practicing each individual question endlessly without knowing the patterns and logic behind it, please work with these hidden patterns.

SSAT Absolute Patterns Elementary Level 8 Practice Tests
10 Absolute Patterns in the Reading Section
The entire 28 questions in the reading section, both literary and informational passages, can be categorized into two parts: Category A: Content Question; Category B: Technique Question. These two categories can be subcategorized into 10 Absolute Patterns.
The 10 Absolute Patterns—mostly one pattern per question—will be absolutely the most effective and systemic way to improve your scores.

Published in 2018 by Rockridge edu. enterprise & services. inc.
ALL RIGHTS RESERVED.
COPYRIGHT @2016
BY SAN YOO

NO part of this book may be reproduced in any form, by phtosat, Microfilm, PDF or any other means, or incorporated into any information retrieval system, electronic or mechanical, without the written permission of the copyright owner

All inquiries should be addressed to:
Rockridge edu. enterprise & services inc.
869 SEYMOUR BLVD. NORTH VANCOUVER B.C. CANADA V7J 2J7
satvancouver@gmail.com

UNAUTHORIZED COPYING OR REUSE OF ANY PART OF THIS PAGE IS ILLEGAL

Made in the
USA
Middletown, DE

76587972R00172